Praise for
GIRLS ON THE EDGE

"The best book about the current state of girls and young women in America."

—Caitlin Flanagan, *The Atlantic*

"Packed with advice and concrete suggestions for parents, *Girls on the Edge* is a treasure trove of rarely seen research on girls, offering families guidance on some of the most pressing issues facing girls today. Dr. Sax's commitment to girls' success comes through on every page."

—Rachel Simmons, author of *Odd Girl Out,*
The Curse of the Good Girl, and *Enough As She Is*

"Crucial. . . . Parents of tween and teen girls would do well to check this book."

—*Chronicle of Higher Education*

"Dr. Sax once again combines years of experience with compelling research and common sense to intelligently challenge the status quo of what it means to raise a healthy daughter. *Girls on the Edge* offers skills parents can incorporate to feel more competent with our girls and young women."

—Florence Hilliard, director of the Gender Studies Project,
University of Wisconsin–Madison

"The world is way different from what it was a couple of years ago; this is essential reading for parents and teachers, and one of the most thought-provoking books on teen development available."

—*Library Journal*

"Fortunately, [Leonard] Sax is up to more here than pronouncing young women irrevocably doomed. . . . *Girls on the Edge* doesn't dramatize the self-destructive behavior it describes . . . [and it] speaks exclusively to parents and offers concrete ways to help their daughters cultivate stronger personal identities."

—Slate.com/Double X

"In clear, accessible language, Sax deftly blends anecdotes, clinical research, and even lines of poetry in persuasive, often fascinating chapters that speak straight to parents. . . . Warning that 'a 1980s solution' won't help solve twenty-first-century problems, Sax offers a holistic, sobering call to help the current generation of young women develop the support and sense of self that will allow them to grow into resilient adults."

—*Booklist*

"Turn off your cell phones and computers and read this book! You will connect with your daughter in new ways, and she will thank you."

—Rabbi Sandy Eisenberg Sasso, author of
God's Paintbrush and *In God's Name*

"Written through real stories and supported by strong evidence in the fields of education, psychology, and the sciences—a must-read."

—Margaret M. Ferrara, PhD,
associate professor, University of Nevada–Reno

"Leonard Sax brings together a rare combination of psychoanalytic training with a deep empathy for girls and their stories in this important book. His argument that girls are struggling to find their centers will resonate and his recommendations for how to locate them will inspire."

—Courtney E. Martin, author of
Perfect Girls, Starving Daughters

"Dr. Sax's deep commitment to girls developing a positive 'sense of self' is woven into the fabric of this book. *Girls on the Edge* is a must-read for every parent of a girl as well as for every adult who teaches girls."

—Dr. Mary Seppala, head of school,
Agnes Irwin School, Bryn Mawr, Pennsylvania

"I made *Girls on the Edge* required reading for all administrators at Woodlands Academy of the Sacred Heart, and I strongly recommend the book to all of our parents. Leonard Sax explains to parents and educators of girls just what is going on in the cyberbubble of instant messaging, texting, and social networking sites. There is a way to help girls navigate this world and find their centers—centers of genuine humanness and authenticity and, yes, spirituality. Readers will find out much they don't know, and that is more than they might guess. A must-read."

—Gerald J. Grossman, head of school,
Woodlands Academy of the Sacred Heart,
Lake Forest, Illinois

"Leonard Sax sounds a crucial warning to parents of teenage girls. No matter how attentive and savvy you are, the lives of girls today are like nothing you ever knew. The obsessions are worse, nastiness is rampant (especially on the web), drinking is up, and sexuality keeps creeping down the age ladder. 'Girls need girl-specific interventions,' Sax insists, and *Girls on the Edge* explains why—and also how to do it."

—Mark Bauerlein, PhD, professor, Emory University

GIRLS ON THE EDGE

ALSO BY LEONARD SAX

Boys Adrift

Why Gender Matters

The Collapse of Parenting

GIRLS ON THE EDGE

WHY SO MANY GIRLS
ARE ANXIOUS, WIRED, AND
OBSESSED—AND WHAT
PARENTS CAN DO

LEONARD SAX, MD, PhD

BASIC BOOKS
New York

Basic Books
Hachette Book Group
1290 Avenue of the Americas, New York, NY 10104
www.basicbooks.com

Printed in the United States of America

Originally published in hardcover and ebook by Basic Books in April 2010
Second Trade Paperback Edition: August 2020

Published by Basic Books, an imprint of Perseus Books, LLC, a subsidiary of Hachette Book Group, Inc. The Basic Books name and logo is a trademark of the Hachette Book Group.

The Hachette Speakers Bureau provides a wide range of authors for speaking events. To find out more, go to www.hachettespeakersbureau.com or call (866) 376-6591.

The publisher is not responsible for websites (or their content) that are not owned by the publisher.

Print book interior design by Amnet Systems.

Library of Congress Control Number: 2020938917

ISBNs: 978-1-5416-1780-3 (trade paperback), 978-1-5416-4709-1 (ebook)

LSC-H

Printing 4, 2025

For my wife, Katie, and our daughter, Sarah

Dig into yourself...
...find out how deep is the place from which your life springs;
at its source you will find the answer to your question...

RAINER MARIA RILKE

contents

GIRLS ON THE EDGE

introduction

three girls

emily

When Emily[1] was five years old, she brought two lifelike miniature gorilla dolls, one big and one small, to kindergarten for show-and-tell. She used the dolls to explain dominance hierarchies to the other children using terms like "alpha male" and "dominant." Each succeeding year, she was always anxious the first few weeks of school. "I have to make sure the teacher knows I'm smart. It's hard to change first impressions if you say something dumb the first week," she told her mom in fifth grade. She need not have worried. Emily seldom said anything dumb. The teachers were quick to recognize that Emily was, indeed, the smart one.

Her dream was to be accepted at an Ivy League school, preferably Princeton. "Everybody talks about Harvard, but Princeton is actually more selective," she told her mom—in ninth grade. Three years later, she was crushed when she was rejected by both Harvard and Princeton. That's when her sense of self began to crumble.

She was accepted at the University of Pennsylvania. She expected that she would be the smartest kid there. But she wasn't. Not even close. She found herself struggling just to pass her courses. And that's when the bottom fell out.

melissa

Melissa and Jessica were best friends from way back in kindergarten. "We were like clones," Melissa told me. The two girls liked to wear the same clothes; they read the same books and went wild over the same movies. "We could read each other's minds."

For eight years—from the spring of their kindergarten year right through eighth grade—the girls shared a unique bond. Then in ninth grade, everything changed. Jessica suddenly turned on Melissa. Jessica invited everyone to a party—but not Melissa. Jessica told all her friends not to sit with Melissa at lunch and to ignore her if she approached. Jessica managed to get the other girls to deploy the full silent treatment. "All of a sudden, I was invisible," Melissa told me.

It really became nasty when Jessica and her coconspirators began using social media and texting to harass Melissa 24-7. "It was awful," Melissa said. "I didn't want to turn on my tablet or my cell phone. I didn't want to see what they were saying about me. I seriously wished I could just die."

avery

Avery's dream was to win *ANTM: America's Next Top Model*. From her ninth birthday until around thirteen years of age, Avery was the prettiest girl, and she knew it.

Then something happened with her hormones and the acne came out. Avery's parents told her to be patient and the acne would go away, but it didn't. It got worse. At Avery's request, they went to their family doctor, who prescribed minocycline, but that didn't help. They went to the dermatologist, who wanted to prescribe Accutane. Avery's parents read about Accutane causing suicidal depression and birth defects. They told Avery, "Absolutely not." A major battle ensued.

That's also when her weight became a problem, at least in Avery's unforgiving eyes. At five foot three, she went from 97 pounds to 124 pounds between her thirteenth and fourteenth birthdays. She was no longer the cute slender girl with perfect skin. Who was she? She no longer knew. She struggled with clinical depression. So her parents brought her to see me. I prescribed Lexapro, which helped but caused even more weight gain, so I switched her to Adderall.

Adderall seemed to be a godsend at first. It not only improved her mood but also helped her to get her weight back down to 107 pounds in about eight weeks. But Adderall sometimes made her heart pound so hard she felt as though it would jump right out of her chest. Nevertheless, she pushed for a higher dose. When I refused, she claimed to have lost her pills and needed more.

Avery defined her value in terms of her appearance. She was worth something only if she were cute, and "cute" meant "slender with clear skin." Once she no longer fit that ideal, she no longer knew who she was.

"Dig into yourself . . . find out how deep is the place from which your life springs," wrote the German poet Rainer Maria Rilke.

If your daughter can develop a sense of self that is deeply rooted, then she has improved the odds of growing up to be a resilient and self-confident woman. Age is no guarantee of a secure self-concept; conversely, some young kids are remarkably mature. I've met a few eleven- and twelve-year-old girls who have achieved a secure sense of self and retained it through adolescence and into young adulthood. I know many adult women who have never achieved this.

A sense of self is about who you *are*. It's not about how you look or what kinds of grades you get or who you're friends with. Emily defined herself as the smart kid. Melissa was Jessica's BFF. Avery was the cute one. Take that away, and each girl's sense of self collapsed. My friend and colleague, pediatrician Meg Meeker, writes in her new book *Raising a Strong Daughter in a Toxic Culture*: "You don't want to trap your daughter into assuming that her inherent value relies on her performing well at a skill or a competition. Kids hate feeling that their parents only give them attention when they succeed at school or extracurricular activities." We don't want girls to "sense that their parents don't really know them for who they are—only for what they do—and if they fail in a game, in a performance, or in a test, then they fail completely."[2] The human experience is about more than performance, about more than the accomplishments of the mind and the feats of the body. Each one of us also has a spirit, or a soul if you like, that must be acknowledged, nurtured, and cherished. We will talk more about nurturing the spirit in Chapter 7.

I began writing prescriptions for children during my pediatrics rotation at the Children's Hospital of Philadelphia

(CHOP). After earning my MD at the University of Pennsylvania, I completed a three-year residency in family practice at Lancaster General Hospital in Lancaster, Pennsylvania. Next I spent eighteen years practicing family medicine in a suburb of Washington, DC. For eighteen years I had the privilege of being a part of the lives of more than a thousand kids, seeing some of them from infancy right into middle school and high school; others I followed from age ten or twelve into adulthood. I have since moved to Chester County, Pennsylvania, about forty-five minutes west of Philadelphia, where I continue to see patients of all ages.

More than thirty-five years have passed since my first pediatrics rotation at CHOP. I've seen some big changes over my three decades as a family doctor. Thirty years ago, even twenty years ago, it was rare to see a girl who was anxious and depressed at thirteen years of age. Today it's common.

Some of the girls I have come to know have grown up in secure homes with two parents who love them. Others have grown up in less fortunate circumstances. But circumstances don't tell the whole story. I know many girls who have been raised by single parents with no money, and yet some of those girls have grown up to be rock solid and resilient. I know a girl who was raised by loving parents in a comfortable home, yet she was hopeless and suicidal by the age of fourteen.

Developing a sense of who you are isn't about how much money your parents have. It's not about how you look or how many followers you have on social media. It's about connecting with yourself, developing a sense of your own personhood. Over my three-plus decades as a family doctor, I have seen a growing proportion of girls whose sense of self is defined only in terms of superficials. As a result, those girls are fragile, susceptible to a meltdown with the mildest of jolts. They may tell you that everything's great, but they are perpetually on the edge of the abyss.

I wrote the first edition of *Girls on the Edge* in 2009. It was published in 2010. Since then, the problems I described have become more widespread; 2009 now almost seems like the good old days. The latest numbers from the National Institutes of Health show that fully 20 percent of adolescent girls in the United States have suffered a major depressive episode just in the past year. That's one girl in five, which is roughly triple the rate for boys (6.8 percent).[3] Many researchers, using different methods, find that girls today are much more likely to be anxious and depressed compared with girls from the same demographic ten or twenty years ago.[4]

When I share these figures, some parents ask whether the increase in the prevalence of depression might just reflect the destigmatizing of mental illness. I think that's unlikely for several reasons, one of which is the statistics on suicide. The rate of suicide among adolescents decreased slightly from the mid-1980s to the mid-2000s. Since 2007, the rate of suicide among young people has increased 56 percent.[5] The rate of increase for girls has been roughly double the rate of increase for boys.[6] Suicide is now the second leading cause of death among young Americans age ten to nineteen years of age (accidents are the leading cause of death).[7] Kids don't commit suicide because mental illness has been destigmatized. They commit suicide because their suffering is so severe that they see no other way out. But if we can't attribute the increase in suicide among adolescents to destigmatization, then we can't reasonably attribute the corresponding increase in depression among adolescents to destigmatization.

The first edition of *Girls on the Edge* was based first and foremost on the girls I had seen in my own practice in Maryland, trying to understand what was driving these girls to the brink. In the years since, others have written about this growing epidemic of anxiety, depression, and fragility among American girls. A few examples, in chronological order, are Nancy Jo Sales's *American Girls: Social Media and the Secret Lives of Teenagers*, Peggy Orenstein's *Girls & Sex: Navigating the Complicated New Landscape*, Rachel Simmons's *Enough As She Is: How to Help Girls Move Beyond Impossible Standards of Success to Live Healthy, Happy, and Fulfilling Lives*, and Lisa Damour's *Under Pressure: Confronting the Epidemic of Stress and Anxiety in Girls*. These books emphasize one or more of the factors I described in the first edition of *Girls on the Edge*: obsessions (Simmons), the depersonalization of sexual intimacy (Orenstein), and social media (Sales and Orenstein and Simmons and Damour and and and . . .). Curiously, no mainstream writer has picked up on the relevance of environmental toxins to the growing prevalence of anxiety and depression among American girls, although the evidence for such a link is stronger today than it was ten years ago. That's our topic in Chapter 4.

By many objective standards, girls today ought to be happier than their grandmothers were at their age. Girls today have choices and opportunities their great-grandmothers would not have dreamed of. Medical school, law school—fifty years ago, those were still mostly for men. When my mom graduated from medical school in Cleveland, Ohio, she was one of only two women in her class. Your grandmother probably did not imagine ever becoming a surgeon, a Supreme Court justice, a combat infantry soldier, or president of the United States. Your daughter knows that all these options are possibilities for her.

And yet many girls today are failing to develop a robust inner life, the sturdy core of personality, the ballast that every human needs in order to navigate the storms of life without capsizing. Their brothers also are often failing to develop that grounded connection to the real world. But the boys' problems and the girls' problems manifest differently.

This book began in part because I was trying to understand lazy boys. Beginning in the 1990s, I saw more and more families from every economic condition in which the daughter was hardworking and motivated while her brother was a goofball—more concerned about getting to the next level in his video game than about getting a good grade on his Spanish final. In 2001, I began visiting schools and communities around the United States as well as in Canada, Mexico, Australia, New Zealand, England, Scotland, Germany, and Spain to get a sense of what is going on. I have now visited more than 460 schools. I have talked with the boys, talked with the girls, and listened to their parents and their teachers. I have found that this phenomenon of lazy boys and hardworking girls is pervasive.[8] The years I spent trying to understand what is going on with the boys led me to write my second book, *Boys Adrift*, originally published in 2007; the second edition of *Boys Adrift* came out in 2016.

Early on, I understood that the girls are not the winners in this story. Both girls and boys are disadvantaged, but they're disadvantaged in different ways. More and more boys are developing a great ability to enjoy themselves—to binge on video games, pornography, food, and sleep—but they often don't have the drive and motivation to succeed in the real world outside their bedroom. More and more of their sisters have that drive and motivation in abundance—but they don't know how to relax, how to have fun and enjoy life. For some of these girls, each accomplishment is only a stepping-stone to the next goal. The treadmill never shuts off. The performance never ends.

In writing the books, I came to understand that the boys' laziness and the girls' obsessive drive are two facets of the same dysfunction, the same failure to develop a healthy and grounded sense of self. Many of those unmotivated boys are content in their cocoon, with their video games and their pornography, reassured in their normalcy by the guys they hang with who are just like they are, by the online communities of guys just like them. The girls are more likely to have some insight into their own situation and to know that something is wrong—but they don't know what to do about it.

Not every girl is struggling. Some girls are turning out fine. They are confident but not narcissistic, self-assertive without being self-centered. They know who they are. They know their own strengths and weaknesses. They are comfortable in their own skin. So why are some girls doing so well while others are having a tough time? Success isn't random. Parents make a difference.

Unfortunately, parents with the best intentions may do their daughter little good if they don't understand their daughter's situation. These parents are sometimes bringing a 1990s solution to a twenty-first-century problem. That's not going to work. The current era has created some girl-specific issues that didn't exist twenty or thirty years ago.

In the first part of this book, I will outline the four factors that I believe are putting girls at risk. In Chapter 1, I will talk about how our culture is pushing girls to present themselves sexually at earlier ages than ever before. We will see how the affirmation of the sexuality of women in the 1960s (a good thing) has led to the sexualization of girls (a bad thing). We will figure out what you and I, as parents, must do to help our daughters define themselves by who they *are* rather than by how they *look*.

In Chapter 2, we'll take up the questions raised by the growing dominance of social media in the lives of girls. While these girls may be hyperconnected with their peers, they are becoming disconnected from themselves. Again, the focus will be on what you and I as parents need to know, and do, to help our daughters to use these technologies appropriately.

There has never before been any culture in which girls have had so many opportunities and yet receive so little structured guidance. As a result, many girls fixate on one activity or one dimension of their lives: Being the top student. Being a star athlete. Being the girl who's really thin. In Chapter 3, we will hear the stories of these girls' dreams and obsessions, and we will learn how parents can determine whether their daughter's interest in sports or good grades or fitness is healthy or destructive—and how to intervene before a girl goes over the edge.

In Chapter 4, the focus shifts to toxins in the environment: in the lotions and creams your daughter puts on her skin, or in the food she eats and the beverages she drinks. We will consider evidence that those toxins may be contributing to some of the problems of accelerated girlhood discussed in the earlier chapters. In recent years, new evidence has emerged of the link between these toxins and anxiety, depression, and overweight.

In the final three chapters, I will share what I have learned over the past twenty years, meeting with parents and teachers and girls across North America and around the world, about how to nourish and nurture your daughter's mind, body, and spirit while helping her to become part of a larger community.

Parenting is an art, not a science. Although we can learn from happy, well-adjusted girls, the exact strategies that worked for those girls might not work for your daughter. But by sharing the stories of girls who prevailed alongside the stories of girls who struggled, my hope is that we can help our daughters become women who are happy, productive, and at ease in this new world.

chapter 1

first factor: sexual identity / sexualization

We are gradually penetrating the highest levels of the work force.
We get to go to college and play sports and be secretary of state. But
to look around, you'd think all any of us [girls] want to do is rip off
our clothes and shake it.

ARIEL LEVY[1]

A teenager who pretends to be an adult is still a teenager. If you
imagine that getting high at a party and sleeping around is going
to propel you into a state of full adulthood, that's like thinking that
dressing up as an Indian is going to make you an Indian. . . . It's a
really weird way of looking at life to want to become an adult by
imitating everything that is most catastrophic about adulthood.

MURIEL BARBERY[2]

Girls are getting sexier earlier. That's not a good thing.

Kathy has a fond memory of one particular Halloween from her childhood. "My grandmother came to America from Bavaria as a young girl. So one year when I was a little girl myself, trying to decide what I should be for Halloween, she suggested that I should dress up like a Bavarian immigrant girl. She spent a month sewing a genuine Bavarian dirndl for me.

She taught me how to wear it. My mom helped. Looking back, I can see that it was a chance for three generations—me, my mom, and her mom—to do something together. Grandma even taught me how to say *'ee be a bairishe maydl'*—'I'm a Bavarian girl.' I was so proud.

"When my daughter was ten, I told her that we could have a dirndl made for her Halloween costume just like the one I had worn. She looked at me like I was crazy. 'I *know* what I'm going as, Mom,' she said in this how-could-you-be-so-stupid tone of voice. She'd already picked out her costume at the party store. It was a French maid outfit, with fishnet pantyhose and a frilly miniskirt. This was an outfit marketed to ten-year-old girls. They even had it in smaller sizes, for even younger girls! Unbelievable. I told my daughter, 'No way.' She threw a fit. So we compromised on a cheerleader outfit.

"And here's what's weird," Kathy continued. "The boys' costumes haven't changed that much from what boys wore when I was little. When I was a girl, boys would dress up as Darth Vader or a Jedi knight or a Teenage Mutant Ninja Turtle. And they still do. But so many of the girls today, nine- and ten- and eleven-year-old girls, seem to feel as though they have to dress up in something really skanky. How come? I've never heard of a boy who wanted to dress up like a Chippendale's dancer."

It's not just Halloween. In many ways, our popular culture now pushes *elementary* school girls to dress and act today in ways that would have been pushing the envelope for *middle* school girls twenty years ago. Skintight leggings, camisoles, and midriff tops are now common dress for girls in third grade.

Girls who are dressing in camisoles and tight leggings prior to the onset of puberty are not expressing their sexuality. Prepubescent children do not have, and should not have, a sexual agenda to express. Dressing sexually in the absence of sexual desire is simply conformism. And it may create long-term problems. As Berkeley professor of psychology Stephen Hinshaw observes, "If girls pretend to be sexual before they really *are* sexual, they're going to find it much, much harder to connect to their own sexual feelings."[3]

There's been a big change in what's expected and what's acceptable. If a girl in 1995 came to school wearing skintight leggings, no skirt, and a midriff-baring top, she probably would have been told to go home and put on something decent. But girls today are bombarded with the notion that revealing your body is a valid means of self-expression, even a manifestation of girl power. As parents, we must reject the notion that girls have to reveal their bodies in order to empower themselves. Boys don't have to take off their clothes to empower themselves. Girls shouldn't either.

Sexuality is good, but *sexualization* is bad. Sexuality is about your identity as a woman or a man, about feeling sexual. That's a healthy part of being human, a healthy part of becoming an adult. But *sexualization* is about being an object for the pleasure of others, about being on display for others. Sexuality is about who you are. Sexualization is about how you look.

The American Psychological Association published a monograph about the sexualization of American girls.[4] The authors concluded that girls today are being pushed to wear "sexy" clothes at age nine and ten—well before these girls have any adult sexuality to express. The authors of the monograph observed that in our contemporary culture, "girls are encouraged to *look* sexy, yet they know little about what it *means* to be sexual, to have sexual desires, and to make rational and responsible decisions about pleasure and risk within intimate relationships that acknowledge their own desires."[5]

underage girls dancing in lingerie?

The video went viral in a hurry. According to *The Early Show*, one online version of the video received 2 million hits within a few days, and multiple versions were soon streaming from dozens of websites, although the copyright owner kept shutting them down as fast as they sprang up on YouTube.[6] The videos show five girls performing at a dance competition in Pomona, California. The girls are dancing a choreographed routine to Beyoncé's song "Single Ladies," wearing nothing but bras, hot pants, and knee-high stockings with black boots. They gyrate their hips, they kick their legs high, they do pelvic thrusting in unison.

But these girls are seven, eight, and nine years old.

Well, what's wrong with that?

Apparently nothing, according to some. The parents of two of the five girls went on national television to defend the dance. Melissa Presch, the mother of one of the Pomona Five, told *Inside Edition* that she was "shocked" that anybody would object to the routine.[7] *Inside Edition*'s Jim Moret asked Cory Miller, the father of another of the girls, whether the routine might perhaps be "overly sexualized." Mr. Miller said no, it's just "really high energy."

Pretending to be sexual when you're seven years old makes you an object on display for others. It's not who you really are. It's not healthy. As we will see, it sets up girls for depression, anxiety, and an unsatisfying sex life later. "Dare to bare!" is a common exhortation on Pinterest pages targeting girls and young women.[8] Where did this crazy idea come from, anyhow?

the mixed-up legacy of germaine greer

In 1970, the feminist writer Germaine Greer published her influential book *The Female Eunuch*. Greer's best seller dissected sexual roles from ancient times to the 1960s. She made a good case that throughout most of recorded history, in a wide variety of cultures all around the world, "good girls" have been portrayed as sexually naïve and lacking in sexual desire. In most of these traditional cultures, men are expected to be the experienced agents and initiators of sex, while women are supposed to be inexperienced and reluctant. In almost all of these cultures, girls are sheltered from the sexual attentions of boys until the girls are of marriageable age. Supposed exceptions to this rule, such as Margaret Mead's famous Samoan Islanders, turn out to be not so exceptional after all.[9]

A cultural anthropologist writing on this topic might reasonably ask, "If we see this pattern in so many cultures, then perhaps it has some adaptive value. Maybe it's there for some good reason. What value might such a cultural paradigm have?" But Greer, writing with the airy self-confidence that characterized so many writers (both female and male) in the 1960s and 1970s, disparages the notion that previous cultures might have anything worthwhile to teach us. Just because most cultures have done it this way doesn't mean that there might be any value in doing things that way. "The new assumption [should be] that everything that we may observe *could be otherwise*," she wrote.[10]

Greer's book was published five decades ago. Her main assertion—that female *modesty* is a consequence and manifestation of the patriarchy—has achieved the status of established fact in contemporary gender studies. The corollary—that female *immodesty* is a sign of liberation—is now widely accepted. Girls today are coming of age in a culture in which teenage girls strip off their clothes at the beach or compete in wet T-shirt contests for the amusement of teenage boys, or to win more followers on social media. What's especially weird about those competitions is that both the girls and the boys seem to believe that the girls' parading their unveiled bodies is somehow modern, hip, and contemporary.[11]

By chastising feminine modesty as a symptom of patriarchal oppression, Greer provided support to the idea that pole dancers are truly liberated women. Her argument became so intrinsic to contemporary feminism that many people today don't even know where it came from. If you hint at an objection to *Girls Gone Wild*, you may find yourself labeled as a reactionary who favors the patriarchy.

To be fair, there was a moment in second-wave feminism when card-carrying feminists dared to question whether liberated women should wear stiletto heels and skintight leggings. Gail Collins, a regular columnist for the *New York Times*, remembers that moment: "There was one minute back in the late 1960s when the women's movement tried to convince everyone that being liberated involved wearing sensible shoes.

It was not a success," she writes.[12] Germaine Greer's vision of feminism triumphed.

But that vision is out of sync with reality, because women's sexuality is simply different from men's. Many teenage boys can be sexually aroused just by looking at a picture of a naked woman whom they have never met. A photograph of a woman's genitals or breasts, omitting the face, can be exciting for some teenage boys. But very few teenage girls will be sexually aroused by a picture of the penis of a man whom they will never meet. A photograph of an erect penis is actually a turnoff for some girls.[13]

For boys and young men, sexuality is often the driving force behind a relationship. But for most girls and young women, it's usually the other way around: the relationship has to drive the sex—otherwise the sex won't be any good. The most fulfilling sexual experience for most teenage girls, and for most young women, is physical intimacy with someone with whom they have a meaningful and ongoing relationship. Those differences were not constructed by the patriarchy. The origins go much deeper than that.[14]

"dress like what?"

Ask an American girl wearing a midriff top with skintight leggings whether she really wants to dress like that. "Dress like what?" is the most common answer I have received. That's just how the cool girls dress. It's just how *normal* girls dress. After dozens of conversations like this, I realized that no other perspective seems real to them. Laura Kipnis, a professor at

Northwestern University, recently wrote about "the armies of young women tottering around the nightclub district of any American city in camisoles and stilettos every weekend night of the year even in the dead of winter (aren't they freezing?) because that's what sexiness looks like onscreen."[15] Choosing to wear an ankle-length skirt with matching blouse and cardigan, for example, is simply inconceivable. Exercising such a choice would open them to charges of being a prude, or simply being an alien visitor from another planet.

The same mentality applies to sexual intimacy itself. After a sixteen-year-old girl told me that she has provided oral sex for "maybe a dozen" guys, I asked her whether she enjoyed doing it.

"I don't know. It's OK, I guess. It's really no big deal," she said.

I'm not the only person who has heard girls talk like this. Dr. Stephen Hinshaw, former chair of the department of psychology at the University of California–Berkeley, describes a similar experience interviewing a young woman. He kept asking a girl named Randi whether she enjoys this kind of impersonal sexual activity, specifically providing oral sex to boys she doesn't know very well. "Randi seems more and more puzzled. It's almost as though I were asking her whether she enjoyed any of the individual drinks she had at the party. It's fun to drink, it's fun to get drunk, it's fun to hook up—or if it isn't . . . [if there is] a sense of, well, boredom, so what? Hooking up is what you do." Dr. Hinshaw concludes that many young women today are "likely to view sex as relatively joyless and impersonal, something that's part of frantic, drunken social activity rather than a source of pleasure, intimacy, or fulfillment."[16]

"it's no big deal"

Remember Avery, the girl I mentioned in the introduction, the girl who was obsessed with being slender and hot? Many girls like Avery are faking it. They don't even know that they're faking it, because they started faking it before they were old enough ever to have experienced from the inside the sexuality they are pretending to manifest. They are dressing to look hot, but most of the tween and teen girls who are wearing skintight leggings are not actually trying to lure boys into sex. Like most young people, they want attention. They want to feel special. They have figured out that one sure way to accomplish that is to look good in the eyes of the boys. The boys rush to compete for the favors of the pretty girl. The other girls notice that, so the status of the pretty girl goes up in the eyes of the other girls.

As a result, the girl wearing the skintight leggings can easily confuse her desire for attention with her desire for sex. She wears the sexy outfit and enjoys the attention she gets from the boys. Or she wears a T-shirt that says "yes, but not with u" or "Behind Every Great Girl . . . Is a Guy Checkin' Her Out." That's the image many tween and teen girls want to present: I'm sexy, I'm *potentially* sexually available, but I'm not a slut.

The mixed message here can create problems. Girls who dress in sexy outfits may eventually have to perform sexually or risk being labeled a tease or a prude. But they often don't feel the desire for intercourse. Hence the popularity of oral sex, with the girl servicing the boy. I have been stunned by the detached tone in which some girls describe oral sex. "It's no big deal" is the recurring refrain. A girl who knows how to give "good" oral sex can raise her status in the eyes of the boys, without risking pregnancy or even making eye contact.

I have talked with many girls and young women whose main sexual experience, from age fourteen onward, has been providing oral sex. One woman, age twenty, told me, "To be honest, I wouldn't mind if I never see another [penis] as long as I live." Many of these girls seem to believe that sex is a commodity that girls provide to boys. Some of them regard sexual intimacy—and especially giving oral sex to boys—as a chore, something you do more because you have to than because you really enjoy it.

In my book *Why Gender Matters*, I devoted a full chapter to research on why girls and boys engage in sexual intimacy. Researchers find that girls and boys approach sexual activity with different motivations. For teenage boys and young men, sex is often about obtaining relief from an urge that can be overwhelming. "It's just something I have to do sometimes. When I need sex, I can't think about anything else until I get it," one boy told me. Only a few teenage girls feel that kind of overwhelming need for a sexual outlet. Instead, providing a boy with a sexual outlet may give a girl the feeling of being wanted, desired, and somehow in control.

Even girls who insist that they enjoy sexual intimacy for its own sake often want the intimacy more than the sex. In a classic paper entitled "The Need or Wish to Be Held," Dr. Marc Hollender described how even young women who labeled themselves as sexually voracious actually craved the closeness—being held, being hugged. The sexual act was their way of getting that closeness.[17]

This is a fundamental difference between female sexuality and male sexuality. For many boys and young men, sex is primarily about achieving a sexual climax and release. For most girls and women, satisfying sex is about intimacy, being desired by someone you like, feeling loved. Orgasm is great, but for most girls and women, it's best when it comes in the context of closeness with a caring person. "Second-wave feminism accomplished sweeping, grand social change," writes Courtney Martin. Nevertheless, she observes, "we still can't be authentically sexual—only raunchy like our brothers or asexual like our mothers."[18] More than five decades after the sexual revolution of the 1960s, young women are still struggling to figure out what it means to be female and sexual in their own frame of reference.

Ignoring these gender differences doesn't help girls; it disadvantages them. I discussed this problem with Dr. Laura Irwin, professor of obstetrics and gynecology at the Medical College of Georgia. She told me about young women in their mid-to-late twenties who have come to see her, all with the same kind of question: "I'm twenty-seven years old," one woman told Dr. Irwin. "I've had sex with lots of different guys. But I've never had an orgasm. At least, I don't think I have. I would know if I had an orgasm, right? Is there something wrong with me?"

Dr. Irwin then proceeds to do a thorough evaluation. In each case, Dr. Irwin told me, she found nothing wrong with the woman's anatomy. "There's nothing wrong with you," she told this particular woman. "It's the men you've been with. They have no idea that 'sexual intercourse' is supposed to be intercourse *between* two individuals. These young men are basically using your body as an aid to masturbation. They do their business and then they're done. They don't have a clue about what you or other young women want or need."

beauty products for tweens . . . and younger

Once upon a time, it was unusual for nine-year-old girls to go to a beauty spa for a full facial, manicure, and pedicure. Not anymore. As Jessica Bennett wrote for *Newsweek*, "This, my friends, is the new normal: a generation that primps and dyes and pulls and shapes, younger and with more vigor. [Some] girls today are salon vets before they enter elementary school." As recently as 2005, the average age for first use of beauty products was age seventeen.[19] No longer. In the past fifteen years, a new market sector has emerged: salons and spas targeting girls between the ages of five and twelve. There's Sweet & Sassy, Girlz Time Boutique, Little Princess Spa, Sassy Princess Spa, Toadly Kool Me, the Seriously Spoiled Spa, the Klumsy Moose Girls Spa. According to the *New York Times*, 25 percent of the country's roughly twenty thousand spas now offer services for "young children."[20]

Birthdays are big business. Sweet & Sassy invites you to book "a fashionista runway party you'll never forget"—for your five-year-old.[21] Anna Solomon, a social worker, told Bennett that her eight-year-old daughter is "so into this stuff it's unbelievable. From the clothes to the hair to the nails, school is like number ten on [her] list of priorities."

In one study, researchers asked girls six to twelve years of age to draw pictures of girls who owned makeup and girls who did not, and then to describe their pictures. Girls who owned makeup were described as being more attractive, happier, and more popular than girls who did not own makeup. Or to put it more simply: Beauty = Good. Quoting Tolstoy, the authors wrote: "It is amazing how complete is the delusion that beauty is goodness."[22]

When I speak to parents on this topic and I advise them *not* to allow their nine-year-olds to go to the spa or to use makeup, I sometimes get pushback. "Why so much fuss?" one parent asked. "What's the harm in letting nine-year-old girls go to a spa?" Here's the harm: allowing a nine-year-old to spend half a day at a spa, worrying about which kind of makeup is best for her face, is another kind of self-objectification, another way of communicating to girls that what really matters most is how they *look* instead of who they *are.*

"will you love me forever?"

Fifty years ago, the lines were clearly drawn. "Good girls" didn't have sex before marriage—well, not until just a few months before marriage, perhaps. In the 1950s, the average age at first intercourse for young women was nineteen years, and the average age of marriage for young women was twenty.[23] Today a girl may commonly have her first sexual experience (including oral sex), at thirteen, fourteen, or fifteen years of age,[24] but she may not marry until her late twenties, if she marries at all. That means she may have a decade or more where she is a sexual agent outside of the context of a lifelong commitment. "Getting married to a guy without having sex with him first would be like buying a dress without trying it on first," a college woman told me. There has never previously been a culture in which young women have had so many years of unconstrained sexuality. In the long perspective of the past four thousand years of recorded human history, this is unprecedented.[25] Whether you view this development as good or bad depends on your personal values. What's clear is that girls today have more freedom and more choices, but less guidance from adults, than any generation of girls in history. Most girls are not getting the guidance they need to navigate this uncharted territory. Many don't have any applicable moral compass.

It's no longer clear to girls today what it means to be a "good girl" or even whether a girl would want to be "good." Consider one of the most basic questions of teenage behavior: Have you ever had sex?

year

Figure 1 shows how teenage girls and boys answered that question, from 1950 through 1999. Back in 1950, nearly two-thirds of boys reported having had sex, but fewer than one girl in six had had sex. The teenage boys were having sex either with the few "bad girls" their age or with older women, some of whom may have been paid sex workers. The proportion of boys getting some action actually declined slightly between 1950 and 1999. The proportion of girls roughly quadrupled.[26]

But the changes go even deeper than these numbers might suggest. Fifty years ago, girls were the gatekeepers for sexual activity. The boys had to at least pretend they liked the girl in order to get physical. Today, girls often engage in sexual activity with boys, particularly oral sex, without any promise of relationship.[27] Being hip, being cool, means not insisting on a romantic commitment prior to sexual intimacy. Being hip means being a guy as far as sex is concerned: sex with no strings attached. As Ariel Levy put it, with regard to female sexuality, "We are all Tarzan now, or at least we are all pretending to be."[28]

Fifty years ago, the dividing line between good girls and bad girls was clear. Good girls didn't have sex before marriage. Bad girls did. In that era, it was good to be a good girl and bad to be a bad girl. Today, Bad is the new Good. An issue of *Cosmopolitan* magazine had a banner on the cover, in large type: "Bad Girl Issue—For Sexy Bitches Only."[29]

The culture of fifty years ago encouraged romance without sex. Today's culture encourages sex without romance. For many girls, the result is profoundly depressing, literally. Pediatrician Meg Meeker, whom I mentioned in the introduction, has suggested that girls who engage in sex in their early teenage years are at higher risk for depression compared with girls in their peer group who don't. Dr. Meeker has gone so far as to assert that depression in teenage girls may often be a "sexually transmitted disease," by which she means that having sex may *cause* some girls to become depressed.[30] Researchers at the University of North Carolina–Chapel Hill have reported evidence that supports her idea. They found that girls who engage in sex are indeed more likely subsequently to become depressed. That's not true for boys.[31] Most boys aren't wracked with regret if they lose their virginity to the wrong person. But your daughter may be.

As journalist and author Laura Sessions Stepp observed, for girls, "losing your virginity is closing the door on childhood and stepping into adulthood. If you're not ready for it and do it anyway, it can feel 'like death,' as one young woman put it. You just want to put it behind you, except that you can't." Stepp has also observed that today's hook-up culture, free of commitment, is "gravy for guys." So, she asks, how much have women really won?[32]

There's the irony. In an era that preaches gender equity, young men today can have sex not merely without marriage but without any sort of romantic relationship. Most cultures in most times and most places have frowned on premarital intercourse. Our culture now expects it. Indeed, teenage girls today are often ashamed to admit that they are virgins, in much the same way that girls fifty years ago would have been ashamed to admit that they were *not* virgins.

This change has taken place with remarkable speed. When I was a teenager myself, forty-some years ago, Meat Loaf had a popular song titled "Paradise by the Dashboard Light." The song describes a teenage girl and boy getting hot and heavy in the front seat of a car. They are on the verge of vaginal intercourse, when the girl interrupts the action, saying:

> *Stop right there!*
> *I gotta know right now!*
> *Before we go any further!*
> *Do you love me?*
> *Will you love me forever?*
> *Do you need me?*
> *Will you never leave me?*
> *Will you make me so happy for the rest of my life?*
> *Will you take me away, will you make me your wife?*

I have played this song for teenagers all across the United States and Canada. They giggle when they hear the questions being asked in the song. But their giggles hide their underlying confusion. "It's obviously just a hook-up," one girl said. "Why is she making such a big deal about it? If she doesn't want to have sex, fine, no big deal. Why would she want the guy to marry her, I mean, that's really weird."

I explain that in ancient times—back in 1977, when this song was a hit—girls often wouldn't agree to go all the way without a promise of marriage.

"But why?" the girl insists. "Didn't they have birth control back then?"

Yes, they had birth control back then (and running water and television too), I explain. It wasn't about birth control. It was the idea that sex was something precious that even cool girls, like the girl in the song, wouldn't give away without a promise of a lifelong commitment.

"Lifelong," the girl mutters. "Weird."

I wrote an op-ed for the *Washington Post* about the growing confusion surrounding gender roles, the pressure girls feel to be sexual, feminine, and brilliant all at the same time.[33] One blogger objected to my article. She insisted that she saw no tension between wearing sexy clothes and being an excellent student. "We can be hot and still come out on top in the classroom," she wrote.[34]

Is she right? Does wearing sexy clothes not affect a girl's ability to be a top student?

"that swimsuit becomes you"

Barbara Fredrickson and her colleagues at the University of Michigan had a wacky idea for an experiment. They recruited college women and men, then randomly assigned each volunteer to wear either a bulky sweater or a swimsuit. The men wore swim trunks, and the women wore one-piece bathing suits. Each volunteer sat in a dressing room: no windows, no observers. Each volunteer was then asked to take a math quiz while sitting in the dressing room. Fredrickson and her team then compared how women wearing swimsuits performed on the quiz compared with women who were wearing bulky sweaters, and likewise for the men.

Figure 2 shows the results. The men who were wearing swim trunks did slightly better than the men who were wearing bulky sweaters. The women who were wearing one-piece

swimsuits did significantly worse than the women who were wearing bulky sweaters.[35] And remember, the women in this study were in a closed room with no windows and no observers. It's a good bet that this effect would have been even greater if the young women were in a classroom with young men.

"Self-objectification." That's the term Dr. Fredrickson and her colleagues used. They found that these women were objectifying themselves. Just wearing a swimsuit made these young women focus on their own bodies as objects to be evaluated and rated. That's distracting, not to mention degrading and dehumanizing. If your daughter goes to school wearing a midriff top and skintight leggings, she's putting herself in a situation similar to the swimsuit condition in Fredrickson's study. At some level, she's going to be thinking about and judging her own body when she ought to be thinking about geometry or Spanish grammar.

This is where you come in. Parents have to be willing to assert their authority. Parents have to be willing to overrule their daughter's decision regarding what she is wearing to school.

"But all the other girls are wearing it! And you should have seen what Ashley wore yesterday: skintight leggings and a clingy top. And nothing else," your daughter says.

"I'm sorry. I'm your parent, and I'm telling you that you can't wear that to school."

"What is *wrong* with you, you are so clueless, you are going to like totally *ruin* my whole *life*! I hate you!" your daughter screams.

You have to stand your ground. When your daughter goes to school wearing an outfit that is not as revealing as what some of the other girls are wearing, you can't expect her to say, "I chose to wear this outfit so that I can focus on my schoolwork rather than worrying about my appearance." It's not reasonable to expect any girl to say that today. But she *can* say, "My evil witch mom made me wear this ridiculous outfit."

You have to be willing to be the evil witch (or the evil wizard, if you're Dad).

Of course it's hard to ask your daughter to wear a modest outfit when "all" the other girls are wearing clingy tops and skintight leggings. A better solution may be to find a school where all the girls are expected to dress appropriately, or to work with other parents at your school to ensure that your school's dress code is sensible and that it is enforced. School uniforms can be helpful in this regard.

lesbian chic

Fifty years ago, the gay rights movement was mostly about men. Male homosexuality was in the news, for example with the Stonewall riot in 1969 and the film *Boys in the Band* in

1970. There were no similar iconic cultural events for lesbian or bisexual women in that era. Sex between women was not a prominent feature of American culture in the 1960s.

What a difference a generation makes. Today, girl-girl sexual intimacy is everywhere: on TV shows, in popular music, and online. When actress Megan Fox asserted that everyone is born bisexual, nothing she said was controversial; on the contrary, her interview had a politically correct ring to it.[36]

According to one nationwide survey conducted by researchers at Cornell University, the proportion of girls and women who have engaged in lesbian sex or had lesbian fantasies is now 14.5 percent. That's slightly more than one girl in seven. For boys and men, the proportion who have engaged in homosexual sex or had homosexual fantasies is 5.6 percent, less than half the proportion for females. Other surveys suggest that the proportion of girls and young women who identify as bisexual or lesbian today may range from 15 percent to 23 percent.[37]

What's going on?

And what does all this have to do with your daughter?

Point number one is that even straight girls are comfortable being physically intimate with other girls in ways that straight boys today are usually not comfortable with other boys. Two girls might snuggle under a blanket to watch a movie, or give each other hugs and kisses, but they'd think you're being silly if you interpreted that behavior as evidence of lesbian attraction. It is much less common in North America today to find two straight boys snuggling under a blanket to watch a movie.

Point number two is that sexual orientation is more fluid for girls than it is for guys. Let's suppose a seventeen-year-old male tells you he's 100 percent gay; he has no interest in sex with females. If you return ten years later and interview the same guy, chances are very high that he will still identify as a gay man. But that's not as true for females, whether they are lesbian, straight, or bisexual. Whatever her sexual orientation at age seventeen, there's a good chance that it may be different ten years later. If she's lesbian at age seventeen, she may be bisexual or straight ten years later. If she's straight or bisexual at age seventeen, she may be lesbian or bisexual ten years later. Psychologists call this "erotic plasticity."[38]

According to one of the leading investigators of sexual orientation in women, Professor Lisa Diamond, a straight woman may in some cases just be a woman who hasn't yet met the right woman.[39] When a woman finds her "soul mate" and her soul mate happens to be another woman—someone she can really open up to, share secrets with, be comfortable with—then that emotionally intimate relationship may become physically intimate as well.

Now we're getting close to understanding the relevance of all this to your daughter. Fifty years ago, girl-girl sexual intimacy was taboo. Now it's the stuff of number one hit songs[40] and reality TV: *The Bachelor* franchise had its first lesbian marriage proposal (which was accepted) in August 2019.[41] Lifting the taboo may have opened the door to girls discovering a different sexual orientation they would never have discovered in an earlier, more repressive era.

But here's the problem: What is genuine and what is fake? I have already mentioned how today's girls often confuse their desire for attention with their desire for sex. One mother told me how some of the sixth-grade girls will kiss other sixth-grade girls in front of the boys. The boys hoot and holler their approval, so the girls do it again, this time with some tongue action, to even louder applause. This mother was worried because she believes that if a girl pretends to be lesbian, she is more likely to explore lesbian sexuality. And Professor Diamond's research provides some support for that view.

I'm concerned that some girls might be pretending to be lesbian when they don't really feel lesbian sexual attraction. They're putting on a show for the boys. Ariel Levy heard similar stories in her interviews with teenage girls. "Definitely girls hook up with other girls because they know the guys will like it," according to one of the girls she interviewed. These girls think, "'Then the guys are going to want to hook up with me and give me a lot of attention' ... definitely. If they think a guy's going to like it, they'll do it."[42]

I am not suggesting that lesbian girls or bisexual girls should pretend to be straight. I am suggesting that our popular culture is pushing girls to put on a girl-girl show for the boys—a show that may not be in sync with who they really are.

"maybe men just don't satisfy"

One possible explanation for the increase in the visibility of bisexual or lesbian women may be that our culture now encourages bisexual and lesbian behavior for girls and young women—behaviors that were out-of-bounds two generations ago. But there's another possibility. I asked June, a young woman, why she thought that the visibility of lesbian and bisexual women has increased so much in recent years. She immediately answered, "Guys today just don't know how to satisfy a woman. The guys just want 'wham, bam, thank you, ma'am.' They don't care about building a relationship. Maybe girls who love other girls are more careful to nurture a relationship. Maybe the girls are less focused on the physical aspects."

I think June may be on to something. I have already mentioned how many young women describe their sexual encounters with young men as being joyless chores. Because both girls and boys are having sex several years earlier today than was the case fifty years ago, the boys are less mature themselves, and more egocentric. In addition, there has been a cultural shift, with boys today feeling less of an obligation to care about the girls. As I said earlier in this chapter, we have moved from a culture of dating to the culture of the hook-up. Popular music, particularly hip-hop and rap, often depicts sex as something that girls provide for boys, for the pleasure of boys, with girls subordinate to boys. This music affects the attitudes of both girls and boys. Girls and boys who listen to this music are more likely to agree with statements such as "sex is for guys."[43] Even in country-music videos, girls are usually on display for the guys, rarely vice versa.[44]

The growing influence of porn culture plays some role here as well. The majority of young men today will tell you that they visit online porn sites. Some of them will even enthusiastically describe to you the features of their favorite sites.[45] Given the choice between masturbating over online pornography and going out on a date with a real girl—that is to say, a girl who doesn't look like a porn star and who isn't wearing lingerie—more and more young men tell me that they prefer online porn. "Girls online are way better looking," one young man said to me. In an interview for *Rolling Stone* magazine, pop superstar John Mayer made a similar comment, boasting that he was "the new generation of masturbator"—that is, a man who *prefers* online pornography over actual sex with real women.[46] Mayer is himself handsome, wealthy, and popular. But this is the new normal for many young men, even for some superstars. More than a few young women have told me how their "boyfriends" have suggested that they shave their pubic hair so that they look more like porn stars. The lesbian subculture may seem like a welcome oasis of connection and caring in comparison with impersonal heterosexual sex. In other words, a growing proportion of girls may be choosing a bisexual or lesbian identity in part because the guys are such creeps.

We are *not* debating whether your daughter "should" or "should not" become a lesbian. The problem I see is that our culture is pushing girls into adopting a sexual identity—and to becoming sexual agents and sexual objects—too soon. And that's unhealthy, regardless of whether your daughter will ultimately be straight, bisexual, or lesbian.

before its time

The biblical Song of Songs is a love story—quite passionate and unbelievably explicit in the original Hebrew. Not once, not twice, but three separate times, the woman at the heart of the narrative gives a command to the other women in her circle: "I charge you, daughters of Jerusalem: *do not awaken love before its time.*"[47]

That's the key lesson to be learned from everything we have discussed here, from Halloween costumes to skintight leggings to bisexuality. *Do not awaken love before its time.* Girls today are being pushed to present a sexy façade, to put on a show for the boys, before they are ready to decide whether that's even something they want to do. The result too often is sexual confusion: they are alienated from their own sexuality.

Let girls have a chance to be girls. Don't push them to be women and sexual agents before they have had a chance to be girls for as long as they need to be.

chapter 2

second factor: social media

The way we live now, where we're forever sending off e-mail and texts, fielding cell phone calls: where we're no longer any one place but everywhere—and nowhere—at once.

JEFFREY EUGENIDES[1]

The most precious gift we can offer others is our presence.

THICH NHAT HANH[2]

Describe yourself in two words.

"Party animal" is how Caitlin answers that question. Fifteen years old, just starting tenth grade, Caitlin plans her life around parties. Getting invited to the cool parties. Then hopping from one party to the next. And most important of all, uploading photos to her various social media pages, illustrating her exploits at the various parties.[3]

I spoke with Caitlin and her mom, Karen, together. Karen says she doesn't mind her daughter's passion for parties. "As long as she's not drinking or doing drugs, and I know where she is, I really don't have a problem with all the parties," Karen says. "When I was in tenth grade, that was all I wanted to do. What bugs me is how obsessive she is about putting it all on her social media. It's like the whole point of the party for her is to upload a photo. She spends at least an hour every day, and more on weekends, editing photos for her social media."

"But you kept a diary, too, when you were my age," Caitlin interrupts. "You told me you used to spend hours writing in your diary."

"But that was private," Karen says. "I wasn't putting it on display."

"So how does that make it better than what I do?" Caitlin answers. "If you're going to spend so much time on yourself, why not share it with other people? It seems kind of weird to spend all that time writing about yourself, just for yourself."

"But you spend so much time on the pictures," Karen replies. "You're not even writing."

Caitlin gives a shrug and shakes her head with her eyes almost closed. It's a perfect "I don't expect you to understand" gesture. "They didn't *have* Instagram when you were growing up, remember? They didn't even have the *internet*," Caitlin says, with a mix of disdain and disbelief. "You didn't share photos online because you *couldn't*, not because you didn't want to."

Caitlin's argument might seem persuasive. But here's the problem: when tweens and teenagers write and post photos online, they are seeking to please/entertain/amuse/impress their friends. It's a kind of performance. When you are writing in your bedroom in a diary no one else will ever see, you can write whatever you want, at whatever length you want. You can explore your own thoughts and feelings through your writing. It's not a performance. It's just for you.

When you are performing, you are wearing a mask. You are trying to amuse or impress the audience. When your daughter is posting on social media, she may not be expressing what she really feels. She may instead be writing what she thinks will entertain or amaze her peers who read it. She might not even be aware of the difference. She may not realize that what she *says* she is feeling isn't what she actually *is* feeling. She subtly adjusts what she is writing to suit what she thinks her friends want to read. After a while, she may gradually become the girl she is pretending to be.

Or maybe not. I am encountering more and more girls who are well aware that the *persona* they are presenting on their social media is not genuine. They are creating a mask. They are marketing a brand. They are performing, putting on a show to amuse others. One of the most powerful of these stories was told by a young woman, Clara Dollar, when she was an undergraduate at New York University. She described how she spent eight years polishing her online brand via social media. In her online posts, she always flipped her hair to the right. She ate ice cream only out of mugs. She wore a black leather jacket. Her online persona was witty and creative, "always detached and never cheesy."

> That version of me got her start online as my social media persona, but over time (and I suppose for the sake of consistency), she bled off the screen and overtook my real-life personality, too. And once you master what is essentially an onstage performance of yourself, it can be hard to break character.
>
> And so it was a validation of sorts when Joe fell for her, the me in the leather jacket. He was brilliant, the funniest guy in our TV writing program, and my ideal cool counterpart. I could already see us on screen; we made sense.

Best of all, he thought he liked me more than I liked him, and that was perfect too, because it gave me the upper hand. I was above love, above emotional complication, dedicated to higher pursuits.

[But] the truth was that I wasn't removed at all. Over the many months we were together, as we went from being friends to more than friends, I had fallen for him completely. . . . But I was reluctant to change my character midseason and become someone who was more open and, God forbid, earnest about love. He had fallen for the cool, detached me, so that's who I remained. And he got bored.

Like an allergic reaction to becoming unloved, my Instagram account went into overdrive, all aimed at one audience member: Joe. . . . But he didn't like me, and each time he didn't, the heartache felt like a warm bullet exploding in my gut. . . . Day by day, hour by hour, my Instagram feed became more manic, nasty, and petulant. Posts that were once meant as romantic gestures became tiny, pixelated middle fingers.

A girl who follows me, with whom I've spoken only a handful of times, told me it was so "on brand." My brand, specifically: funny, carefree, unromantic, a realist.

I'm like the chief executive of my own company, so I'm familiar with my branding, but its success doesn't thrill me the way it used to. Instead of feeling validated by her comment, I felt deflated. I barely know this girl, and yet she knows me, knows my "brand," and I am overwhelmed by the desire to tell her that I am fake, that I am heartbroken . . . clinging to continuity has made my skin crawl and itch, as if I superglued a mask over my face. I thought every day about peeling back that mask, but I couldn't; the girl it represented was everywhere, and I feared that her insides were completely mechanized.

If you spend eight years building a house (no matter how uncomfortable or ugly it may be, no matter how impractical or poorly lit), it becomes nearly impossible to knock it down. That is about how long I put into building my social media presence, into becoming the cool girl I showcase on Instagram and Facebook.[4]

The pogo stick I was riding, made out of all my coolest, documented moments, upgraded itself to a jackhammer beneath me. I was bounding down the street, loudly drilling into everyone's head that I was unemotional and funny and that's all, folks! It got away from me. I became everything I was online, and that everything wasn't much.[5]

social media can make you sad

The more time kids spend on social media, the more likely they are to *become* depressed. That's true for both girls and boys, but it's a much bigger effect for girls than for boys.[6] How come?

Research suggests several reasons why girls may be more vulnerable than boys to the toxic effects of social media.[7] First, girls spend more *time* on social media than boys do, and girls are more *invested* in social media than boys are. The average boy spends more time playing video games than he does photoshopping his selfie for social media.[8] Boys report that playing video games is their favorite online activity, while girls report that playing video games is their *least* favorite activity. Social media ranks among girls' favorite online activities, while social media is boys' *least* favorite online activity.[9]

Second, girls use social media differently than boys do. Boys are more likely to post a photo where the emphasis is on something the boy has *done*; girls are more likely to post a photo where the emphasis is on how the girl *looks*.[10] If you don't like Jake's selfie showing off his big new trophy, he may not care. But if you don't like Sonya's selfie of her at the beach in her new bikini, she's more likely to take it personally.

Third, boys post a wider variety of their lived experience on their social media. A boy and a girl both get sick. They both throw up. The boy posts a photo of his own vomit on his social media. Girls hardly ever do that. Girls are less likely than boys to post the disgusting or yucky parts of their lives. Jason, looking at his friend Brett's vomit on Brett's social media, is unlikely to envy Brett or to want to be Brett. But Sonya, looking at Vanessa's cute puppy or Aisha having a great time at the party or Avery in her bikini at the beach, may understandably envy Vanessa or Aisha or Avery.

I am not suggesting that boys are immune to the toxic, envy- and depression- and anxiety-producing characteristics of social media. I myself have counseled teenage boys who are struggling with these issues. But I am saying that girls, on average, are more vulnerable than boys are to these toxic effects. (Boys are more susceptible than girls, on average, to the addictive characteristics of video games. That's a topic I explore at length in my book *Boys Adrift*.)

When I speak to parents about the dangers I see for teens in the new world of social media, some parents push back. "Kids need to be comfortable in the digital world," one father said to me. "This is the technology they will use at college and in the workplace. Why shouldn't my daughter develop her proficiency?"

For many parents, this father's comment seems reasonable. But this father is mistaken. Posting on social media is not the best way to develop skills that will be useful in the workplace. Emory University professor Mark Bauerlein reviewed the available research on this point, and he concludes that the writing teens do on social media "sticks to the lingo of teens— simple syntax, phonetic spelling, low diction—and actually grooves bad habits."[11] Professor Bauerlein found that spending time on social media "doesn't impart adult information; it crowds it out. . . . To prosper in the hard-and-fast cliques in the schoolyard, the fraternities, and the food court, teens and 20-year-olds must track the latest films, fads, gadgets, YouTube videos, and television shows."[12] Bauerlein concludes that "success in popular online youthworlds breeds incompetence in school and in the workplace."[13]

too hard, too soft, just right

The late psychologist Diana Baumrind spent most of her life studying what makes for good parenting. Over more than thirty years, she and her colleagues interviewed families, getting to know the parents and the children, so that they understood how those parents were raising their kids. Then they watched to see how those kids turned out.

Dr. Baumrind identified three basic parenting styles, which she called "authoritarian," "permissive," and "authoritative." I've always found it confusing that she used two similar words, "authoritarian" and "authoritative," to describe two very different parenting styles. Author Judith Rich Harris shares my confusion, so she refers to Baumrind's styles as

"Too Hard," "Too Soft," and "Just Right."[14] I will borrow Harris's nicknames here.

Authoritarian (Too Hard): This is the ultrastrict parent. Any deviation from the rules is penalized, sometimes with corporal punishment, regardless of any mitigating circumstances. This parent seldom shows love or affection to the child and is not reliably responsive to the child's needs. He or she may be hypercritical of the child's behavior and may make excessive and unrealistic demands.

Permissive (Too Soft): These are the laid-back parents, very good at expressing love and affection for their child, not so good at enforcing the rules.

Authoritative (Just Right): This parent is firm but not excessively rigid. Rules can bend to accommodate special circumstances. Though these parents communicate their love for their child, they also enforce the rules in a fair and consistent manner. Over Dr. Baumrind's three decades of research, she accumulated overwhelming evidence that the healthiest parenting style is the authoritative style: firm but not rigid, loving but not permissive. Most of us are striving to get it "just right": not too hard, not too soft.

Parenting is an art, not a science. You can't give Siri or Alexa the details of your situation to find out what the "Just Right" parent should do. Well, I suppose you could ask Siri or Alexa, but there's not much likelihood that the first answer given will be the right answer for your situation. Reasonable parents with good intentions may differ about what's "Just Right" in a particular situation. I find many parents who are striving to be "Just Right" parents in most areas but who make no effort to exercise parental authority over their child's use of twenty-first-century technology. These parents may not understand social media very well. Their children don't want them looking over their shoulder. Some parents feel that they are violating their daughter's privacy by watching what she's doing online.

How do you balance privacy concerns with safety concerns? How can you and I know what is "just right" with regard to social media? Or more generally, how are we supposed to figure out what's the best course of action in our role as parents? One way is to think back to the way our parents raised us. But that won't help when we're talking about social media. Kids didn't have smartphones when we were growing up. Social media, as we know social media today, didn't exist when we were growing up.

Another way is to look to our peers and neighbors. How are other parents handling these challenges? As a practicing physician, I can tell you: *don't do that*. Lots of parents are screwing up. Big time. Your neighbor doesn't know what to do any more than you do.

So what's a parent to do?

social media: more like food, or more like booze?

What should parents do regarding their kids' use of social media? Let's try to come up with some evidence-based guidelines. Broadly speaking, there are two ways of thinking about how kids (and grown-ups) use social media. One school of thought is that social media are like food. We all need it. But if you consume too much, or too little, you won't be healthy.

The opposing school of thought maintains that social media are more like booze. We know a lot about the association between alcohol consumption and health. Strict teetotalers are less healthy, on average, compared with people who drink in moderation. That may be because strict teetotalers are outliers: they may be socially isolated or otherwise on the margins of society. Or, alcohol may have some health benefit in low doses. But beyond a low level of consumption—at most two drinks a day—the risks of alcohol accumulate steadily and inexorably. Optimal consumption is not zero, but some amount slightly above zero.

These two schools of thought make different predictions about what we should find when we study teens' use of social media. The "more like food" prediction would be an inverted-U curve: bad outcomes at low usage and high usage, optimal outcomes with in-between usage. This is sometimes called the Goldilocks prediction: the best outcomes are associated with not-too-much, not-too-little, but just-right usage.

The "more like booze" prediction would be an asymmetric curve, with a little notch upward on the left—signifying that the best outcomes occur at low (but not zero) levels of use—and then a steady downward trend with increasing use. This is sometimes called the "dose-response" or "exposure-response" prediction: beyond a very low level of consumption, outcomes get continually worse with increasing exposure.

Figure 3 illustrates the differences between the two predictions.

Perri Klass, a pediatrician who writes regularly for the *New York Times,* has made up her mind about these two perspectives. Dr. Klass writes that "we should teach kids to think

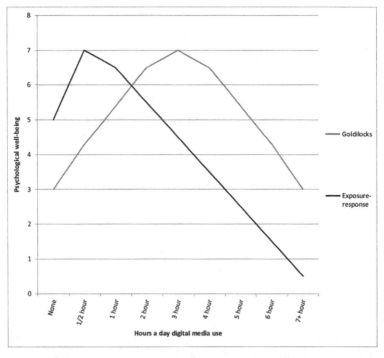

Figure 3: Two different predictions regarding the effects of social media. Reproduced by permission of Springer Nature.

of screens as something to handle in moderation, like food."[15] According to Dr. Klass, the right approach to social media is the Goldilocks approach: not too much, not too little, but just right. Use of the term "addiction" is not appropriate, according to Dr. Klass and her preferred experts. Someone who over-eats is not addicted to food. A girl who spends three hours a day on social media is not addicted to social media. She just needs some counseling and redirection.

There is another possibility in addition to the "Goldilocks" and "exposure-response" predictions: you could predict that social media has no effect on kids, period. The leading advocate of this position is Andrew Przybylski, professor at Oxford University in the United Kingdom and director of research at the Oxford Internet Institute. The notion that social media has *any* negative effect on kids is, according to Przybylski, nothing more than "a projection of our own fears."[16]

These three perspectives correspond to different predictions about what you will find when you actually look at how much time kids spend on social media and how well they are doing in terms of anxiety, depression, and other measures of well-being. Jean Twenge, a professor at San Diego State University and author of the book *iGen*, recognized that we have large, nationally representative datasets that correlate kids' use of social media with multiple measures of well-being, both from the United States and from the United Kingdom. She and her colleague Keith Campbell set out to study whether there was a relationship between the amount of time kids spend on social media and their psychological well-being.

Her findings were clear. In each of the datasets, the pattern of the data fit the exposure-response predictions perfectly. Psychological well-being was highest for kids with low levels of social media use, around thirty minutes a day. Beyond thirty to sixty minutes a day, psychological well-being declined. Two hours a day is worse than one hour a day. Three hours a day is worse than two hours a day, and so forth.[17]

I am not suggesting a complete ban on social media. I realize that for many girls, social media is now a major mechanism for communicating basic information such as where the party will be Saturday night. I have no objection to kids using social media to *facilitate* their social life in the real world. My concern is the growing proportion of kids who are using social media to *replace* their life in the real world, spending hours a day photoshopping their selfie for Instagram or perfecting a short video for TikTok. When you limit your daughter's time on social media to thirty minutes a day, or less, you enable her to use social media to facilitate her social life but make it less likely that her use of social media will grow into an addiction that *replaces* her social life. (Incidentally, although I used the word "daughter" in the previous sentence, these rules of course apply to your son as well. It's just that boys are more likely to be addicted to video games and less likely than their sisters to be addicted to social media. I address the issues of boys and video games in my book *Boys Adrift*.)

Some parents are reluctant to put limits on their daughter's use of social media, because they fear that their daughter will be ostracized or excluded if she has to cut back on her time online. In most cases, I have found that these fears are unfounded, as long as the girl makes clear that her parents are responsible for the new limits. It's easy for a girl to say, "I'm so sorry I didn't see your post yesterday; my evil parents have installed this horrible app that automatically logs me out of social media after twenty minutes, and I got logged out before I had a chance." It would be much harder for a girl to say, "I think it's more important for me to get a good night's sleep than to stay up late on social media, so I went to bed rather than look at your post." In most cases, girls will be OK with a friend who blames her lack of involvement in social media on limitations set by her parents. The other girls just say, "You know her—she has those crazy parents who put that ridiculous app on her phone."

In the previous paragraph, I twice said "in most cases." Gabriela, thirteen years old, was at a school where almost all the other girls were on social media, constantly talking about social media, sharing memes and dances they had found on social media, looking at their phones every available moment, including in the classroom. Her parents did not allow her to be on social media at all, and Gabriela was OK with that. (I do not recommend such a strict prohibition for most families, but it seems to be working for this family.) But it was difficult for Gabriela to be the *only* girl in her grade who wasn't on social media, who wasn't able to follow the conversations about social media, who couldn't understand the references to the latest memes or dances.

So Gabriela and her parents made the decision, as a family, to move to a different school, where the school leadership is more serious about not allowing kids to use phones in school, and where the school culture doesn't revolve around social media: a school where kids still hang out with other kids after school rather than rushing home to post something online. The parents found this school after listening to friends, visiting the school, and talking to unselected teens they encountered in the hallways on a full-day visit. And it has worked out well. Gabriela has flourished. "I really look forward now to car line, just hanging with the other kids waiting to be picked up," she told me. "At my old school, just about every other girl was looking through her social media, or texting, in car line. I was the weird kid because I didn't have a smartphone, just a basic phone to call my parents. At my new school, we all hang together, talk, or just chill. Nobody's on their phone. It's just way better."

Our society is performing a massive experiment on kids. Most American teens now are trying to figure out on their own, with little input from parents, how much time to spend online—while immersed in a teen culture that is all about being popular online—and how to structure a social life when their world is dominated by the new dynamics of social media. Many grown-ups haven't figured this out yet. Is it reasonable to expect teenagers to know how to limit and govern their use of social media when even some grown-ups are struggling and when the most popular kids are (usually) the kids who are fully invested in their online persona?

Let's say your thirteen-year-old daughter goes online to poke around some teen-friendly websites. She encounters a funny, friendly thirteen-year-old boy named Jake from Spokane. They exchange jokes. He shares a photo: sure enough, the photo shows a good-looking thirteen-year-old boy. Your daughter shares one of her photos. The boy sends another photo. Your daughter sends another photo back. The boy asks for something "fun." Your daughter knows what that means. It means something more revealing. She sends a topless photo. Why not? After all, that's what all the cool girls do.

Jake then demands more revealing and more explicit photos. Your daughter protests. Jake now makes it clear that he knows all about your daughter: he knows her favorite social media sites, the school she attends, even some of her passwords. If she doesn't send the photos he is demanding, he will post her topless photo to the school website. It turns out that "Jake" is not a thirteen-year-old boy in Spokane. He is a thirty-one-year-old man named Richard and living in New York. Or maybe a forty-year-old man in Texas. Or maybe a fifty-year-old man in Russia.

Adult men are posing as kids on sites that are popular with kids, tricking real kids into sharing photos, then blackmailing the kids for more explicit photos. Authorities call this "online sextortion." Six years ago, a federal clearinghouse documented just sixty such cases nationwide. Last year, they documented more than fifteen hundred, and they believe that figure may underestimate the true number by a factor of one hundred or more. The great majority of these cases are never reported. Even when they are, expensive computer forensics may be required to track down the offender. These men know how to hide their tracks. And there is currently no federal statute that clearly criminalizes such behavior. On the contrary, a 1994 federal law specifically protects websites from any liability. If local authorities can track down that young man in New York—or Texas, or Russia—then they may be able to bring charges to bear. But extradition issues can be problematic, and such cases are rarely a high priority for local law enforcement.[18]

When a thirteen-year-old is online with an adult who is masquerading as a kid, that's dangerous. It is not reasonable to expect the thirteen-year-old to recognize that the kid is not a kid and to outwit the adult. It is irresponsible for parents to put their kids in jeopardy in that way. As a *New York Times* article on this topic stated: "The solution many game developers and online safety experts return to is that parents need to know what their children are playing. . . . Sometimes it means monitoring the games as they are being played." But it's crazy to expect a parent to look over a kid's shoulder every moment the kid is playing. A good parental monitoring app is the only reasonable way to "monitor the games as they are being played." The app can do that.

limits

Once you decide that you should set limits on what your daughter is doing on social media, the question arises: How?

The first step is to sit down with your daughter and explain the rationale behind the limits. Start with extremes. Ten hours a day on social media would be too much, right? There wouldn't be enough time for sleep. Share the information in this chapter that provides evidence-based guidance: the evidence shows that social media use beyond thirty minutes a day increases the risk of bad outcomes. Explain that you want her to prioritize her real life—meeting friends in the real world, getting homework done, sports, music, hobbies, etc.—above performing on social media.

Explain, but don't negotiate. Don't yield to threats. One teenage girl was enraged when her parents announced that they were going to start limiting her to no more than thirty minutes a day on social media. "That is child abuse!" she shouted. "I'm going to call Child Protective Services!"

"Fine," her mom responded, and handed her the house phone. "Here's the phone."

Next: you will have to install monitoring software on every device your daughter uses to access the internet. The monitoring software will tell you, first, what sites your daughter is visiting. That's essential, because new sites are always emerging.

Most of these apps make it easy to limit the amount of time your daughter spends on any one particular site as well as the total amount of time online. And almost all of them will alert you if your daughter is engaging in the kind of interaction with "Jake" described above, the kind of interaction that can lead to sextortion.

"I don't think I need to install monitoring software," one father said during Q&A at one of my presentations. "Maybe that's a good choice for other parents. But my daughter gives me the password for her Instagram, and she's fine with me occasionally checking what she's doing. I think that installing parental monitoring software would be too intrusive."

I explained to this father the many problems with his approach. First of all, lots of kids have more than one Instagram account. They may have one "official" Instagram account for parental consumption, but the real action is happening on a "finsta"—a fake Instagram account. Second, kids are constantly moving between apps and changing the apps they use. If you are monitoring Instagram but your daughter is doing something inappropriate on TikTok, you may be the last to know. You might not even know that she is *on* TikTok. The monitoring software will show you every app she is using. Most leading monitoring apps make it easy to set time limits, app by app or by category. Of course, you can also block certain categories, such as pornography. All the leading apps allow you to customize controls for each child. It might be reasonable to allow your teenager twenty or thirty minutes a day on social media, but your eight-year-old should not be on social media at all.

Third problem with that dad's approach: as I mentioned above, you don't have the time to be clicking on all your kid's apps every day. Nor should you. The monitoring apps provide a dashboard on your own phone that shows you the highlights of how your daughter is spending her time. Most of the monitoring apps will also flag suspicious or inappropriate activity.

One word of warning about parental monitoring apps. Most of these apps do *not* work on iPhones or iPads or any Apple device. Any iPhone user can uninstall the app without administrator privileges, then reinstall the app after they've done whatever they don't want you to see.[19] You have no way of knowing what happened. My recommendation: junk the iPhone and get an Android or Google phone instead. (I have no affiliation with Android, Google, or any maker of mobile phone hardware or software.)

On Android and Google phones, these apps really do work. The app can show you every text and will flag suspicious texts, which you will see on a dashboard on your own phone.

In addition to setting limits on how much time your daughter spends on social media, you also need to limit *where* and *when* she uses her device. No devices in the bedroom after bedtime. Your daughter needs to *sleep* at night. If there's a phone in the bedroom, she may be tempted to check for a text at two in the morning. No phones in the bedroom! (And of course that goes for your son as well.)

I was speaking to a group of parents. One father said, "Dr. Sax, there's no need to remove the phone from my daughter's bedroom, because she always puts it on airplane mode when she goes to bed. That way she won't be awakened during the night, and she won't check her phone for a text during the night."

"How do you know that she *keeps* it on airplane mode?" I asked. "Do you go into her bedroom at midnight to check?"

Dad was clearly offended by my question. "Dr. Sax, you are suggesting that my daughter might lie to me. My daughter would *never* lie to me."

"Sir, I don't know you, and I don't know your daughter," I said. "But the research suggests that your daughter is more likely to lie to you, and to her mother, than to anyone else, because she doesn't want to disappoint you. She doesn't want to let you down. Don't put your daughter in that situation. Don't allow a phone in the bedroom after bedtime. At nine at night the very latest, you switch the phone off and you put the phone in the charger, which stays in the parents' bedroom."

Help your daughter to understand that real-life, face-to-face communication is more important than performing on social media. And practice what you preach. Declare the family dinner table to be an electronics-free zone: no use of the mobile phone allowed at the dinner table. Not for you either, Dad. Or you, Mom. No electronic devices at mealtime.

There are no guarantees in parenting. But if your daughter has years of practice doing it the right way, the odds that she will do it the right way at college are better than if she does not have that practice.

mean-girl cyberbully

Sometimes friends become enemies. Even the best of friends.

Remember Melissa and Jessica from the introduction? They were best friends starting in kindergarten. They were both friendly, athletic, and good students. Melissa was brunette and Jessica was blonde. Aside from that, they might have been clones. They liked to wear the same clothes, read the same books, and listen to the same music. "We were inseparable," Melissa told me. "We were more than best friends. We were way better than most sisters. We were like those identical twins you read about. We could read each other's minds. We didn't even need to talk. If somebody said something silly, we could just look at each other and then laugh hysterically for an hour."

It was a unique bond. Both girls agree that it lasted for an amazingly long time: from the end of kindergarten right through eighth grade.

Then in ninth grade, in a matter of days, it was over. Jessica suddenly developed an insatiable need to make new friends. Because Jessica and Melissa were so alike in so many ways, they occupied the same social niche. At some not-quite-conscious level, Jessica seems to have decided that there wasn't room for two athletic/smart/pretty girls in the same niche. Jessica turned on Melissa. It started with the usual sort of nastiness. Jessica hosted a huge party. She invited practically the whole class—but not Melissa. Next, Melissa found that she no longer had anyone to sit with at lunch. If she tried to sit with Jessica or with any of Jessica's friends—which now seemed to include most of the girls—they ignored her. None of the girls would speak to her. "It was like I wasn't even there," Melissa told me.

Then Jessica and her collaborators went online.[20] Girls posted mysterious comments on Melissa's Instagram like "We know what you did with Justin on Saturday." Justin was a boy Melissa barely knew, and she hadn't even seen Justin that

Saturday. Another comment read, "Melissa—please get help for your drinking problem. We care about you!" Melissa didn't have a drinking problem. She didn't drink. Jessica sent her an instant message late one evening that read, "I can't believe how nasty you are. I don't want to be friends with you anymore." Melissa immediately sent a message back: "What did I do? Why can't we talk?" She received no reply.

"It was relentless," Melissa recalls. Girls would text her, inviting her to nonexistent parties, or send her messages like "y r u so mean?" She would try to send a text message in reply, but she would receive only cursory responses such as DIKU—Do I know you?—or no message at all.

"By the middle of tenth grade, not a single girl at school would even talk to me," Melissa told me.

"How did you survive?" I asked.

"I started making friends with the boys," Melissa said. She had previously been shy around boys, preferring to hang with the girls. But "the boys were totally oblivious to what the girls were doing," she said. "They had no idea that the girls were boycotting me. They had no clue that they were rescuing me, but they rescued me." She started hanging out with the boys, even watching ESPN with them.

This made the girls even more malicious. The comments on Instagram grew more hateful. Melissa deleted her Instagram. Someone else, claiming to be her, created an Instagram page with her name on it. The cruel comments and photos proliferated—only now Melissa could no longer delete them. "It made me physically sick just to look at that page online and see all the horrible things they were saying about me. I couldn't stand to go to school. I couldn't make eye contact.

I could only wonder, 'Is this girl one of the girls who's been saying those awful things about me?'" There was no safe place.

Melissa and her parents spoke with the school's guidance counselor and the assistant principal. They said there was nothing they could do. There was no way to determine who was behind the cyberbullying, even though Melissa is sure to this day that Jessica was the ringleader. So Melissa arranged to take all her senior-year courses at the community college. "I just had to stop caring," she said.

One thing Melissa really needed, and didn't have, was an alternative community of girls and women who could have given her a hug and told her not to care what those mean girls were saying about her. Boys can't provide that. The boys Melissa had befriended were fine, but when a teenage boy hugs a teenage girl, a different message is being sent, and a girl needs to stay on her guard. What Melissa needed was another place where she could feel at home, where she could get a hug without any boy-girl sexual messaging poking in. (I will have more to say about alternative all-female communities in Chapter 7.)

There is nothing new about girls being mean to other girls. What's new is the technology that allows cyberbullies to inflict their pain 24-7. Bullying on social media differs from the bullying of previous generations in two important respects. First, it's nonstop with no escape. Even when your daughter is alone at home, she is still being victimized online, and she knows it. Her cell phone is buzzing with nasty texts whether she checks them or not. And she can't help wondering: Who's sending them?

The second difference: cyberbullying can be completely anonymous. Twenty years ago, if a girl wanted to spread rumors about another girl, everybody would know who was doing it. That knowledge constrained what the bully might say. If you got too nasty, your nastiness could reflect badly on you. But now you can pretend to be a boy who's just received sexual services from Leeanne, then post something crude and vicious about Leeanne online, and nobody will ever know that you are actually a girl who invented the whole story to make Leeanne look bad.

There's nothing illegal about one girl posting an anonymous note, allegedly from Jason, saying that another girl tried to give Jason a blow job but Jason laughed at her. As Montgomery County detective John Reinikka told the *Washington Post,* calling other girls names is not against the law. "It's so frustrating," he said. "There's nothing positive about [some of these sites]. Young girls are coming home crying."[21]

That's why you *must* know what is going on when your daughter is online. You have to know whether she is being bullied. You have to know whether she is a bully. Remember, even nice girls can be bullies.

the invention of alcohol—in 2018?

Imagine that alcohol had just been discovered a few years back. Imagine that the human race had existed for all these millennia, and then suddenly in 2018 somebody discovered how to ferment grapes to make wine. Within just a few years, let's imagine, beer and whiskey and gin were developed as well. It wouldn't take long to understand the risks of drunkenness. But it might not be immediately obvious that these beverages should generally be prohibited to fourteen-year-olds.

That's the situation we are in with regard to these new technologies. As reporter Emily Nussbaum observed after interviewing teenagers and young adults on these topics, "We are in the sticky center of a vast psychological experiment, one that's only just begun to show results. . . . We're living in frontier country right now. We can take guesses at the future, but it's hard to gauge the effects of a drug while you're still taking it."[22] We are going to learn the hard way what happens when kids are allowed to immerse themselves in this technology before their sense of self has had a chance to form.

Adult guidance is essential. To continue the analogy, some countries allow teenagers to drink alcoholic beverages, but most countries that allow sixteen-year-olds to drink permit this drinking only in the company of a parent or other responsible adult. And most such countries don't allow sixteen-year-olds to buy alcohol, only to drink alcohol that has been purchased by an adult. Maybe that tradition can provide a rough template for us. Maybe young teenagers who want to use these sites should do so only under the auspices of an adult who takes responsibility for them. This is a discussion that we, as parents, need to have. We haven't even begun.

In Chapter 1, we considered some of the evidence that more and more girls are confused or unsure about their sexual orientation. Now it's time to consider how social media interacts with, and often compounds, that confusion and that uncertainty. In Chapter 1, we discussed how girls often feel pushed to self-objectify, to focus on how they look to others instead of on who they are inside. That push now makes social media really toxic for many girls. As Dr. Hinshaw observed, social media exacerbates the "culture of self-objectification; girls turn themselves instantly into images, meant to be viewed from the outside in, actively inviting viewers to watch, judge, admire. Experience itself becomes an object to display."[23]

After the pop star Rihanna broke up with her boyfriend Chris Brown, someone—perhaps Brown or one of his allies—published naked photos that Rihanna had texted to Brown when they were a couple. Rihanna described the release of the photos as "humiliating" but later shrugged off the incident, saying, "If you don't send your boyfriend naked pictures [of yourself], then I feel bad for him."[24] For Rihanna, as for many other girls and young women today, sexting photos of yourself to your boyfriend is just part of the job description.

What is your daughter supposed to do when her girlfriend says, "Hey, how about I take pics of you taking your clothes off, and you take pics of me taking my clothes off, and we'll send the pics to our boyfriends?" What is your daughter supposed to say?

Make it easy for her to do the right thing. Install parental monitoring software on her phone that ensures every photo taken with her phone goes immediately to your phone, in real time. So when her girlfriend proposes taking seminaked photos, your daughter can respond, "I can't do that, because my evil parents have installed this horrible software on my phone, and they see every photo I take as soon as I take it! And if my parents find out that anybody else has taken photos of me with my clothes off, they will take my phone." We are living in a culture that promotes self-objectification for girls. You have to be willing to take the blame in order to safeguard your daughter.

A teenage girl I know was asked by her girlfriend to engage in the scenario I just described: they would each take pictures of each other taking off their blouse and skirt and send the photos to their boyfriends. The girl I know said she couldn't take such pictures because of the parental monitoring app her parents had installed on her phone. The girl who had *proposed* the striptease then said, "Wow, I wish my parents cared about me that much. They have no idea what I do with my phone." And the striptease did not happen, although the girls could easily have used the other girl's phone, which had no monitoring software installed. The striptease didn't happen, I think, because neither girl really wanted to do it. The fact that the one girl had a parental monitoring app installed on her phone gave *both* girls an excuse not to do it.

Most girls get no great pleasure out of sharing explicit photos of themselves. In one study, researchers asked high school students how they felt when friends asked them to share explicit photos of themselves. Girls were nine times more likely than boys to say that such requests bothered them "a great deal." Boys were five times more likely than girls to say that such requests bothered them "not at all."[25] It's not unusual to find a high school boy who gets a genuine thrill out of taking a photo of his own erect penis and sending that photo to a girl he knows. Very few girls get a comparable thrill from taking a photo of their own private parts and sending the photo to a boy.

When I tell parents that they shouldn't allow their daughters to share such photos, some disagree. They say to me, "Who am I to tell her not to, if that's what she wants to do?" Those parents need to understand that in most cases, the girl who is sharing that explicit photo doesn't really want to. She's sharing the photo because she feels like she *has* to, in order to remain popular, in order to be cool, but not because she really *wants* to.

So what's a parent to do with regard to girls' use of social media? I've been wrestling with these issues for more than ten years now, ever since I wrote the first edition of *Girls on the Edge.* I've listened to girls. I have counseled their parents. I've heard the parents' stories of what works and what doesn't seem to work. I acknowledge that every one of us, as a parent, has a hard choice to make here. On the one hand, if you install parental monitoring software, your daughter may well say, "Don't you trust me? If you trusted me, you wouldn't install this software." On the other hand, I have seen firsthand how easily girls' lives can be derailed, with permanent consequences, when parents step back.

I was doing a presentation for parents at a school. During Q&A, one mother said, "Dr. Sax, there is no way that I am going to install any kind of monitoring software on my daughter's phone. I respect my daughter's privacy. If she doesn't want me to see her photos, that's fine with me. I don't *want* to see her photos if she doesn't want me to see her photos. I respect her privacy."

I gently suggested to this mom that one important lesson she needs to teach her daughter is that there is no such thing as privacy to any photo that is shared electronically. Privacy is great. If your daughter wants to share a photo privately, here's what she needs to do: Print the photo out on photo paper. Go over to her friend's house and show the photo to her friend. Then put the photo in a shredder. That's privacy.

To illustrate this point, I have found it useful to share the story of the world's richest man, Jeff Bezos. Mr. Bezos shared private photos of himself with his girlfriend, Lauren Sanchez. But the photos did not remain private. Instead, Mr. Bezos was humiliated when the photos turned up in a front-page story for the *National Enquirer*.

How did the photos become unprivate? Federal prosecutors have evidence that Lauren Sanchez shared the photos with her brother Michael, who then sold them to the *Enquirer* for $200,000.[26] But for our purposes, the details of how the photos became public don't really matter. The take-home message is that if the world's richest man, who certainly understands the internet (Bezos invented Amazon, remember?), can't protect the privacy of his photos, then neither can your daughter.

There is also a growing awareness of how often jilted boyfriends engage in "revenge porn." Logan and Sonya are boyfriend/girlfriend. Logan asks Sonya to send him some photos of her wearing a bra and panties, or less. He promises that he will never share the photos with anybody, ever. So she sends him the photos. A few weeks later, she dumps him. He posts her photos online, with her true name beneath each photo. It's extremely easy to do this anonymously. Actually, Logan created a fake Instagram account *in Sonya's name* to make it look as though Sonya was sharing the photos herself. In a matter of days, the photos had received thousands of views and had been reposted on other sites.

Sonya was sure that Logan was behind the fake Instagram account. But she couldn't prove it. Those photos are still out there. If you Google Sonya's name—with "safe search" turned off—those photos will come up as one of the top hits. (Of course, her real name isn't Sonya.)

"Revenge porn" is already illegal in forty-six states, but successful prosecutions are rare.[27] A boy can buy a cheap "burner phone," create a fake Instagram account from that phone, post the photos using that phone, then throw the phone in the nearest dumpster. For less than $100, he's ruined a girl's life. The girl may suspect him, but proving that he is the guilty party—with evidence sufficient to meet the "beyond a reasonable doubt" standard in a criminal court—is another matter. In one survey, 51 percent of revenge porn victims reported considering suicide.[28]

Don't put your daughter in that situation. Explain that girls today find themselves in a toxic culture, a culture in which it's easy for a boy to destroy a girl's life and difficult, if not impossible, for the girl to fight back. The parental monitoring software gives your daughter an excuse to say no.

your daughter the (micro)celebrity

Columnist Clive Thompson says that we have entered the age of "microcelebrity." When real celebrities like Angelina Jolie or Reese Witherspoon go to a party, they know that somebody may take their photograph. They know that the photograph may appear within a matter of minutes online. They know that if they say something dumb, someone at the party might call them out on social media. These celebrities know they have to be careful about what they say and about how they look. They know that they must always be on their guard.

Girls nowadays learn that they must exercise much the same caution. As Nussbaum wrote in her interview with some of these blogger girls, the girls have "to be constantly aware that anything you say can and will be used against you." Nussbaum observes that these girls, just like real celebrities and like politicians, must "learn to parse each sentence they form, unsure whether it will be ignored or redound into sudden notoriety. In essence, every young person [on social media] has become, in the literal sense, a public figure. And so they have adopted the skills that celebrities learn in order not to go crazy."[29] Watch what you say. Be witty—but don't offend your friends. Be cute—but not skanky. Be spontaneous—but not stupid. And if you make a single mistake, it could go online and stay there, forever.

Thompson writes that "we're learning to live in front of a crowd." That's precisely the problem. The strain of living in front of a crowd 24-7, 365 days a year, is what causes real celebrities to fall apart. Remember Britney Spears shaving her head and attacking that car with an umbrella? Spears was twenty-five years old at the time. She wasn't a teenager. She was (or was supposed to be) a mature adult. She was the mother of two children.

How much harder is it for teenagers? When today's teenage girls go to a party, Thompson says, "they make sure they're dressed for their close-up—because there *will* be photos, and those photos *will* end up online. In managing their Web presence, they understand the impact of logos, images, and fonts."[30] But do they? Is the average teenage girl better able to manage her web "brand" than, say, Britney Spears at age twenty-five? *Should* she be? Should we be expecting teenage girls to manage their "brand" with the slick sophistication of a public relations professional?

Many girls are trying their best. That's part of the problem. Theresa Senft teaches media studies and was one of the first to investigate this phenomenon of microcelebrity. "People are using the same techniques employed on Madison Avenue to manage their personal lives," says Senft. "Humans are getting corporatized."[31]

That's what concerns me. It's one thing for an adult woman who has chosen the life of a celebrity to use slick filters to promote herself to those watching. But we are talking about tween girls and teenage girls. These girls are not yet adults. They are packaging a product—their own self—that has not yet had a chance to develop.

In the previous chapter we discussed how girls are being pushed to present a sexual identity before their sexual identity has been formed. As a result, many girls are confused about who they are sexually. Social media is pushing a similar process but with respect to the sense of self, who you are as a person.

Every child and every teenager needs to have a "sense of place."[32] They need to know where they came from, where they are, and where they want to go. Tweens and teens who get sucked into the world of social media will find it harder to acquire that sense of place. Instead of feeling at home with who they are, they will try to corporatize their image, to make their brand slick and cool. Even adult celebrities have trouble keeping themselves straight in their own heads, distinguishing who they really are from who their publicity people say they are. And those are the grown-ups.

It's all happening way too early in the lives of these girls. The end result of both these factors—confused sexual identity and the claustrophobic world of social media—is girls who don't know who they are. Because they don't know who they are, they are all too ready to seize anything real to define themselves: something tangible and solid and sharp. Even if it's a razor blade they use to cut themselves. Or a bottle of gin. Or a finger down the throat. Or a straight-A report card combined with an incredible list of extracurriculars.

Obsessions.

chapter 3

---

third factor: dreams and obsessions

One of the trademark perfect-girl talents is this ability to ignore and overcome the body's weakness in pursuit of a goal. We quickly condition ourselves to tune out our own internal signals, our aches and pains, our hungers, and tune up our plans, our determination, our control. What works in the short term, however, eventually leads to burnout.

COURTNEY MARTIN[1]

thinspiration

I first met Lauren while I was doing a medical consultation on the psychiatric ward. She was fourteen years old. She looked as though she were made out of translucent porcelain. She spoke softly, as though she might crack into pieces if she raised her voice. Lauren, who was five foot five inches tall, had been hospitalized when her weight dropped to eighty-seven pounds.

Lauren and I shared an interest in Japanese language and history, so it was easy for us to talk. "The Japanese are so disciplined," she said. "I really admire that." When I asked about her other interests—friends, hobbies—she smiled a Mona Lisa smile, as though she had a secret no one else could ever know. "I guess I don't really need them," she said. "I used to, but I'm way past that now."

Lauren told me that she and the other girls used to compare themselves to see who was thinner. But soon after her twelfth birthday, something had kicked in. "I just—I discovered that I could turn on this tremendous willpower, like pushing a button."

"Like pushing a button?" I asked.

She nodded. "All of a sudden, it felt good not to eat," she said.

"I don't understand," I said. "When I'm hungry, I want to eat."

Lauren gave me that smile again, and a little shrug. "When I haven't eaten for a while, my mind gets really clear. I stop caring about what the other girls think or what the boys say. I just feel calm and relaxed and at peace."

Calm and relaxed and at peace. What can I say to that? Who wouldn't want to be calm and relaxed and at peace?

There have been many useful books written about eating disorders. What's missing from many of those books is an awareness that eating disorders are just one manifestation of a larger problem affecting girls and young women today. As Courtney Martin observed in her book *Perfect Girls, Starving Daughters,* "Eating disorders are more extreme versions of what nearly every girl and woman faces on a daily basis—a preoccupation with what they put in their mouths and how it affects the shape and size of their bodies. . . . Almost every girl I know lives as if how she feels about her body is representative of how she feels about everything else. It doesn't matter how successful or in love or at peace she is in the rest of her life, if she feels overweight, she is unhappy."[2] If you conquer that fear by becoming thin, really thin, then maybe at least that part of the anxiety might go away.

For some girls, like Lauren, the anxiety really does go away. The popular notion that most anorexics are unhappy is false, in my experience. I have met a number of anorexic girls who seemed genuinely happy—in an odd, ghostly sort of way—when they were concentration-camp skinny. After those girls were put on medications and/or force-fed in order to gain weight, they seemed less happy. Healthier, certainly, but not happier. Part of that might have to do with loss of control: nobody likes to be force-fed. Nobody likes to be compelled to take medication. But another part of the loss of happiness I have seen some anorexics experience as they go through treatment is that they lose their sense of self. The anorexic girl may have come to define herself as the thin girl, the girl who has actually accomplished what the other girls talk about but never achieve. Take that accomplishment away from her, and she doesn't know who she is.

There has been an explosion in the number of websites that are collectively termed "pro-ana"—sites that unapologetically promote anorexia.[3] According to the creators of these websites, anorexia is a lifestyle choice, not a psychiatric disorder. These sites are filled with photos of ultrathin girls and young women, glamorizing anorexia. In addition to photos, these girls share motivating quotes that they call "thinspiration." Here's a sample:

- "Other girls will want to look like me and look up to me."
- "I can run on sheer mind power alone."

- "Self-denial shows strong willpower."
- "Thin people look good in *any* kind of clothes."

Doug Bunnell, PhD, an advisor to the National Eating Disorders Association, is alarmed by these websites. "Imagine if there were web sites encouraging people not to get treatment for cancer, or celebrating how great it is to have diabetes," he says. These sites "promote a myth that eating disorders are choices, rather than a physical and mental illness." He adds that they "are really damaging. Patients are . . . encouraged to stay ill by these web sites."[4]

How can you tell whether your daughter might be at risk for developing an eating disorder or might already have one? I have listed some clues below. If even one of these is true of your daughter, then I would encourage you to schedule an evaluation with a qualified professional. Here's the list:

- Your daughter is obsessed with dieting even though she's not overweight.
- She is preoccupied with food and cooking: for example, she makes a batch of chocolate brownies from scratch but then won't eat any.
- She insists that she's not hungry, even when she hasn't eaten all day.
- Her hair is falling out.
- Her resting heartbeat is less than sixty beats per minute, although she's not an athlete.
- Her menstrual periods stop.
- She complains that the room is cold when it's not.

This last clue merits some additional comment. If your daughter complains that she feels cold when nobody else feels cold, then she should be evaluated by a physician. That symptom can be a sign of a low thyroid condition as well as anorexia. Anyone who has worked with anorexic girls knows that they like to wear layers of clothes: a sweater on top of a blouse on top of a T-shirt. Though some counselors claim that these girls do this in order to hide how skinny they are, in my experience these girls are wearing layers of clothing mainly because they feel cold. As humans, we rely on our subcutaneous fat to help keep us warm. Once that fat is gone, the world's a cold place.

How different is anorexia from bulimia? The traditional distinction is that while anorexics engage in fasting or extremely low-calorie eating in order to lose weight, bulimics eat normal amounts, or even binge, and then make themselves throw up. Twenty years ago, it was common to pigeon-hole anorexic girls in one category and bulimic girls in another. Anorexic girls were supposedly hyperachieving skinny loners, whereas bulimic girls were gregarious average-weight girls who were terrified of gaining weight. Although some girls do fit these stereotypes, there is growing awareness that many girls who are obsessed with their weight and have unhealthy eating habits may not fit neatly into either category. And girls can shift categories over time. Girls who are anorexic this year may become bulimic next year. When researchers followed one group of 216 girls and young women for seven years, they found that more than half the anorexic girls subsequently went on to have problems with bulimia or binge eating.[5] (Binge-eating disorder refers to individuals who engage in binge eating, which they later regret, but who do not then make themselves vomit.)

If you think your daughter may be struggling with an eating disorder, remember that successful treatment of anorexia has to include much more than just gaining weight. Likewise, treating bulimia involves more than stopping the purging. The key to lasting success in treating eating disorders is for your daughter to develop an authentic sense of self that doesn't depend on how she looks or how much she weighs.

I have found that anorexia is a paradigm for many other problems that I see and hear about so often now in girls and young women. In each case, the girl seizes on one aspect of her identity—her weight, or her grades, or her sports—and she focuses on it to the exclusion of everything else. Her life is out of balance, but she doesn't care as long as she achieves her goal in that one realm: Her dream. Her obsession.

"running helps me relax"

Chloe always enjoyed sports. Even as a little girl, she loved to chase the other kids around the playground or to be chased. She was on MSI, the Montgomery County (Maryland) after-school soccer program, beginning in second grade. She quit soccer three years later, at age ten, when the coach yelled at her to stop hogging the ball. She tried softball but never really cared for it.

Her private school offered competitive track beginning in seventh grade. Chloe signed up. Almost immediately, something connected. Chloe wasn't the fastest member of the team, but she was the most motivated. She soon discovered that her motivation paid off for the longer-distance events such as the eight-hundred-meter race. "I'll never be the fastest in the sprints, because I wasn't born to be a sprinter," she explained to me. "But the long-distance events are all about training and hard work. The girl who trains the hardest can win in the long-distance events."

Chloe soon proved how true that was. Even as a seventh grader, she was competitive in the eight-hundred-meter. At her first meet as an eighth grader, she came in third. At the next meet, she won the event. "That was such a high," she told me later. "It was the first time I won. My first victory. I felt like I was queen of the world. My parents told me how great I was. Even Coach said something nice, which doesn't happen very often. But I didn't really need it. I *knew* how great I was. After that, I got serious about running."

Chloe was soon running almost every day, between fifteen and twenty miles a week, while she was still in eighth grade. Her parents brought her to see me when she started complaining of shin splints. I explained to Chloe how and why shin splints develop. "You're accelerating your training faster than your legs can handle," I said. "It's great to be serious about your running, but you need to build up more slowly. Take two weeks off, then start back up at one mile a day, and no more than five miles per week. From that point on you want to build up gradually."

"Five miles per *week*?" Chloe said. "Can't you just give me something for the pain?"

"Pain is your body's way of telling you that you're overdoing it," I replied. "You don't want to cover up the pain. You want to listen to it. Get rid of the *cause* of the pain."

"But I'll get out of shape. I'll turn into a blob!" Chloe protested.

"Go swimming," I said. (Chloe's school has an indoor swimming pool.) "You can swim as much as you want to. Swimming will keep your fitness level up, and it's great cross-training for runners. It's December. Take two weeks off from your running, swim at the pool as much as you can. Then start your five-mile-a-week program in January, add one mile per week, and you'll be all set when track season starts in the spring."

Chloe agreed to do as I suggested. She threw herself into swimming. I learned later that she briefly considered becoming a long-distance swimmer. But when the weather warmed up she was back outside running, following the program I had set out for her. By April she was running fifteen miles a week.

In ninth grade, she started to lose her edge in the eight-hundred-meter. Her times were still good, but the other girls had caught up to her. So she switched to cross-country and much longer distances. That way her edge in motivation could still translate into victory.

The high school required yearly doctor visits for all athletes. When I met with Chloe the summer before tenth grade, she admitted to lots of pain: in her feet, her legs, her knees, and her lower back.

"Do you remember what I said to you, a long time ago, about how pain is your body's way of telling you that something is wrong?" I asked.

She remembered, but she didn't agree. "Working through the pain is what this sport is all about," she said. "That's what Coach says. Besides, running helps me relax."

I tried to talk to her about balance. It's great to be disciplined, to push yourself hard, to test your limits, I said. But when that drive squeezes everything else out of your life, it's not healthy. The dream has become an obsession. Many of Chloe's friendships had withered due to neglect. Her only friends now, she acknowledged, were the other kids on the track team. She had invested all her resources, both physical and emotional, in running.

For a teenager, that's life out of balance.

I'm not against girls competing hard in sports. In Chapter 6, I will discuss some of the benefits associated with competitive sports for girls. Girls' sports, done right, can really help girls to focus on who they *are* rather than on how they *look*. But sports can become an obsession for some girls, and when that happens you have to intervene—just as the parent of an anorexic girl has to intervene. You can't wait for your daughter to decide that she's too obsessed with sports, just as the parents of an anorexic girl shouldn't wait for their daughter to decide that she's too skinny. As Courtney Martin points out, there are many characteristics shared by the girl who's anorexic and the girl who is obsessed with her sport: "Overexercising, undereating, a reluctance to listen to the body's signals that it's tired, hurt, hungry. And the destination—the thin, muscular, perfect body—of the parade of scantily clad athletes also looks strangely similar. Athleticism was supposed to empower us, and in so many cases it has; but in others, it has created another giant cover-up."[6]

Chloe had a good relationship with both her parents. Her father often accompanied her jogging, although by the time she was in tenth grade he had to run as hard as he could in order to keep up with her. Dr. Margo Maine has seen many girls who are trying too hard to please their fathers through their sports. She finds that these girls are "exercising excessively, with their dads or independently, pushing their bodies to the point of exhaustion. They strive for a hard, lean body, believing that their dads will accept them if they achieve this. Often they pursue sports hoping to please their father rather than to fulfill any personal desires of their own."[7]

Courtney Martin shares the story of a young woman she knew named Heather, who had built her life around competitive cross-country running. Things were going fine until Heather literally started to fall apart. "Slowly but undeniably, Heather's body started to break down. She suffered from stress fractures, from fatigue, from a pulled hamstring. . . . Running was her entire identity, so when her coach recommended she take a couple of days off, it felt like a death sentence. Who was she if she wasn't maniacally circling the track or pounding through the woods around campus?"[8]

Female athletes are famously prone to the "athletic triad": (1) loss of the menstrual period associated with (2) disordered eating and (3) brittle bones. Teenage girls who exercise too much may throw their endocrine systems out of whack. Excessive exercise can lead to lower estrogen levels, which in turn can cause brittle bones and irregular or absent menstrual periods.[9]

The physical consequences for girls who exercise too much are important, but in my firsthand experience with teenage girls, trying to frighten them about the risks is not an effective strategy. Instead, you have to understand your daughter's motivations. Where is the hole in her soul that she is trying to fill?

In eleventh grade, Chloe came to see me again. This time the pain in her shin was much more severe and persistent than her shin splints had ever been. The diagnosis was easy: a tibial stress fracture. The MRI scan showed it clearly. Chloe's brittle bones, weakened by years of overexercising and undereating, had taken their revenge. The prescription was intolerably difficult: crutches. No weight-bearing on that leg. I told her that she would have to be off her feet for at least four weeks. Chloe was furious with me. Her parents were skeptical.

"We want to see an orthopedic surgeon," they said.

I gave them the names of several good surgeons. I even made a phone call to arrange for the specialist they chose to see Chloe the very next day. He concurred with my diagnosis, but he didn't agree with my recommendation of four weeks off her feet. He insisted that she would have to be off her feet for *eight* weeks.

Chloe wanted to get still another opinion, but at this point her parents had begun to understand the situation. Chloe's career as a long-distance runner was in jeopardy. More important, her sense of self was on the verge of a major crack-up. She had defined herself as a runner. If she wasn't able to run anymore, then who was she?

anorexia of the soul

Emily was the smart girl. She had never been the pretty girl, but that didn't bother her. Even in elementary school, she would shake her head in disgust when other girls would talk excitedly about outfits they wanted to buy.

She wasn't the popular girl, but that didn't bother her either. She had a few close friends, most of whom happened to be the children of recent immigrants: Emiko from Kyoto, Jaswinder from Bangalore, and Xiu Li from Shanghai. Beginning in eighth grade, the four of them would meet at one another's homes to study and to share their dreams of attending elite universities. Xiu Li wanted to go to Stanford. Jaswinder wanted to attend Harvard. Emiko wanted to go to either Oxford or Cambridge. Emily's sights were set on Princeton.

"Everybody talks about Harvard, but Princeton is actually more selective," Emily told her mom, Annette. A few weeks later, Annette asked me whether it was normal for a girl in ninth grade to know or care so much about college admissions. I told her I didn't think there was necessarily anything wrong with Emily being so interested in college admissions, as long as she was engaged in a healthy mix of different activities.

Annette answered, "She's a reporter for the school newspaper. She's also on the school yearbook, the debate team, and she's in the Spanish club."

"That's great, but what does she do for *fun*?" I asked.

Annette shrugged. "She's really busy with all her activities," she said.

Emily and her clique—Emiko, Jaswinder, and Xiu Li—dominated the top academic ranks in their grade. All of them were nearly straight-A students. Their friendship was closest when they were in ninth and tenth grades. In eleventh grade, they each became more competitive as college admissions became dominant in their minds. Although they remained friends, there could be only one valedictorian (Xiu Li eventually won that slot) and one editor of the school newspaper

(Jaswinder). Their friendship rekindled briefly when Emily, Jaswinder, and Xiu Li began attending the same SAT prep class together, and they would go out to a restaurant for a snack afterward. Emiko, who was being privately tutored for the SAT, joined them once or twice.

I was vaguely concerned about Emily throughout her high school years, although I didn't see her often. Her mother wasn't concerned in the slightest. On the contrary, she was proud. "I hear all these horror stories about other girls who are obsessed about their weight, or spending a zillion hours on social media online, or demanding the most expensive clothes—and I'm just so thankful that Emily has turned out so well. So sensible," Annette said to me.

I nodded, but I was thinking of the old proverb "Do not praise a day until it is over, or a sword until it has been tested, or a man until he is dead." A girl at age seventeen still has a long way to go.

Emily came in for her yearly physical at the beginning of her senior year. "So tell me, what do you do for fun?" I asked her.

She gave a snort. "I don't have *time* for fun," she said. "Between volunteering at the soup kitchen and taking four AP courses and writing for the newspaper and doing most of the layout and formatting for the yearbook, I'm lucky if I have time to sleep at night."

Jaswinder was accepted at Harvard, but each of the three girls in their group had to make do with a respectable second choice. Xiu Li was accepted at UCLA. Emiko was accepted at the University of Sheffield.

Emily's mom paged me through the answering service the evening that Emily got her letter from Princeton. "When she saw that it was a thin envelope, she burst into tears," Annette said. Annette sounded as though she were on the verge of tears herself. "Emily opened the letter and it was a rejection, not even a deferral or a waitlist. She kept saying to me, 'But I did *everything*! What more do they want?'" It was past midnight and Emily was still crying, Annette said. "She's shaking and shivering like she's cold."

I called in a prescription for Xanax, a nerve pill, to the twenty-four-hour pharmacy near their home. Emily could take one pill immediately and another in the morning. It was a Saturday, so she could stay home and grieve. Xanax can be addictive, so I called in just seven pills to tide her over the next few days. I told Annette that if Emily wanted a refill, she would need to come in and talk with me first.

At least in the academic realm, Emily appeared to be the perfect girl. But trying to be the perfect girl can be dangerous. As Anna Quindlen writes in her essay about trying to be perfect, the danger is likely to strike when you fail "at something at which you badly wanted to succeed. And sitting there, you will fall into the center of yourself. You will look for some core to sustain you. And if you have been perfect all your life . . . chances are excellent that there will be a black hole where that core ought to be."[10] Emily didn't fall apart, not completely, when she got the rejection letter from Princeton. But the black hole was lying in wait for her a few months down the road.

Emily had her friends and her parents fooled. She even had herself fooled. She had no idea how close she was to the edge. Her minor breakdown when she received the rejection letter from Princeton, and her major disintegration the following fall, came as a surprise not only to her family and friends but also to herself.

These girls "can present as models of competence and still lack a fundamental sense of who they are," writes psychotherapist Madeline Levine. "Psychologists call this the 'false self,' and it is highly correlated with a number of emotional problems" including depression and anxiety.[11] Emily had created a false sense of self. She had built her life around being "the smart girl"—but as she was to discover over the next seven months, that wasn't who she truly was. It wasn't even who she *wanted* to be.

The *New York Times* devoted front-page coverage to this topic in an article entitled "For Girls, It's Be Yourself, and Be Perfect Too." As the reporter, Sara Rimer, observed, these girls' "quest for the perfect résumé" conflicts with their search for a sense of who they really are. Rimer found

> girls by the dozen who are high achieving, ambitious, and confident.... Girls who do everything: Varsity sports. Student government. Theater. Community service.... But being an amazing girl often doesn't feel like enough these days when you're competing with all the other amazing girls around the country who are applying to the same elite colleges that you have been encouraged to aspire to practically all your life....There is something about the lives these girls lead—their jam-packed schedules, the amped-up multitasking, the focus on a narrow group of the nation's most selective colleges—that speaks of a profound anxiety.[12]

Rimer interviewed many of these "amazing girls" along with their parents. One mother expressed concern that the obsession with achievement could give rise to "anorexia of the soul." I think that's a powerful metaphor.

The problem isn't ambition or even perfectionism per se. Dr. Levine makes a useful distinction between healthy perfectionism—the drive to do better and be your best—and what she calls *maladaptive* perfectionism. "Maladaptive perfectionism is driven by an intense need to avoid failure and to appear flawless," Levine writes. "Maladaptive perfectionism hides deep-seated feelings of insecurity and vulnerability."[13] Levine believes that maladaptive perfectionism has its roots "in a demanding, critical, and conditional relationship with one's parents."

I don't agree with Levine that parents are always to blame. I have seen girls who are prototypes of the maladaptive perfectionism Levine describes whose parents are not at all demanding or critical. Instead, I think that the pressure often comes from the larger society—or more precisely, from the niche the girl has made for herself within the larger society, the niche of being "that amazing girl."

In any case, the notion of "perfectionism" doesn't quite get to the core of the issue. "Anorexia of the soul" comes closer. There is reason to believe that a similar dynamic underlies the growing number of girls who are abusing alcohol and the growing proportion of girls who are deliberately cutting themselves. It's a search for a sense of self, an attempt to relieve the anxiety that comes from the fear that there may be only a black hole at the core of your self. In some girls, like Emily, that search for a sense of identity can morph into a frantic and ultimately self-destructive perfectionism. In other girls it can become a relentless focus on sports, or on being thin.

Emily came to see me on Tuesday morning, a little more than seventy-two hours after her mother called me. Emily had told the receptionist she just needed a quick visit for a prescription refill. "Thanks for the Xanax. It was a lifesaver," she said. "I felt like I couldn't breathe. But half an hour after I took that pill, I was able to take a deep breath."

"I'm sorry to hear about Princeton," I said. "What's your plan now?"

Emily explained that she had been accepted to the University of Pennsylvania. "It wasn't my first choice, but it's an Ivy League school and it's got a strong premed program."

"You still want to be a doctor?" I asked.

"A trauma surgeon," she said. "Absolutely. I'm not going to give that up just because I didn't get into Princeton. You know, maybe it's not so bad that I didn't get in. I've heard that lots of snobby rich kids go there. Penn sounds more normal. And I'll probably be the smartest kid there."

I nodded.

The following November, Emily's mom called again. "Emily's used up all the Xanax you prescribed for her. Could you please call in a refill?"

I explained that I would need to speak with Emily directly. After all, she was eighteen now and away at college. Mom gave me her number.

Emily was polite when she answered her cell phone. "I'm sorry to bother you, Dr. Sax. I just need a refill on the Xanax."

"What's going on?" I asked.

Emily at first sounded composed as she explained how she had worked hard on an assignment in her philosophy class. "Compare and contrast Nietzsche and Kierkegaard" was the assignment. She read the textbook entries for each philosopher carefully, skimmed their Wikipedia entries, and looked up related essays at SparkNotes.com. She then wrote what she thought was a thorough twelve-page essay answering the question, being careful not to plagiarize the essays she had read online. She got a C. "I looked around to see what other kids got," Emily said. "I saw one A, mostly Bs. I didn't see anybody else who got a C. I was totally freaking out, thinking, 'What did I do wrong?' I went to meet with the instructor. He said that there was nothing original in my essay. He said I had just 'regurgitated' what was in the textbook. He seemed to enjoy telling me how awful my paper was.

"If it was only him, I could probably have blown it off, but I actually expected philosophy to be my easy class. Organic chemistry has been a total disaster. I don't understand it at all. I got a five on my AP exam in high school chemistry. How come I can't understand organic chemistry?"

"Organic chemistry is really tough," I said. "The concepts are so different from high school chemistry."

"Right now I barely have a passing grade in organic," she said. "I have something around a C-minus or a D-plus—" Suddenly her voice broke. "What—what am I going to do?" she said, and she began sobbing.

The crisis was about more than organic chemistry. It was existential. Emily was discovering that she wasn't as smart as she thought she was. Her sense of self, which was so dependent on being the smart girl, was collapsing.

I spent half an hour listening to her and talking with her. I asked her to promise me that she would see a counselor on campus, which she did. Just once.

Two weeks later, Emily dropped out of school and came home.

Emily's parents at first wanted to blame Penn, but the university was not at fault. Emily didn't belong at an elite, highly competitive university—but Emily didn't understand that until she got there. Emily's sense of self was based too narrowly on academic achievement—just as Lauren's was based on how much she weighed, and Chloe's was based on her speed in the eight-hundred-meter.

You have to help your daughter connect with who she is in a way that doesn't depend on what grades she gets, or how well she does in a track meet, or how much she weighs. I think Emily's parents might have had more of a clue what was happening if they had shown interest in something other than her academic achievement and her extracurricular activities. Ask your daughter questions like, "What do you like to do for fun?" If a girl answers that question, as Emily did, by saying that she doesn't have time for fun, that's a red flag.

Ask your daughter, "What three words describe you best right now?" If those words include "hyper" or "anxious" or "wired" or "sleepless" or something similar, dig deeper. Try to understand the source of your daughter's anxiety. Is she worried about something she thinks the other girls are saying about her? Is she worried about her grades? Is she worried about her weight? You need to know what keeps your daughter awake at night.

Be a good listener. Don't be in a hurry to make recommendations. Just nod your head, and keep your mouth shut until your daughter has had her say. As Levine observes, "When we

listen to our friends it is usually with the purpose of understanding their dilemmas, of helping them clarify how they feel,
and of letting them know that we care. We listen long enough
to know what it feels like to be in their shoes. Too often with
our children, we rush in and offer suggestions, propose alternatives, or solve problems."[14]

Emily's parents were astonished and horrified when she
returned home that November without even completing her
first semester. "How could you do that?" Annette asked.

"I'm not as smart as I thought I was," Emily answered.

"How can you say that?" her mom replied. "Maybe if you
had a tutor . . ."

"I don't want a tutor, Mom," Emily answered.* "What's
the point? Why should I go on pretending to be something
I'm not? Why should I kill myself trying to learn this stuff if
I'm going to be at the bottom of the class? Why should I waste
a hundred thousand dollars getting a degree in subjects I
hate?"

Defining yourself in terms of how you rank relative to others is always dangerous—and ultimately immature. It doesn't
matter whether the rank has to do with your grades, your
weight, or where you finished in the eight-hundred-meter
race. Becoming a mature adult means, among other things,
that you define yourself relative to your *own* potential, not relative to somebody else's standard. The well-meaning praise
and encouragement from her parents to "go for the dream" of

---

* This conversation is Emily's version. I never heard her parents' take on this
conversation. Emily's parents were angry with me after Emily decided to drop
out, because I would not cooperate with them in pushing Emily to return to her
university.

getting into Princeton all throughout middle school and high school actually helped to set her up for a fall.

Instead of encouraging Emily to put all her emotional investment into the dream of getting into Princeton, Emily's parents might have tried to help her broaden her horizons. Emily was focused on one dream, a dream based not on her own likes and dislikes but on impressing *other* people: getting into Princeton. Emily's parents might have tried to help her discover something she really enjoyed for its own sake. All through middle school and high school, Emily never really gave much thought to questions such as "What do I love to do?" without regard to whether that activity might be prestigious in the eyes of others.

Emily's parents wanted her to return to Penn, but Emily refused. Instead, she became a full-time volunteer at a sanctuary for abused farm animals. Working with the sheep and goats, a few cows, and a retired race horse, she began to find a new way back to herself.

Emily soon became friends with Carol, a middle-aged woman at the sanctuary. Carol took Emily under her wing and taught her how to work with the animals. "It's all about patience," Carol said. "These animals expect the worst of people because that's what they've experienced. You have to show them that people can be gentle and loving. You have to move slowly. Take one step toward the animal and then wait five minutes if you must. If you approach them too quickly, they may panic. You have to wait for them to be ready."

Emily was fascinated by Carol's calmness and focus. She wanted to find out Carol's secret. Eventually, Carol shared it with her: Carol had spent seven years as a Catholic nun, and she still meditated and prayed for an hour or more almost every day.

"I thought meditation was just something Buddhists did," Emily said.

The next week, Carol lent Emily two books by Thomas Merton: *The Seven Storey Mountain* and *The Seeds of Contemplation*. This was a completely new world for Emily. She devoured those books. The following week, Carol lent Emily her copy of Omer Englebert's biography of St. Francis of Assisi. Emily had never heard of St. Francis, but she was so inspired by his life that she started talking with Carol about possibly becoming Catholic herself.

Another fortysomething woman at the barn, Rachel, overheard Carol and Emily talking one afternoon and joined in their conversation. Rachel was a great fan of books about mindfulness, and she began sharing these books with Emily. Rachel suggested that the three of them meet for lunch one Friday at the Corner Café, a coffeehouse that was right next to my office in Montgomery County, Maryland, where patrons are welcome to linger around tables and chat for hours. The Friday lunch soon became a regular feature for the three women.

At this point, Emily told me, her parents were getting seriously annoyed. "The Catholic thing was amusing to them because they never took that seriously. But when I started talking about mindfulness, especially Friday afternoons when I came home after coffee with Rachel, my dad would get really steamed. 'You dropped out of college in order to become some kind of New Age hippie?' was the sort of thing he would say. He was really riled."

Her parents still didn't get it. They couldn't see any other standard of value besides earning a degree from a prestigious university and then landing a high-paying job. But Emily continued, and continues, to resist her parents' pressure. "I'm trying to figure out who I want to be rather than what would impress other people."

Will Emily ever earn a four-year college degree? I think she probably will, eventually. Emily would say that's not the most important thing. Meanwhile, she is taking courses at the local community college, one or two at a time, trying to figure out what she really enjoys.

She laughed when I asked her whether she still wants to be a trauma surgeon someday. "I don't think I ever really wanted to be one," she said. "That is just *so* not who I am. I can't stand the sight of blood! And I don't like to do anything in a hurry. I'd be a pretty pathetic trauma surgeon. I'll figure it out," she added. "I'm not in a rush anymore."

Emily was fortunate that she did finally connect with herself after less than one semester at the wrong university. Author Liz Funk shares the stories of many girls like Emily in her book *Supergirls Speak Out: Inside the Secret Crisis of Overachieving Girls*. Funk describes girls who don't discover until well into their college experience that they don't want to be the supergirl scholar they previously tried to be. As one young woman told Funk, "I didn't get into Yale, [so] now I'm a little bit like, 'Screw it.' I wasted high school studying to try to achieve something that clearly wasn't possible, and I'm not going to do that again for college."[15]

Other women don't hit the wall until their midtwenties. The years after college graduation, when the woman has landed her first job, are often the time when the existential crisis finally occurs. Psychologist Robin Stern says, "Sometimes there is just so much disparity between what young women are told to expect and what actually happens that they get disillusioned. The ones who blame themselves tend to get depressed."[16] The contrast between imagining yourself as the next Jennifer Lawrence, the next Billie Eilish, or the next Sheryl Sandberg and the reality of life for a twentysomething woman in the workplace can come as a shock.

As I said a moment ago, it's helpful to periodically ask your daughter some open-ended questions about herself: "Describe yourself in four sentences or less," that sort of thing. These questions don't have right or wrong answers. The point is to explore what the answers might mean. For example, if you ask your daughter to describe herself, she might give very concrete answers: "I'm tall. I'm thin. I'm really smart. And I hate sushi." Those answers are fine as far as they go, but they are superficial. They are great answers if your daughter is eight years old, not so great if she is seventeen. By age seventeen your daughter should have a sense of herself that is multidimensional. When I asked Emily that question after she started working at the animal refuge, she answered, "I really care a lot about animals, so I've thought about being a veterinarian. But veterinarians sometimes have to put animals down, and I couldn't do that. And I really don't care for the blood-and-guts aspect of being a vet. So I think I might prefer to run an animal shelter. But it would have to be a shelter like this one, where they never kill any of the animals." That's a good answer. It's substantive. It tells me something about who this girl is, not just her surface. As girls move from childhood through adolescence, the answer to "Tell me about yourself" should evolve from con-crete descriptors to more abstract ideas about what they want and how they see themselves now compared with their past and their future.

smashed

Alicia was thirteen years old when she took her first illicit drink.

According to the most recent report from the Centers for Disease Control (CDC), 37.9 percent of American high school girls now report drinking alcohol. Among high school girls who drink alcohol, more than half (54.6%) report binge drink-ing, which the CDC defines as drinking five or more drinks in a row in the past thirty days.[17]

Like her parents, I was astonished when we learned about Alicia's drinking problem. Nobody saw it coming—certainly not her parents or me. She was doing well in school, she was on the cheer squad, she had lots of friends. When I asked her about cheer squad and other school activities, though, she was dismissive. "Those are just things I *do*," she said. "That's not who I *am*." Alicia had come to define herself through her drink-ing. Being a drinker had become a core feature of her identity in her own mind. That made it much more difficult for her to stop. To paraphrase her earlier comment, with a twist, drinking wasn't just something she *did*; it had become part of who she *was*. Giving up drinking would mean giving up her sense of self.

Koren Zailckas began drinking at age fourteen, one year later than Alicia. In her memoir, *Smashed*, Zailckas describes how a teacher told her class about the rites, the *sacra*, in different cultures, to mark a girl's transition to adulthood. Koren wondered what her sacred rite, her *sacra*, would be. "I have been waiting for something sacred to present itself," she wrote. "Even though I haven't had sex yet, I know it can't be the sacred thing I am waiting for, either. For girls sex is seen as a fall, not a triumph. When word got out that Sara Dohart messed around with Trent Cooper in the athletics closet, he rose to the status of teen heartthrob, and she was called 'Sara Blows Hard' so often her parents had to put her in private school.... It only makes sense for the *sacra* to be the bottle."[18]

Unlike Alicia, who was always outgoing, Koren Zailckas was shy. She initially hoped that alcohol might help her to be more comfortable in groups, might help her true personality shine through. But she soon realized that drinking alcohol actually

makes me act *less* like myself. For all intents and purposes, it should make me more comfortable being regular old Koren . . . but instead I, too, conform to a beer-ad version of myself. I kick off my shoes and pirouette in the sand. I agree to drink beer from a funnel, even though I know the boy channeling it through will pour too fast, and I will end up wearing the thick tar of beer and wet sand. When Natalie and the other girls strip down to their underwear, I do too. . . . I concede to shifting my personality, just a hair, to observe the standards I think the situation calls for. From now on, every time I drink, I'll enhance various aspects of myself, willing myself into a state where I am a little bit brighter, funnier, more outgoing, or vibrant. The process will be so incremental that I'll have no gauge of how much it will change me. I will wake up one day in my twenties like a skewed TV screen on which the hues are all wrong. My subtleties will be exaggerated and my overtones will be subdued. My entire personality will be off-color.[19]

Alcohol doesn't give teenagers personality; more often, alcohol takes it away. Just as social media pushes girls to conform to the conventions of Instagram and Snapchat, so Zailckas discovered that alcohol pushes girls to conform to the conventions of beer commercials and television sitcoms. "That's the thing about social drinking," she writes. "In the end, it's the drinking that creates the scene, not the other way around. You grow to relish the buzz, regardless of the situation. Once you're there, really there inside that moment, with its neighborly warmth and conversation, it's hard to tell what's responsible for producing emotion. What's responsible for the light-headed feeling? Is it the Molson, or the boy [Greg] who is running his fingers through the ends of your hair? . . . When you're fifteen and female, when you experience these feelings . . . only when you are drinking, it becomes a question of which came first, the liquor or the Greg?"[20]

Koren was searching not only for a *sacra* but for a sense of self, something to combat the nihilistic urge. "Other girls my age steered into that urge with starvation diets or razor blades, but I chose alcohol because it seemed far less fanatical. On nights when I felt sad, particularly, I could feel my drinking accelerate. . . . Drinking is a visible sign to the world that you're hurting, in the same way that starving and cutting are for some girls."[21]

Many parents misunderstand the reasons why girls begin drinking. It's generally not peer pressure, in my experience, but rather the sort of mixed motives that Zailckas describes: the desire to do something associated with adulthood, mixed in with the desire to find one's true self. As mature adults, we know that there is no surrogate, no shortcut to discovering your true self. You can't find it in a bottle or a razor blade. But your daughter may not know that yet.

Gender matters. Throughout the 1970s, 1980s, and 1990s, most research on alcohol use and abuse by children and teen-agers was not gender specific. In that era, gender was regarded primarily as merely a "social construct." Nobody guessed that the determinants and consequences of alcohol use might be fundamentally different for girls than boys.

Those days are past, at least for anybody who has been paying attention to the research. As the leadership of the National Center on Addiction and Substance Abuse has emphasized, girls and young women use alcohol "for reasons different from boys, their signals and situations of higher risk differ, and they are more vulnerable to substance abuse and addiction and its consequences."[22] Whether you are male or female is much more than a social construct: it is a biological reality, with substantive consequences regarding the meta-bolic effects of alcohol. Drink per drink, alcohol is more dan-gerous to young women than it is to young men.[23] That's not a function of differences in height or weight. It's because female physiology differs from male physiology. Binge drink-ing damages girls' brains differently and more severely than binge drinking affects boys of the same age.[24]

The prefrontal cortex is the part of the brain involved in decision-making, balancing risk and benefits.[25] Teenage girls who drink alcohol have significantly smaller prefrontal cortex volumes compared with teenage girls who don't drink alcohol. But teenage boys who drink alcohol actually have slightly *larger* prefrontal cortex volumes compared with teenage boys who don't drink.[26] Other studies have confirmed and extended these findings: alcohol affects girls' brains differently from boys' brains.[27] In yet another study, researchers followed teenagers who drank alcohol from age seventeen through age twenty-nine. They found that even if a girl stopped drinking completely in her twenties, that girl who had been a drinker at age seventeen was more likely than a boy who had been a drinker at age seventeen to have long-term issues with drug use, more psychiatric problems, and poorer adjustment to life in general.[28]

These sex differences are now well known among researchers who study alcoholism, but they are not well known to the rest of us. I have found that some people are uncomfortable with this information. To them, it seems sexist to suggest that alcohol is more toxic to women than to men. But pretending that girls are no different from boys puts girls at risk. Nowhere is that clearer than when we are talking about alcohol abuse.

For some girls and young women, alcohol becomes a way of defining themselves, a kind of obsession, even a kind of salvation (or so they hope). They may believe that getting buzzed will help to alleviate their anxiety. As Zailckas writes, "People with substance-abuse issues like to think that changing physical states [getting buzzed] is the equivalent of changing emotional states [feeling less anxious]."[29] I find that same confusion is also common among anorexic girls and among girls who are obsessed with fitness.

Here's an interesting finding: girls and young women who drink coffee regularly are much more likely to drink alcohol. Among girls and young women who drink coffee regularly, 70 percent also drink alcohol; among girls and young women who don't drink coffee, only 29 percent drink alcohol.[30] Why is this? I think that many girls and young women who drink coffee regularly may have learned to fix one problem, namely fatigue due to sleep deprivation, by drinking a certain beverage, namely coffee. Once you have the mindset that you can fix a problem by taking a drink of something, it's not a big jump to the notion that you might fix a different problem—such as anxiety or insomnia or depression—by taking a drink of a different beverage, maybe two shots of vodka.

Do girls drink because they're depressed? Or are girls depressed because they drink? A study from the Harvard School of Public Health suggests that the arrow may point in both directions. Depressed teens are more likely to drink, and teens who abuse alcohol are more likely to become depressed.[31] Other researchers have found that for young women in particular, the likelihood that drinking will lead to depression is especially strong—much stronger than it is for young men.[32]

Community matters—especially for girls. That's the finding of a survey in which researchers compared the likelihood of binge drinking in permissive communities, where there was little or no stigma attached to bingeing, with the likelihood of binge drinking in communities with strong norms, where binge drinking was severely frowned upon.

Figure 4 shows the results. For men, community standards had a barely significant effect. But for women, the effect was large. Women in communities with weak norms were

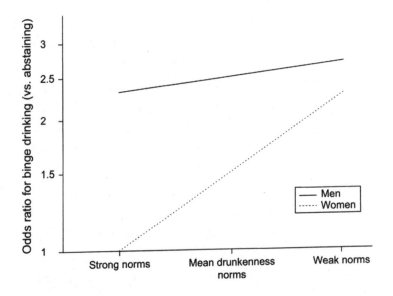

more than twice as likely to engage in binge drinking, compared with comparable women living in communities with strong norms.[33] Asian American girls are somewhat less likely than black, Latina, or white girls to drink alcohol and to binge drink,[34] perhaps in part because Asian American parents may be more likely to teach their girls that drinking can be very risky.

So it helps to tell girls in no uncertain terms that teens shouldn't drink. And you should start early to educate your daughter about the dangers of drinking. Girls have one great advantage over boys: as a rule, girls don't want to fry their brains just for the sake of frying their brains. That's not true for some boys. I've seen more than a few boys and young men who take pride in getting totally wasted. It's their twisted idea of macho. But there's nothing feminine about throwing up all over the front lawn. As Zailckas observes, "Drinking confirms men's gender role, whereas it diminishes women's. We are meant to believe that men who drink heavily are men's men. Beer ads play strongly to the idea that men drink because they like shooting pool, watching ESPN, and bonding with other men. . . . By contrast, a girl's drinking makes her less feminine."[35]

The perils of drinking include sexual risks. A boy who is drunk may do stupid things—things he wouldn't do when he is sober. And if you're drunk, you will be less able to stop him. Alcohol is involved in the majority of all rapes, including date rape.[36] As Zailckas wrote after a semiconsensual sexual act that occurred while both she and the young man were drunk, "I can't let myself feel abused. He was drunk, which makes him less blameworthy; and I was drunk, which makes me more so. I don't need anyone to explain this equation to me."[37]

Several readers criticized me for including this quote from Zailckas in the first edition of this book. In the era of #MeToo, it seems wrong to quote a statement that endorses a double standard with regard to teens drinking and having sex. I get that. But the reality that Zailckas describes is still very much with us. The fact that the girl now has a somewhat better chance of getting the boy disciplined or expelled from school after the fact—and maybe even prosecuted for rape—doesn't change the reality of what happened and the trauma that your daughter suffered. You don't want your daughter to be in that situation to begin with.

The perils of drinking include the risk of being in a car with a drunk teen driver. This risk is especially high for "nice girls." Nice girls don't like to make trouble, so if a boy is a little bit drunk, a nice girl is less likely to take his car keys away, less likely to refuse to get in his car. Nice girls don't make a fuss. I know a nice girl in my own practice who ended up in the hospital for three weeks with broken ribs and a collapsed lung after being out with a young man who had been drinking. She warned him that he shouldn't drive. She offered to drive for him. He insisted on driving. A sensible girl would have refused; a sensible girl would have called her parents for a ride home. But nice girls aren't sensible girls. She got in the car. A few minutes later, they were in a head-on collision.

But you have to use your judgment as a parent. Don't threaten to ground your daughter for a year if she has a drink. If you do, and your daughter has a drink, she may be terrified to tell you about it. If your daughter is sixteen years old and has a glass of beer at a friend's house, she has to be able to call you and tell you to come pick her up and drive her home. If you've been authoritarian ("Too Hard") rather than authoritative ("Just Right"), then she won't make that call, because she's afraid you'll be angry. She'll try to drive home even when she knows she shouldn't.

Here's a tip: have a code word or phrase that you and your daughter agree on in advance. I recommend this for any occasion when your daughter will be separated from you, even if she's only nine years old. The code word might be "brownie," or it could be a phrase, such as "bake some brownies." If your daughter calls you and asks, "Mom, are you going to bake some brownies?" that means "Come get me right away." You don't want your daughter to have to explain, with her friends listening, why she needs you to come pick her up. All you have to say is, "Are you still at Avery's house?" When she says, "Yes, I'd love some," you say, "I'm on my way." When you get there, just swoop in and collect your daughter. She's allowed to say, "Mom, what are you doing here?" You answer, "I'm taking you home right now, no more questions please." A little playacting is OK. You and your daughter are on the same team with the same objective: to get her out of a potentially dangerous situation without her losing face in the eyes of her friends. It's not reasonable to expect your daughter to say in front of her friends when you arrive, "I'm so glad to see you here, Mom. This party was getting a little too wild for me." It's perfectly fine for you and her to put on a little show, to give her some cover, to allow her to leave without embarrassment.

Don't be reassured just because your daughter is a good student or is involved in lots of extracurricular activities. I can't tell you how many parents of "good girls" have told me, "I never thought this would happen to my daughter." Their daughter was earning good grades; how could she possibly have a drinking problem?

Koren Zailckas herself struggled with a drinking problem for years, but nobody understood how bad it was, not even her parents, who were as loving and caring as any daughter could ask. As Zailckas observes, "Too many people rely on outward signs of aggression to indicate their daughters or girlfriends or sisters have problems with alcohol. They wait for fights, or DUI charges, or destruction of property, when girls who drink are far less apt to break rules in [such] overt ways. As a gender, we are far more likely to turn our drunken destructiveness inward, to wage private wars against ourselves."[38] Girls can be subtle.

The core intervention you have to undertake as a parent is to ensure that your daughter develops a strong sense of self and that she develops confidence in her identity that doesn't depend on what her grades are or how well she is doing in sports or any other extracurricular activities. If there's anything I have learned from my conversations with girls who struggle with alcohol, it's that girls begin using alcohol to compensate for something that's missing in their lives. If they have a strong sense of self, then they don't need to drink.

girls on the edge

On the table there was a roll of batting, a glue gun, a doily, a 1997 Krafty Kitchens catalogue. Next to the catalogue was a special craft knife.... It was sleek, like a fountain pen, with a thin triangular blade at the tip. I picked it up and laid the blade against the doily. The little knots came undone, just like that. I touched the blade to a piece of ribbon draped across the table and pressed, ever so slightly. The ribbon unfurled into two pieces and slipped to the floor without a sound. Then I placed the blade next to the skin on my palm.

A tingle arced across my scalp. The floor tipped up at me and my body spiraled away. Then I was on the ceiling looking down, waiting to see what would happen next. What happened next was that a perfect, straight line of blood bloomed from under the edge of the blade. The line grew into a long, fat bubble, a lush crimson bubble that got bigger and bigger. I watched from above, waiting to see how big it would get before it burst. When it did, I felt awesome. Satisfied, finally. Then exhausted.

That's a passage from the opening chapter of Patty McCormick's *Cut*, about a young girl named Callie. Callie was doing poorly after four miles in a cross-country race. She was in last place and couldn't even see the runners in front of her. Instead of finishing the race, she ran home—where she found the knife.

McCormick's description of Callie's first cut rings true for me, based on my own conversations with girls who have cut themselves. In particular, the dissociation—the sense of being detached from her body, watching herself from up above—has been a central feature of the experience for many of the girls with whom I've spoken. "I knew the pain was there, but I didn't really feel it, because I was like not really *there*, I was *high*—literally, I felt like I was up in the sky." That's how one girl explained it to me.

Cutting used to be rare. In the early 1980s, psychiatrists announced the emergence of a new clinical syndrome, the "deliberate self-harm syndrome."[39] The preferred term today is NSSI, nonsuicidal self-injury. Back in the 1980s, estimates of the prevalence of this "syndrome" were well under 1 percent of the population. Today it's so common that some researchers have argued we should no longer consider girls who cut themselves to have a psychiatric problem at all; rather, these girls are basically normal girls engaging in a "voluntarily chosen deviant behavior."[40] For these researchers, deliberately cutting your skin with a razor blade is not so different from dyeing your hair purple. After all, these researchers point out, many of these girls "feel positive about their self-injury" and don't seek treatment, so who are we to say that they have a psychiatric disorder?[41]

I disagree. These girls are struggling. A girl who dyes her hair purple may be indulging a playful whim. But every girl

I have met who is deliberately taking a blade to her own skin has major issues, and cutting herself is her way of dealing with these issues. I don't think it's the best way.

Estimates of the prevalence among teenage girls have been rising steadily; most recent surveys find that at least one in five adolescent girls now report a history of deliberate self-harm.[42] Almost all studies agree that girls are at much higher risk than boys. Most studies find that the average teenage girl is at least twice as likely to cut herself compared with a teenage boy in the same community.[43] It's important to keep that in mind when you read scholarly articles on this topic. For example, if researchers interview kids at a high school that has a roughly fifty-fifty mix of girls and boys, the researchers may report an overall prevalence of cutting as, say, 12 percent. But that number may be misleading if only 4 percent of the boys are cutting themselves compared with 20 percent of the girls.[44]

Furthermore, the significance of cutting appears to be different depending on whether you're talking about girls or boys. When you find a boy who is cutting himself, he is often the outcast, the loner. But you will find girls who cut themselves among almost every demographic at the school, including the popular girls, the star students, and the athletes.

When I wrote the first edition of *Girls on the Edge*, back in 2010, I said, "Most girls who are cutting themselves do NOT want you or any other adult to know about it. If they cut themselves on their arms, then they wear long sleeves or baggy sweaters." I quoted psychotherapist Madeline Levine, who said that when she sees a girl wearing "a long-sleeve T-shirt pulled halfway over her hand," she has found that "such T-shirts are almost always worn to camouflage an array of self-mutilating behaviors: cutting with sharp instruments, piercing with safety pins, or burning with matches."[45]

That was true enough in 2010. It's not true today. I was leading a workshop for professionals who work with troubled teens in northern Ontario. Brittany Begin, an intervention specialist east of Sault Ste. Marie, told me that she is seeing more and more girls who are cutting themselves on their forearms and then wearing short-sleeved blouses so that everybody can see the cuts. "All the 'cool' girls are doing it," she told me. "They show off their cuts to the other girls, as a sign of how cool they are. It's spreading like crazy."

When Brittany told me that, in 2016, I was surprised. I remember thinking, "Wow, Sault Ste. Marie must be really weird." I don't think that anymore, because I'm now seeing the same behavior at home in Pennsylvania and across the United States and Canada. Sault Ste. Marie was ahead of the curve. Cutting is now cool.

Emily Greene, an English teacher in San Antonio, Texas, emailed me this comment: "Something that I'm witnessing at an unprecedented level is the number of students who have slashed their arms to ribbons. Last year, we had two girls (they were a romantic couple) who went 'live' on Facebook and started cutting their wrists together. That triggered a torrent of students on campus cutting themselves on their arms, the inside of their thighs, their stomachs, etc. It almost became a point of pride to have scars all over one's arms. The culture that I work in is now completely foreign to me."

Why are they doing it? The number one answer: because cutting relieves anxiety. Psychiatrist Armando Favazza has been studying nonsuicidal self-injury for more than two decades. He writes that cutting and other forms of self-wounding can begin as "forms of self-help because they provide rapid but temporary relief from distressing symptoms such as mounting anxiety, depersonalization, racing thoughts, and rapidly fluctuating emotions."[46] But when a girl repeats that behavior over and over again, it can—as Dr. Favazza observes—become an "overwhelming preoccupation." That transcendent feeling, the feeling of being above it all, can be supremely satisfying. Researchers have actually found that for these girls, the act of cutting her own flesh may trigger the release of endogenous opioids in her brain, giving her a kind of opiate high.[47] And so the obsession becomes stronger.

All the obsessions we have discussed in this chapter are linked to one another in various ways and with varying degrees of affinity. As Dr. Favazza observes, a girl who is cutting herself for a period of months or years may stop doing that and instead begin abusing alcohol or develop an eating disorder.[48] There is now strong evidence that girls who cut themselves are likely to develop an eating disorder, although the process can also work in the other direction: girls who have eating disorders are more likely to become girls who cut themselves.[49]

Girls who exercise excessively are more likely to be anorexic. Anorexic girls are more likely to be cutters. Girls who are obsessively perfectionist are more likely to abuse alcohol. At some level of analysis, these are all different manifestations of the same problem, which earlier in this chapter we heard one mother call "anorexia of the soul." If you don't know who you are, then you become vulnerable to dreams; and the wrong dream can become a nightmare, an obsession.

Many parents become frustrated when they seek help for a daughter struggling with any one of these problems. The generalist pediatricians and family physicians often don't know much about these topics, and the specialists are over-specialized. One mother told me that she found a psychiatrist who specializes in eating disorders, but the psychiatrist insisted on referring her daughter to a different specialist when he found out that she was also a cutter. Another psychiatrist, widely respected as an expert in helping teens struggling with alcohol abuse, refused to accept a teenage girl I referred to him after I told him that she was a straight-A student. "If she's a straight-A student, then her drinking is not an impairment. She is not impaired. Without impairment, there's no ground for a psychiatric diagnosis." He talked like a robot. *Of course* she's impaired, I argued. She's abusing alcohol, and she talks about suicide. But he wasn't interested. It was frustrating for me as the referring physician, but it was agonizing for the parents, who couldn't find a specialist who would take their daughter's problem seriously just because her grades were impressive.

I am not suggesting that these obsessions are interchangeable. Many girls who suffer from one of these obsessions may never have the misfortune of suffering from any of the others. Each of these obsessions has its own causes, its own risks, and different outcomes. But like so many other parents I have known, I am frustrated by the compartmentalization of our current system of healthcare. This compartmentalization rewards each professional for focusing on one little piece of the elephant without seeing the whole picture. As Mark Taylor, a professor at Columbia University, has observed, "There can be no adequate understanding of the most important issues we face when disciplines are cloistered from one another."[50]

The big picture is a growing proportion of girls who don't know who they are. So they fill the black hole with a dream, and the dream becomes an obsession. Because something is better than nothing.

when treatment becomes trauma

Dr. Tom Hall is a psychologist in Menlo Park, California. He and I first met many years ago when I spoke at a nearby school, and we have stayed in touch over the years (we even visited a Hutterite community in Manitoba together). When I told him that I was writing a revised edition of *Girls on the Edge*, he offered to share a story for the new edition, with permission from the girl—whom we will call Sara—and from her parents. I think the story is important, because it highlights a new, weird dimension of the problems that daughters and their parents now face. Here is Dr. Hall's story:

> During a routine appointment with her pediatrician for a physical, Sara was asked a series of questions. The doctor, reading from her iPad app, came to the mental health section.
>
> "Have you ever felt anxious or depressed?"
>
> "Yes," said Sara.
>
> "Which?" asked the doctor.
>
> "Both."
>
> "Have you ever had thoughts of harming yourself?"
>
> "Yes, actually I have."

"How recently have you had such thoughts?" asked her doctor.

Sara hesitated, then said, "Yesterday."

"Did you act on those thoughts?"

"Actually, I did. I took a pill."

"With the intention of killing yourself?"

"At the time, yes, but I'm better today."

With no other information, and a waiting room full of other children, the pediatrician had the nurse fetch Melinda, Sara's mother. The pediatrician instructed Melinda to take Sara to the Stanford Hospital ER immediately for a mental health evaluation.

Mother and daughter arrived a short time later. It was 10:00 a.m. on a Monday. From 10:00 a.m. until about 4:00 p.m. they waited and watched as an endless procession of humanity passed through with a variety of needs, most requiring urgent attention.

At 4:00 p.m. a mental health clinician, apologizing for the long wait, took Sara into a curtained cubicle for her mental health evaluation. The clinician asked the same questions that the pediatrician had asked that morning. Sara answered just as she had earlier that day. During their long wait, Melinda texted me for advice, and I told her to tell the clinician to call me, as I'm Sara's psychologist and know her well—but the clinician never called. The clinician deemed Sara to be a "danger to herself," filled out the proper forms, and instructed Melinda that she was putting Sara on a seventy-two-hour involuntary hold. Sara was to be hospitalized for observation, and after three days she would be either discharged or kept for an additional period to be determined. However, there was a problem: no beds available.

For the time being, Sara and Melinda would have to stay in the ER until a bed came available.

Around 9:00 p.m. a sympathetic nurse found a temporary room with a bed. Exhausted, Sara went right to sleep, and her mom sat in the room for another four and a half hours before the same nurse stopped in and encouraged Melinda to go home and get some sleep, assuring her that Sara wouldn't be moved before morning.

But sometime during the night there was a shift change, and at 4:30 a.m. Tuesday, there was a sharp knock on the door. Sara woke up disoriented and confused. The new nurse announced that a bed had opened up and that Sara was going to be moved right away. Behind her two men entered with a gurney.

"I don't need that," said Sara. "I can walk."

"Rules are rules," said the nurse as she took Sara's arm to help her onto the gurney. One orderly secured her with a strap across her chest while the other strapped her down just above her knees. She asked for her mom and was assured that she would see her once she was settled in.

But Sara, as it turned out, wasn't being moved to another floor in the same hospital; she was wheeled outside and into a waiting ambulance. Lying on the narrow vinyl-padded plank, Sara realized that the next day was Wednesday, the day that she and her best friend were going to their first concert. It was an early birthday present from Sara's mom who had bought a third ticket for herself, but in a row further back. Got7 is a South Korean boy band and one of Sara's favorite bands. She would explain it all to the staff. "They'll give me a pass, right? How could they refuse me? My mom already bought the tickets, and it's not any band; it's Got7!"

Sara's first view of Saint Mary's Medical Center was looking straight up from the gurney. When the elevator doors opened on the fifth-floor psych unit the first thing Sara heard was a girl screaming.

Released from her restraints, she was handed a pair of regulation purple pajamas and given a room to change in. Before being shown to her bedroom, Sara was interviewed for a third time and again asked the same questions that she had been asked twice the day before. But this time she said that the suicidal thoughts had been weeks ago and that she had considered taking the pill but changed her mind. Sara was learning to game the system, a system that didn't seem interested in her or able to get to the heart of why she had felt so desperate on Sunday, the day before her appointment with her pediatrician. Before being excused, Sara asked the case worker if she might, if she behaved well, be a candidate for a pass to go see Got7. "You know, given that it's my birthday and all."

"Happy birthday," replied the case worker, "but we don't give passes. You won't be going to any concerts, at least not before your hearing on Thursday, anyway."

When I texted Melinda that morning to let her know that no one called me from the ER and to get an update, Melinda wrote back that she had just read a text from the ER that Sara had, in fact, been transferred and she was just leaving for San Francisco, which, with morning traffic, could easily take between two and three hours.

Once more I reminded her to insist that the attending clinician call me. No one called. If they had called, I would have told the clinician that Sara was a sensitive kid who was having difficulty coming to terms with all of the changes brought

on by puberty. She didn't like all the attention she was getting from boys, and especially not from men. I would have
told the clinician that this was only her third menstrual cycle
and so far, each time it had been preceded by an emotional
tsunami.

I would have shared that despite being a conscientious
and hardworking student, and never being one to complain
about having weekend tutors, Sara had just found out that she
had failed four of the six end-of-the-year final exams and that
her elite private school had just notified her parents that they
were strongly recommending that Sara not continue at the
school. Not sure what else to do, her parents had enrolled her
in the local public middle school. That school required that she
have a physical examination—the reason for the visit to her
pediatrician.

I would also have shared with her clinician that on the day
Sara felt suicidal she had come home early from a summertime
class party where she learned that her only friend would be moving to Texas later in the summer. Also, two boys at the party came
to her separately as she lay on a lounge chair in her one-piece
swimsuit and extra-large T-shirt. They confessed their affection
and although flattered, she also recalled how mean both of the
boys had previously been to her. She wondered if their confes-
sions had to do with a change of heart or more to do with this
new and unfamiliar womanish body that she now found herself
wearing. Having told no one, not even her best friend, that she
wouldn't be returning to school in the fall, she left the party
early feeling that she was a fraud and that her classmates had
been right when they said that she didn't belong there. She was
relieved to find that no one was home at her dad's house so she

could sob openly, and during this abreaction she went into the kitchen, saw a pill on the counter, and she swallowed it. The pill she had taken was a baby aspirin that had been left on the counter.

Sara found her clinician and insisted that he hear her out. She explained that her pediatrician had overreacted and that there were other girls who had much greater needs than she had. She told him that she had a therapist (me) and that although he was on vacation, he had made himself available and had been in contact with her parents. The clinician listened. When Sara's story checked out, the clinician said, "I'm going to do something that I've rarely done before. I'm going to recommend that Sara be given an early discharge. But no promises."

The following morning Sara's name came up on the discharge board for 3:00 p.m. At 7:30 p.m. that evening, Got7 had just opened with their lead song "Eyes on You." Sara and her friend marched into the Oracle Arena and into a crowd of nearly twenty thousand people. At one point during the concert Sara stood up and did the dap step. Bam-Bam, the lead singer, took notice of her and grinned. Then he made their signature "finger-heart sign" and pointed to her. Sara did likewise and pointed to him. They both laughed.

The very next day, Sara and I had a long talk on the phone, and toward the end of our conversation, I asked her to summarize the day before. She said, "I woke up in the morning in prison, and that same evening I experienced total freedom. It was both the worst and the best day in my life."

"And how about the whole hospital experience?" I asked. "What's the takeaway?"

"The fact that I survived it."

I share this girl's story to illustrate an unfortunate truth. If you live in the United States, the mental health system is now designed first and foremost to minimize liability for the provider and the institution. As recently as ten years ago, if I were working with a girl in crisis, I might recommend an emergency evaluation at an ER or a psychiatric hospital. I am much less likely to make such a recommendation today, because I have encountered situations similar to the one that Dr. Hall described.

That's why it's so important to have a good relationship with a professional who knows the system. Of course, in Dr. Hall's story, it didn't help that the girl was already known to Dr. Hall, because the clinicians never called him. But I have been involved in similar situations where I was able to make a phone call and "spring" the girl from her jail cell, so to speak.

Of course, there are times when involuntary commitment of a suicidal girl is necessary in the best interests of the girl. If a girl is truly suicidal, then involuntary commitment makes sense. In most people—and this is true for both girls and boys, and for adults and children and teens—the suicidal impulse is transitory. If you prevent that girl from taking her own life on Monday, by the following Friday she no longer wants to kill herself. She may even thank you for saving her life.

But the system in the United States is now out of kilter, driven by the concern over liability. Any girl who answers yes to the question "Have you thought about hurting yourself?" may well find herself committed against her will, even when such a commitment makes no clinical sense.

So be on your guard. Establish a relationship with a clinician who knows your daughter and who is willing to challenge the system on your daughter's behalf, if and when necessary.

life out of sync

Lily Allen, a British pop star who has been an overachiever since middle adolescence, shared her plans with an interviewer: "What I'm going to do is work really hard, trying to make as much money as I can, then retire when I'm thirty and have my childhood. I'll just sit in the countryside, ride quad bikes all day, and have my own paintball course."[51]

That sort of comment is an extreme example of the role reversal that has become typical in the lives of many girls and young women today. More and more girls are trying to be adults too early, while hoping, as Lily Allen hopes, that someday, as adults, they might have a chance to enjoy the childhood they never had. I have listened to an eight-year-old girl of normal weight explain to me why she needs to go on a diet. I have listened to a fourteen-year-old girl tell me why she doesn't have time for even six hours of sleep a night because she is too busy promoting her brand on social media and building her list of followers. I have handed a box of Kleenex to a seventeen-year-old girl who was barely able to breathe because she just found out that she didn't do well on the SAT, which she believed dooms her chances of getting into a top university, which means her life is basically over.

Meanwhile, how have things worked out for Lily Allen? Thirteen years after she announced her plan to retire at age thirty, she is now thirty-five years old, a divorced mother of two young children. Like most single moms, she doesn't have time to "just sit in the countryside, ride quad bikes all day, and have my own paintball course." She's busy.

What all these stories have in common are girls whose lives are out of sync. It's similar to the problems of premature sexualization that we discussed in Chapter 1. Girls who are eight or nine years old trying to dress like teenagers. Teenage girls who want to drink like adults. Girls of every age who are obsessed with dreams that are turning into nightmares.

One key to a healthy, happy, and fulfilled life is to live each stage of your life to its fullest. When you are a child, do the things that children are meant to do. Be silly and carefree. When you become an adult, it's time to put those childish things away, for the most part, and to assume the responsibilities of an adult. By pushing girls to act like adults before their time, our twenty-first-century culture is robbing them of their girlhood and often condemning them to an unhappy adulthood.

How did we get here? Why are girls getting older younger? Part of the answer may have to do with toxins in the food they eat, the beverages they drink, and the creams and lotions they put on their skin.

chapter 4

fourth factor: environmental toxins

The childhoods of US girls have been significantly shortened. . . .
About half of all US girls show signs of breast development by their
tenth birthday.

DR. SANDRA STEINGRABER[1]

bra at eight

Olivia's parents were concerned when she began developing breasts shortly after her eighth birthday. Her mom, Vanessa, was sure that Olivia would be the only girl at school wearing a bra. She worried that the other girls might tease her daughter. So Vanessa was surprised to discover there were two other girls in the class who were already wearing bras. That made a total of three girls, out of twelve girls in the classroom, who had begun the process of puberty.

The parents of the other two girls were not concerned, but Vanessa took Olivia to the pediatrician, who said that Olivia's early development was "within the range of normal." Vanessa insisted on a referral to a pediatric endocrinologist.

The specialist ordered some blood tests. At the follow-up visit to discuss the test results, the specialist confirmed that Olivia had begun puberty, but he said that there was no need to do anything about it. "There's nothing wrong with your daughter," he said. He explained that the definition of "normal puberty" had been revised and that breast development beginning at age eight, or even age seven, is now considered normal for American girls.

The specialist was correct. According to the current guidelines, a girl who has begun to develop breasts at age seven is now considered "normal."[2] Indeed, roughly half of the girls in the United States today will begin breast development before their tenth birthday.[3] But as Dr. Sandra Steingraber observes, "What has become the new norm is not necessarily normal or good. Whether or not a 7-year-old with breasts is labeled with a disorder and treated, the falling age of puberty raises serious public health questions. . . . The fact that 'normality' may have changed does not negate the possibility that the physiological processes leading to these changes are neither normal nor benign."[4]

By the time she was eleven, Olivia could easily pass for a girl of fifteen years of age. She was attracting whistles and comments and other unwanted attention from boys at the mall. Her body might have looked like the body of a fifteen-year-old, but she had the emotional maturity of an eleven-year-old, because she *was* an eleven-year-old. Most eleven-year-old girls who look fifteen are not ready to handle the attention they may attract when they go to the mall or the beach. It's often confusing and embarrassing to them. It may even be frightening.

The downside of early puberty goes beyond an increased risk of sexual harassment by older boys. We're talking about the loss of middle childhood, that special period from roughly age eight to age twelve when girls in previous generations were able to figure out who they were and who they wanted to be. That's the age of Peppermint Patty and Harriet the Spy. That's the age when previous generations of girls were able to develop a sense of self without regard to their sexuality, without being overly concerned about how they looked in the eyes of boys or whether this skirt or that top was too "hot" or not hot enough.

A long childhood is one of the features that define us as a species. In most mammals, the juvenile period is short. Once an infant is no longer dependent on its mother's milk, the objective in most species is to start reproducing as soon as possible. The period between the time when a mouse is weaned and when it is ready to start reproducing is only a few weeks; likewise for a rabbit. Horses—which are larger in size and weight than humans—can begin reproducing at two years of age, although most veterinarians recommend that owners of female horses wait until the filly is three or four years old. A two-year-old female horse is still growing. Pregnancy can interfere with healthy development. A four-year-old mare is ready.

A four-year-old human still has a long way to go.

"Childhood" can be defined from a biological perspective as the period between weaning from the breast and the onset of puberty. Humans have the longest childhood of any mammal on the planet.[5] How come? What is the benefit of a long childhood? One part of the answer seems to be that children need that time in order to expand their potential before the onset of puberty.

Because puberty changes everything.

the price of puberty

Prior to the onset of puberty, the human brain is incredibly plastic. A normal five-year-old can learn any language and become fluent in it, acquire a new physical skill such as riding a bicycle with relative ease, and achieve age-appropriate proficiency in a new sport within a few weeks. After puberty, the potential to learn completely new things is reduced. You can still learn a foreign language in your teens or as an adult, but you will probably speak it with at least some trace of an accent.[6] If you want to speak another language without an accent, your best bet is to learn it before the onset of puberty. There has been much talk about "neuroplasticity," the ability of the adult human brain to rewire itself.[7] But the mental agility of even the most intellectually nimble adult can't compare with a child's.

It's a trade-off. "Pubertal re-sculpting of the brain's circuitry is believed to make possible the emergence of abstract thinking, values, autonomy, adult social behaviors and the capacity to consider alternative viewpoints," writes Dr. Steingraber. But, she adds, "the development of higher-order thought does not come without a price: during the course of sexual maturation, the brain loses plasticity and cognitive flexibility. The ability to assimilate complex new skills—such as playing a musical instrument, riding a bicycle, or achieving athletic prowess—declines dramatically after puberty."[8]

The Philip Pullman trilogy—*The Golden Compass, The Subtle Knife, The Amber Spyglass*—illustrates this point in a poignant way. In the first book of the trilogy, *The Golden Compass* (originally published under the title *Northern Lights*), Lyra Belacqua is twelve years old—and for her, unlike most modern girls, the process of puberty has not yet begun. She discovers that she has an extraordinary talent that enables her to use an ancient instrument, the golden compass, to discover hidden truths about the present and the past, and even to glimpse the future. Her unique ability shapes the plot of the first two books. In the third book of the trilogy, *The Amber Spyglass*, Lyra goes through puberty. She experiences a sexual awakening and falls in love with a teenage boy, Will Parry. As their relationship progresses and Lyra matures, her special ability slips away. She can no longer read the compass. Pullman is careful to make clear that the loss of her gift is not a punishment but is rather an inevitable consequence of her maturity. She gains a great deal as she undergoes the transition from girl to woman, but something precious is irretrievably lost along the way.

Puberty has different significance and different consequences for girls compared with boys. As boys progress through puberty, they become more satisfied with their bodies; as girls progress through puberty, they become less satisfied with theirs.[9] Girls in puberty are much more likely to have problems sleeping compared to boys in puberty or to prepubescent girls.[10] Prior to puberty, there is no difference between girls and boys in the incidence of depression; once puberty is underway, girls are much more likely than boys to become depressed.[11]

Girls who begin puberty earlier are at greater risk for developing anxiety and depression; that's not true for boys.[12] Girls who go through puberty earlier are at greater risk of being sexually victimized as teenagers.[13] For many years it was thought that a girl who began puberty early was more likely to be sexually abused in her home; however, it now appears that the arrow of causality points the other way, with childhood sexual abuse *causing* an earlier onset of puberty.[14] (We will come back to the explanation for this finding later in the chapter.)

Girls who begin puberty earlier are more likely to develop eating disorders.[15] They are more likely to smoke cigarettes and to abuse drugs and alcohol as teenagers.[16] They are more likely to engage in delinquent and criminal activity.[17] They do less well in school compared to girls from the same neighborhood who go through puberty later.[18] They are more likely than other girls to develop cardiovascular risk factors such as high blood pressure, even if they're not overweight.[19] They are also more likely to develop breast cancer as adults;[20] and if they do get breast cancer, their cancer is likely to be more aggressive and more lethal than the cancers that develop in women who experience later onset of puberty.[21]

And then there's fat.

as a matter of fat

There are close links between overweight and early puberty. Girls who become overweight early in childhood are more likely to go through puberty earlier. Girls are heavier today, on average, than they were fifty years ago. In the early 1970s, only 4 percent of American children five to eleven years of age were obese. In 2008, 19.6 percent of American children five to eleven years of age were obese. The proportion of obese kids more than quadrupled—from 4.0 percent to 19.6 percent—in less than four decades. There was a similar quadrupling in the rate of obesity among American adolescents twelve to nineteen years of age, from 4.6 percent in 1970 to 18.4 percent in 2010.[22] In the subsequent decade, rates of obesity remained steady for American children and teens, although the physical *fitness* of American kids appears to have declined.[23]

Could that be the whole story? Maybe girls are going through puberty earlier than girls did fifty years ago simply because girls today are heavier than girls were back then, and/ or less physically fit than girls back then? It seems plausible, but the truth may be more complicated.

Certainly there is a strong association between overweight early in childhood and the subsequent early onset of puberty. Researchers in Louisiana found that heavier girls typically get their first menstrual period earlier than thinner girls.[24] In a study of 181 girls in Pennsylvania, girls who were fat at age five were more likely to begin puberty at age nine, compared to other girls in the group.[25] In another study, researchers at the University of Michigan periodically examined more than three hundred girls for nine years, beginning at age three. They found that the girls who had more body fat at three years of age were more likely to begin puberty earlier. In this study, the girls who gained weight the fastest between ages three and six were at highest risk to have begun puberty by age nine. In this study, nearly half of the girls had begun puberty by age nine.[26]

But an association between overweight and early puberty doesn't prove that overweight *causes* early puberty. In fact, evidence suggests that the association between overweight and early puberty may not be causal at all. In one study, Danish researchers described a group of eleven hundred girls who had been examined in the early 1990s; the same researchers then looked at a different group of about one thousand girls evaluated about fifteen years later, from the same neighborhood and with the same demographics. The average age of breast development for the girls in the early 1990s was 10.88 years. In the group of girls examined between 2006 and 2008, the average age for breast development was 9.86 years of age. That's an acceleration of one full year in less than two decades. But the girls in the later group, in this particular study in Denmark, were not heavier than the girls in the early 1990s. As the Danish researchers wrote, "We do not believe that the increasing incidence of obesity among children can explain our findings."[27] A large study by American researchers, examining girls in California, Ohio, and New York, arrived at a similar conclusion: there has been a continuing acceleration in the onset of puberty among young girls, especially white girls.[28]

Other researchers agree that the hypothesis that early puberty is caused by overweight is "far from compelling."[29] Instead, they believe that some other factor or factors are causing both the obesity epidemic and the acceleration in the onset of puberty—and/or that overweight *mediates* some other factors that are actually causing earlier puberty. What could those other factors be?

In the study I just cited, the Danish researchers suggested that "increased exposure to endocrine-disrupting chemicals...may be involved in the observed trends" of earlier breast development in girls.[30] "Endocrine-disrupting chemicals" are man-made substances that can mimic the action of hormones in the human body. And most of these endocrine-disrupting chemicals mimic the action of *female* hormones.[31] Almost all of the endocrine disruptors are fat-soluble, which means that the more fat you have in your body, the more you will accumulate these chemicals.[32] In addition to concentrating within fatty tissues, these chemicals may actually change the metabolism of fat cells, making them more resistant to shrinkage or breakdown.[33] In other words, these man-made substances not only make it easier for you to get fat, they also make it harder for you to lose the fat once you've gained it.

So if you are overweight, you are likely to have more endocrine-disrupting chemicals in your body compared to someone the same age and height who has less fat on board. That means that heavier girls might go through puberty earlier, not because they are heavier per se but because their extra fat translates into an extra dose of endocrine-disrupting chemicals.

What your daughter eats also seems to make a difference, independent of her body weight. Girls who eat high-fat and high-calorie diets are at higher risk of early puberty, even if they aren't fat themselves. Pediatric endocrinologists Dr. Melvin Grumbach and Dr. Dennis Styne conjecture that this "effect of fat in the diet may be compounded by the effect of estrogen added to commercial beef production cows, which is concentrated in fatty tissue."[34] In the United States, beef cattle are given hormone supplements.[35] In Europe, such supplementation is prohibited. That may be one reason why girls in the United States begin puberty earlier than girls in Europe, even after adjusting for any differences in weight between European and American girls.[36] Conversely, a high-fiber diet appears to postpone the onset of puberty in girls.[37]

Breastfeeding also seems to be a factor in the timing of the onset of puberty. There are at least two possible reasons why. First, formula-fed infants grow up to be heavier than breast-fed infants.[38] The second reason is that babies who are fed with formula are fed entirely with bottles. Thirty years ago, those bottles would have been made of glass. Today, they are often made of hard plastic, or they have soft plastic liners, both of which can be sources of endocrine disruptors.

Even parents who breastfeed their infants often dispense that milk in a bottle with pumped breast milk. If you are such a parent, then you may need to be vigilant about what kind of bottle you are using. Glass bottles are better than plastic, particularly if the milk is warm rather than cold. When you put warm milk or any hot beverage into a plastic liner or a plastic bottle, it's easier for the chemicals to leach out of the plastic and into the liquid (more about that in a moment).

The relatively low rate of breastfeeding in the United States may be one of the reasons why American girls begin the process of puberty earlier than girls in other developed countries. The rates of breastfeeding in the United States are among the lowest rates in the developed world.[39]

So how can you reasonably avoid these endocrine disruptors without fleeing with your family to the wilderness and living in a tent?

what's in your tuna?

Medical experts are famous for disagreeing. The old joke is that if you get five medical experts in a room, they'll give you six opinions. So expectations may not have been high when the National Institutes of Health (NIH) convened a panel of thirty-eight leading medical experts, mostly from around the United States but also from Germany, Italy, Japan, Spain, and the United Kingdom, to see if they could reach any consensus about the medical risks posed by a particular chemical, a substance known as bisphenol A, or BPA.

BPA is used to make many kinds of hard plastic. It's also the main ingredient in the resin that lines the inside of the can in most canned foods such as soup, canned pasta, tuna, and vegetables. Many studies suggest that humans are exposed to BPA in doses that can mimic the action of female hormones.

Remarkably, the expert panel convened by the NIH agreed that BPA acts like a female hormone in the human body at the kind of exposures that normal people encounter in everyday life, such as eating half a small can of tuna fish or eating half a small can of pasta. They agreed that BPA acts like a female hormone in the human body in concentrations of one part per *trillion*. They concluded that at least 90 percent of people in developed countries have BPA in their tissues at concentrations at or above the threshold at which BPA acts like a female hormone.[40] (A Centers for Disease Control study of children and adults in the United States found significant levels of BPA in 92.6 percent of the sample: children had higher levels of BPA than adults, and females had higher levels than males.[41]) The expert panel concluded that there is "great cause for concern" that exposure to BPA is contributing to the "early onset of puberty in girls."[42]

Can we say with 100 percent certainty that BPA is contributing to the early onset of puberty in girls? Maybe not, but the likelihood is high. In 2012, the United States Food and Drug Administration banned the use of BPA in baby bottles and sippy cups, but BPA is still widely used in the United States. Banning BPA in baby bottles and sippy cups is great, but most girls older than three years of age don't drink from sippy cups.

Fortunately, it's easy to prevent your daughter (and yourself) from being exposed to BPA. Here's what I recommend:

- Avoid canned foods, particularly canned pasta, canned soup, canned beans, and canned tuna. In one study, 50 percent or more of these canned foods contained dangerous levels of BPA.[43] Eat fresh or frozen foods instead.
- Never heat food in any kind of plastic container, either in the microwave or in a conventional oven. If you buy a frozen entrée in a "microwave-ready" plastic container, don't use that container. Put the food in a bowl made of ceramic or glass and use that instead. For a conventional oven, use a metal tray or pan.
- Don't put plastic containers in the dishwasher. Wash them by hand instead. The detergents used in dishwashers—even the most environmentally friendly detergents—will increase the leaching of bisphenol A from plastic when you subsequently use that item.
- Don't pour hot beverages like coffee or tea into any kind of plastic cup. Instead, use a cup made out of ceramic, glass, porcelain, or steel.

- Avoid any container with "7" in the recycle triangle (see Figure 5). This number can stand for "other" or for polycarbonate (PC). Polycarbonate is made from BPA. However, certain other containers made out of hard plastic may also leach BPA, even if they don't have the number 7 on them.

Figure 5.

gimme some skin

Phthalates, pronounced THA-lates, are synthetic chemicals used to make lotions and creams softer and creamier (among other uses). Phthalates may be as hazardous as BPA, but they haven't received nearly as much press, perhaps because they are harder to spell. Just remember that these substances used to be called "naphthalates," but then somebody decided to drop the "na," maybe as a prank to confuse kids in spelling bees. Phthalates have a complex action on the human endocrine system, disrupting sexual development and increasing the risk of obesity, possibly via a direct action on fat cells.[44]

In order to avoid the various phthalates, your daughter must be careful about what she puts on her skin. Many lotions and creams on the market today contain phthalates. When you rub those lotions and creams onto your skin, phthalates get into your system. A study of babies from several sites across the United States found that more than 80 percent had *seven or more* phthalate metabolites in their system. As the authors observed, "In the United States, there is no requirement that products be labeled as to their phthalate content. Parents may not be able to make informed choices until manufacturers are required to list phthalate contents of products." These investigators—from the Centers for Disease Control, the University of Washington, and the University of Rochester Medical Center—came to this conclusion: "Until additional information is available on infant care product phthalate content . . . we recommend limiting [the] amount of infant care products used and not to apply lotions or powders unless indicated for a medical reason."[45]

Figure 6.

When you're buying any skin lotion or cream for yourself or for your daughter—or a sippy cup or pacifier for your baby or toddler—I recommend that you look for a label like the one shown in Figure 6, stating that the product is *both* BPA-free and phthalate-free. Fortunately, it's getting easier to find these products. I recommend the website maintained by the Environmental Working Group, online at www.ewg.org/skindeep (and I have no affiliation with the Environmental Working Group). You can type any cosmetics product—shampoo, skin cream, lipstick, sunscreen, etc.—into the search engine, and the database will provide a hazard score—0 is the safest, and 10 is most dangerous—along with detailed information about what's really in the product. Here's a tip for any product manufactured in North America that lists "fragrance" or "parfum" in the ingredients: "fragrance" and "parfum" are industry code for "phthalates." Don't buy that product.

who is PETE?

Just as BPA is used to make *hard* plastic as well as resins, many kinds of clear, *soft* plastics today are made from a substance called PETE: polyethylene terephthalate ethylene. PET, polyethylene terephthalate, is a synonym for PETE. The clear plastic bottles that bottled water is sold in are made from PETE, along with just about every kind of soda and sports drink in a clear plastic bottle, as well as soft, clear plastic squeeze bottles of peanut butter and salad dressing and ketchup and mustard and mayonnaise.

Chemists have found that containers made from PETE can leach phthalates into whatever's inside them, whether it's bottled water, soda, or salad dressing.[46] In one study, the water inside clear plastic bottles made from PETE contained phthalates at levels nearly twenty times higher than water in glass bottles.[47] That leaching is most likely to happen if the container is exposed to sunlight under warm conditions. So don't leave your plastic water bottle in your car.

Conversely, the container is less likely to leach if it is kept cool and in the dark. The problem is, you don't know where that container of bottled water has been on its long journey to your neighborhood store. It may have sat out on a loading dock, exposed to the sun on a hot afternoon. It may have been inside a truck, where temperatures can easily rise above one hundred degrees if the truck is in direct sunlight, even if the temperature is cool outside. The warmer the temperature, the more leaching will occur.[48] "If you heat up [these] plastics, you could increase the leaching of phthalates from the containers into water and food," says Kellogg Schwab, PhD, director of the Center for Water and Health at the Johns Hopkins School of Public Health.[49]

German researchers looked to see whether the water in a clear plastic bottle made of PETE did in fact have estrogen-like effects. They bought bottled water in PETE containers, emptied out the water, and poured in ultrapure water instead. They then put one hundred little snails into the plastic bottles filled with ultrapure water. As a control, they put another one hundred little snails in *glass* bottles filled with the same ultrapure water. The female snails who were in the plastic PETE bottles produced more than double the number of embryos per female, compared with the female snails in the glass bottles. "It is obvious that the observed effects can only be attributed to xenoestrogen leaching from these plastic bottles," these authors concluded. (A "xenoestrogen" is a substance in the environment that acts like estrogen, a female hormone.) They suggested that their findings were just "the tip of the iceberg" regarding the endocrine-disrupting effects of bottled water sold in PETE bottles.[50]

It's easy to tell if a particular container is made out of PETE. Just look at the underside of the container for the "1" in the recycle triangle.

What do you need to do in order to avoid exposure to phthalates and to PETE?

- Pour water directly from the faucet into a glass. If you are concerned about impurities in tap water, install a filter. If you insist on purchasing bottled water, buy it in a glass bottle, not in plastic. Bottled water is available in glass bottles at most health-conscious grocery stores such as Whole Foods and Wegman's. If you must carry bottled water with you, make sure that your bottle is BPA-free and phthalate-free. There are many lightweight stainless-steel bottles available on the market now for just this purpose. That's what I use. I pour the water from the faucet directly into my steel canteen.

- If you want to drink soda, buy it in glass bottles. Yes, Coke and Diet Coke and many other soft drinks are available in glass bottles, though you may have to go to a beverage distributor to get them. (In Chapter 6, I will try to persuade you and your daughter to avoid cola beverages altogether; if you want fizz, drink seltzer water instead.)

- When you microwave food, don't allow the food to come into contact with the plastic wrap you put over the top. Instead of putting the food on a plate, put the food in a deep bowl, so the plastic wrap across the top won't come in contact with the food. Or, instead of using plastic wrap, you can cover the food with a plate or other microwave-safe glass or ceramic.

- Even better, avoid using plastic wrap altogether: use waxed paper or parchment paper instead. You can buy both online if you can't find them at your neighborhood store. (Don't put any kind of waxed paper in a conventional oven or it will smoke; parchment paper is fine in a conventional oven. Both waxed paper and parchment paper are safe to use in the microwave.)

All these warnings about hidden toxins in our food and beverages can be a little overwhelming. But there's actually a simple fix to this problem, which Michael Pollan outlined in his
book *In Defense of Food*. Pollan summarized his book in just
seven words: "Eat food. Not too much. Mostly plants."[51] When
Pollan recommends that you eat food, he means whole foods
your grandmother would have recognized, like artichokes and
asparagus and broccoli and cabbage and cucumbers and oat-
meal. None of those foods are shipped in PETE bottles or BPA
containers. None of them pose any risk of endocrine disruption
if you buy them whole at the store and prepare them yourself.

What about milk? First, we need to clear up some common
misconceptions. Livestock raised for beef in the United States
are often injected with hormones, especially bovine growth
hormone (BGH), to make them grow faster. However, it's illegal to administer any kind of sex hormones such as estrogens
or testosterone to dairy cattle, even in the United States. We
do know that cows' milk contains natural cow estrogens, but
the concentration is so low that it almost certainly cannot
affect a girl's endocrine system. In one study, the highest concentration measured from any cow was ten nanograms per
liter.[52] A nanogram (ng) is one-thousandth of one-millionth
of a gram. That's how much estrogen you would ingest if you
drank a liter of milk at one sitting. It's not much. (And most
of the cows tested had less than that amount—ten ng per liter
was the highest reading.) You would have to drink one thousand liters of milk in order to ingest one-millionth of a gram of
estrogen. Second, the natural estrogen in cows' milk is highly
protein-bound. It's not easily absorbed by the body, and it's

likely to be broken down in the digestive process. Third, there's no evidence that girls who drink lots of milk are at any risk of earlier onset of puberty. Between the 1970s and the 1990s, consumption of milk by American girls fell by 36 percent,[53] and the decline has continued since that time.[54] If milk were a significant cause of early puberty, one would expect that fewer girls would be experiencing early puberty today than was the case fifty years ago—but of course the opposite is true.

How about juice? It's fine to buy *fresh* juice in plastic bottles in the refrigerator section of the grocery store, because fresh juices are shipped in refrigerated containers. Those juices are not allowed to come to room temperature. That means the plastic can't leach into what you're going to drink.

Other juices, such as white grape juice and apple juice, are often sold in clear plastic bottles or even plasticized cardboard boxes and are shipped and stored at room temperature. Don't buy them. Don't buy any beverage in a plastic bottle or plasticized box that has been shipped at room temperature. Maybe that bottle sat in a hot truck for a week. Maybe it didn't. You have no way of knowing.

But we're not finished. There's more to the story of early puberty than just environmental toxins. Another factor may be something that used to be a part of almost every girl's life but has become less common today: a dad in the house.

life with father

Here are two facts:

1. Girls who grow up without their biological father go through puberty earlier. The absence of the mother,

by contrast, does not appear to affect the timing of puberty.[55]

2. Girls today are more likely to grow up without their biological father, compared to girls in the mid-twentieth century. As recently as 1960, only 17 percent of children grew up without their biological fathers; by 1990, that proportion had more than doubled, to 36 percent, and the proportion has risen slightly since that time.[56] A girl today may grow up with a man in the home, but he may not be her *biological* father.

First, some disclaimers. I am not suggesting that mothers aren't important, nor am I suggesting that fathers are more important than mothers. I am just noting that *on this one parameter*—the timing of puberty in girls—the presence of the biological father appears to matter more than the presence of the mother.

Second: I am not suggesting that stepfathers can't do a great job of parenting girls. Indeed, some research suggests that stepfathers, on average, do as good a job, on most objective measures of parenting, as biological fathers do.[57]

Nevertheless, the presence of the biological father appears to have a protective effect, delaying the onset of puberty in the father's daughter. What's going on?

Scientists have been debating the roots of this phenomenon for more than forty years.[58] Back in the 1980s and 1990s, many people thought that a father's absence might merely be a marker for poverty. Poverty, these researchers thought, might be the actual reason why girls raised without their fathers go through puberty earlier. Girls who grow up without their biological fathers are more likely to be in low-income house-holds,[59] and some research suggests that girls who grow up in low-income households may indeed go through puberty earlier.[60] Therefore, girls who grow up without their father go through puberty earlier just because there's less money around, right?

Probably not. In more recent studies, investigators have carefully controlled for household income, and they have found that the father-absence effect is still highly significant.[61]

Others have conjectured that maybe the absence of the father somehow leads girls to be overweight and that it's the overweight—not the absence of the father—that is to blame.[62] Again, subsequent research has disproved that theory: girls who grow up without their father are not more likely to be overweight than girls who grow up with their father.[63]

The quality of the father's involvement matters as well. If a girl has a dad who is loving and physically affectionate with her, giving her hugs, then she will, on average, go through puberty at a later age.[64] If a girl has a dad who is emotionally distant, then she will, on average, go through puberty earlier. If a girl has a father who abuses her sexually or physically, then she is at greatest risk and will go through puberty even earlier.[65]

Dad's presence will protect his daughter against early puberty only if Dad is more or less a normal guy. If Dad is abusive, if he's addicted to drugs, or if he is a violent criminal offender, then there is no protective effect with regard to early onset of puberty associated with Dad being in the home.[66]

Stepfathers don't seem to be able to substitute for the bio-logical father on this one parameter, the timing of puberty. In fact, there is some evidence that the presence of a stepfather may actually *accelerate* the onset of puberty in girls, compared to girls raised without any man in the home.[67]

But we still haven't answered the question of what's going on. How come the presence of the biological father, but not the biological mother, plays a role in the timing of puberty in girls?

Some people think that the answer has to do with pheromones.

something in the air

A pheromone is basically an airborne hormone: a form of hormonal communication wafting in the air between individuals. Many people confuse pheromones with odors. Although some pheromones have odors, and some odors may act as pheromones, pheromones do not necessarily have any smell. There's good evidence that many vertebrates, including humans, have a special cranial nerve that is devoted solely to detecting pheromones, even if we can't detect those pheromones as odors.[68]

Pheromones can influence the pace of sexual development.[69] In laboratory animals, females raised in the presence of an *unrelated* male will reach sexual maturity *earlier* than females who are not exposed to males.[70] Researchers have also found some cases where female animals raised in the presence of their *biological* father will reach sexual maturity *later*;[71] that finding is of course similar to the effect biological fathers have in human families.

Why do adult humans have hair in their armpits? Part of the answer appears to be because the armpit is the number one place where adult humans manufacture pheromones. The armpit is where you find the apocrine glands, the glands that produce most of the substances believed to act as pheromones in humans. Children don't have hair in the armpits until the process of puberty begins, because prepubescent children don't manufacture pheromones. Armpit hair, as one researcher eloquently puts it, "provides a warm environment where the action of commensal bacteria can volatilize the precursor molecules released from apocrine glands."[72] Bacteria in the armpit turn your pheromones into an aerosol, which the armpit hair then wafts into the air.

Makes you want to take a shower, doesn't it?

Researchers Robert Matchock and Elizabeth Susman are convinced that pheromones are the mechanism whereby the presence of the biological father slows down the tempo of his daughter's sexual development. They believe that this phenomenon is hardwired in our species, as it is in many other mammals, in order to decrease the likelihood of a father having sex with his daughter.[73] "Biological fathers send out inhibitory chemical signals to their daughters," says Matchock. "In the absence of these signals, girls tend to sexually mature earlier."[74]

It's a plausible hypothesis. We do know that we humans can distinguish degree of kinship, from close family members to total strangers, by using chemical clues, and we know that males and females process these chemical clues differently. Women can distinguish a male relative from an unrelated man just by sniffing some hair snipped from each man's armpit.[75] (How much did they pay those women to participate in that experiment?)

But there's still a great deal we don't know about why girls are going through puberty earlier. For example, in their study of about two thousand college girls, Matchock and Susman found that girls who grew up in the city went through puberty earlier than girls who grew up in the countryside, even after adjusting for any difference in the father living at home. They aren't sure why. Urban girls aren't any fatter than country girls. My own guess would be that girls in big cities are exposed to BPA and phthalates more than girls in the countryside, but for now that's just a guess.

Another group of investigators found that girls who drink lots of soft drinks are more likely to begin puberty earlier.[76] Maybe that's because girls who drink lots of soft drinks are fatter than girls who don't. Maybe it's because endocrine disruptors are leaching out of the plastic bottle and into the beverage. Maybe it's because biological fathers don't let their daughters drink lots of soft drinks. Maybe it's something else altogether. We just don't know.

what can parents do?

Let's get practical. What can you do to prevent your daughter from going through puberty too early? The following measures may reasonably decrease the likelihood that your daughter will go through puberty before she should:

- Avoid exposing her to the environmental toxins we discussed earlier in this chapter. That means avoiding plastic bottles, avoiding heating any food in a plastic container, and being mindful of what lotions and creams go on her skin.
- Engage her in appropriate exercise programs. "Exercise is protective against early puberty," Dr. Steingraber

observes.[77] Your daughter doesn't have to exercise herself skinny to enjoy this benefit. Girls who are involved
in swimming, for example, decrease their risk of early
puberty, even though girls who swim do not weigh less,
on average, compared with other girls.[78] In Chapter 6,
we will return to the question of what's "appropriate"
exercise.

- If you're a mom, and you live with your daughter's biological father, then encourage her dad to be a warm
and loving father. If you're a mom and your daughter's
father doesn't live with you and your daughter, then try
to create opportunities for your daughter and her father
to have fun together—as long as he's not abusive, alcoholic, or a criminal.
- If you're a dad, be there for your daughter.

Up to this point, we've considered the challenges facing
twenty-first-century girls from the perspective of the four factors that are driving this new crisis for girls. Now we're going
to change direction. Instead of focusing on the problems, we're
going to focus on *solutions*. We're going to consider how other
parents have helped their daughters develop a healthy mind in
a healthy body, and more.

chapter 5

---

mind

*Sticks and stones may break my bones
but words will never harm me.*

Children's proverb

*Wind extinguishes a candle and energizes fire...
You want to be the fire and wish for the wind.*

Nicholas Nasim Taleb[1]

knives for four-year-olds?

On a recent visit to Germany, I had the privilege of visiting a *Waldkindergarten*—a "forest kindergarten" with no building or classroom, where the kids meet outdoors in the woods every day, all year round. What was most striking to me was not the outdoor format but the attitude toward risk and danger, which my hosts and other Germans told me was common throughout Germany. I saw four-year-old girls and boys using sharp knives to whittle sticks they found in the woods. Four- and five-year-old children climbed tall trees without any safety gear or harness and without help from a grown-up. On this trip and on my previous trips throughout Germany and

Switzerland, I have found the general attitude toward risk to be profoundly different from the "culture of safetyism" that is now so prevalent in the United States.

I borrow the term "safetyism" from *The Coddling of the American Mind*, by Greg Lukianoff and Jonathan Haidt. They describe how many American schools now prohibit any activity that might conceivably result in any injury to any child. American parents follow suit. Four-year-olds whittling sticks with sharp knives? Unthinkable. Five-year-olds climbing trees without a harness? Not happening.

But risky play is part of childhood, and kids have always done it. By engaging in risky play, kids develop an awareness of what they can and cannot do. When a girl climbs a tree all by herself, she earns a sense of mastery. No amount of preaching about how "You're special because you're you!" can accomplish that.

What if she falls and hurts herself? As a family doctor, I have evaluated many such injuries. In the great majority of cases, the trauma sustained in a fall from a tree or a jungle gym is minor. My daughter was at the very top of a jungle gym, about nine feet above the ground, when she fell to the ground onto her outstretched hand. She broke her wrist: a nondisplaced fracture of the distal radius. I applied the cast myself. She had a good outcome, with full healing of the broken bone. And she acquired a sense of *resilience*: the knowledge that she can get hurt and recover. No amount of preaching about resilience can do that.

But if you constantly warn your daughter, "Don't do that; you might get hurt!" you are sending an unintended message to your daughter, a message that the world is full of risks and that the only way to stay safe is to avoid risk. Don't say that. Sending that message may actually *increase* your daughter's anxiety, making her more fragile and risk averse. Girls who have never climbed a tree without a harness, or whittled a stick with a knife, and who constantly hear warnings about the dangers inherent in everyday life, may be more likely to become anxious, sometimes without even knowing *why* they are anxious.[2]

Girls are less likely than boys to engage in risky play.[3] Gender stereotypes may be playing a role here. When kids are asked which child—a girl or a boy—is most likely to get hurt when riding a bike, climbing a tree, and so forth, girls and boys agree that the girl is more likely to get hurt. In fact, the reality is just the opposite: *boys* are more likely to get hurt.[4] The majority of our entertainment, of our television and movies and novels and stories, and of our video games, continue to show the boy saving the girl or the man saving the woman. There are some exceptions—such as the character of Rey in the latest *Star Wars* movies—but they remain exceptions. That bias toward depicting males and not females as risk-takers in the majority of programming may be partly to blame for girls' underestimation of their abilities.[5]

What are good ways to get girls to be more comfortable with risk-taking? Margrét Pála Ólafsdóttir, an educator in Iceland, has developed a program for young girls that she calls "dare training." The idea first occurred to her during a field trip for girls only. It was a warm day, and some of the girls took off their shoes and socks. On an impulse, she encouraged *all* the girls to take off their shoes and socks and run around on the stones and pebbles in the park (I wonder whether a teacher in our more litigious American society would have had the cour-age). Then she dared them to dance. One girl moaned when a stone hurt her foot. "What can we do instead of complaining when it hurts?" Ólafsdóttir asked the girls. "Sing," suggested one of the girls. "And so we did," Ólafsdóttir says. "Sang and danced all the way [back to the school]—barefooted. We felt like superwomen."

The girls were "joyful and proud that they had discovered a new world," Ólafsdóttir wrote. Inspired, Ólafsdóttir hauled mattresses into the girls' kindergarten. She stacked the mat-tresses on the floor, put a table next to them, and encouraged the girls to jump from the table onto the mattresses, with an invitation to scream as they jumped. Because "an important part of the [stereotypical] female role is to keep quiet and because noise is not integrated into girls' play, it became obvi-ous that training in making noise and using the voice should be part of the 'daring' exercises," Ólafsdóttir wrote. Soon the girls' room was almost as loud as the boys' room. When the girls said it was too easy to jump from a table onto a mattress, "we just put another table on top of the first one—and at last a chair on top of everything."[6]

"she is looking to you"

Several years ago, I attended a workshop for parents hosted by Donna Lindner, who was then head of the Lower School at my daughter's school. Donna told us about a situation that had recently occurred at the school. A girl—let's call her Bella—had come home in tears. Bella told her mom that *all* the other girls had been invited to a birthday party. She, Bella, was the *only* girl who wasn't invited. Indignant, the mother called the mother of the birthday girl to ask why Bella hadn't been invited. The mother of the birthday girl coolly explained that Bella was mistaken. About half of the girls in the class had been invited. Many other girls besides Bella had not been invited. Bella's mother had to apologize for the call.

Donna told us this: When your daughter comes home from school, and she's upset about something that's happened, *she is looking to you* to teach her: Is this a big deal or not? No child is born knowing what's a big deal and what is not. So what should you do if your daughter comes home and announces that all of the other girls have been invited to a party and that she's the only one who wasn't invited?

Prioritize the parent-child relationship. In my book *The Collapse of Parenting*, I describe how many parents now act as if how your kid is getting along with friends her age is the most important thing in the world. It's not. When kids value friendships with other kids above the relationship they have with their parents, then those kids are at risk. Friendships between kids come and go, and those friendships are fragile. Every girl knows that you can go from being the most popular girl to being the odd girl out in one day. In five minutes. Last month, Sonia and Vanessa were best friends. Now Sonia hates Vanessa and says terrible things about her. That happens all the time in girl world. If your girl builds her world on a foundation of friendships with kids her own age, then she is building on a foundation of sand.

But your daughter knows, or should know, that you will never stop loving her, no matter what. If the parent-child relationship is the most important relationship in her life, as it

should be, then her emotional world rests on a solid foundation, on the bedrock of your love for her.

So how to apply this to the situation Donna described?
Your daughter comes home and says that she's the only girl
who wasn't invited to the birthday party. What should you say?

Here's my suggestion. Look at the calendar. Say, "OK, that's
this coming Saturday. We've been talking about going on that
new bike trail, but we haven't been able to find the time. Let's
write it on the calendar. Bike trail, Saturday afternoon, you
and me." Done. That sends the message that you and me, the
parent-child relationship, is way more important than whatever is going on in the storm and stress of Girl World.

But unfortunately that's not how most parents are react-
ing. It's much more common, in the scenario Donna described,
for a parent to cry, "Oh *honey!* I am *so sorry!* You must be *so
upset!*" And then you both burst into tears.

Think about the unintended messages you are sending
when you say, "I am *so sorry!* You must be *so upset!*" You are
sending the message *Whether or not you get invited to a party
is really, really important.* You are sending the message *If you
don't get invited to a party that other girls got invited to, then
you should be really sad and/or angry.* You are sending the message *When other girls get invited, and you don't get invited, then
you might as well burst into tears.* You are not teaching your
daughter to be strong. You are teaching her to be fragile.

sticks and stones

When I was a child, my teachers told me to recite this line
whenever someone made fun of me: "Sticks and stones may

break my bones, but words will never harm me." Other kids liked to say, "I am rubber; you are glue. Whatever you say bounces off me and sticks to you."

I remember thinking, as a child, that both these sayings made a lot of sense. They seemed wise to me. They still do.

Lisa Feldman Barrett is a professor of psychology at Northeastern University. She wrote an opinion piece on this topic for the *New York Times*. She began by quoting the familiar "sticks and stones" ditty, but she doesn't agree with that old rhyme. On the contrary, she insisted that words *can* be harmful. She then asserted that "certain types of adversity, even those involving no physical contact" can "kill neurons."[7] In support of that claim, she cited an article in which researchers subjected naïve laboratory rats, one by one, to severe stress: being suddenly placed in a cage with two aggressive rats who attacked the naïve rat, usually pinning it down and biting it. Sure enough, the victimized rat showed loss of some brain cells compared with control rats who weren't pinned down and bitten.[8]

Barrett misrepresented this study. An experiment in which naïve rats were pinned down and bitten by aggressive rats is hardly an experiment "involving no physical contact." And in any case, the consequences of being pinned down and bitten by a fellow rat are of doubtful relevance to advising parents about best practices when a child is taunted by a peer. Humans are not rats. We are capable of putting our lives in context, seeking larger purpose and meaning, finding resilience in character, even as children. Rats are not capable of such higher-order thinking, as far as we know.

I am not condoning kids who say unkind things to other kids. I know how much it hurts. I was bullied myself in middle school (a story I shared in my book *Why Gender Matters*, Chapter 9). But I don't think we should overstate the case. Words can hurt. I know that's true from my firsthand experience. But teaching kids that unkind words are a form of *violence* dilutes the meaning of the word "violence." It also suggests that if someone says something unkind to you, then they have violently attacked you, and you are justified if you hit them in the mouth. But if your kid is hauled into the principal's office because someone said something unkind to her, your kid is going to get into trouble. The principal is likely to ask, "Didn't anybody ever tell you that you shouldn't hit unless someone hits you first?" Words are not violence. Yes, words can be cruel, just as violence can be cruel. But words and violence are not the same thing.

Lukianoff and Haidt are not condoning mean kids either. They note that Oberlin College has provided a guide for faculty, urging them to use whatever gender pronouns the student prefers: for example, "zhe" and "zhir" for a student who doesn't want to use "she" and "her," if that's the student's preference. Oberlin could reasonably have justified this recommendation by claiming that using the student's preferred pronouns is simply one way to be appropriately respectful of the student. Instead, the Oberlin guide asserts that a professor who uses the wrong pronoun "prevents or impairs [the student's] safety in the classroom." Lukianoff and Haidt note, "If students have been told that they can request gender-neutral pronouns and then a professor fails to use one, students may be disappointed or upset. But are these students *unsafe*? Are students in any *danger* in the classroom if a professor uses the wrong pronoun? Professors should indeed be mindful of their students' feelings, but how might it change Oberlin students—and the nature of class discussions—when the community is told repeatedly that they should judge the speech of others in terms of safety and danger?"

Again, I am old enough to remember when we encouraged students not to make mountains out of molehills. Lukianoff and Haidt are concerned that contemporary American culture—from K-12 schools and continuing to the leading universities—now encourages students to do just that, to make mountains out of molehills, to be offended even when no offense was intended. To be fragile rather than robust. To be candles rather than bonfires.

Children look to grown-ups to learn about the ways of the world. If you continually tell a child that they will be harmed by unkind words and that unkind words are a form of violence, then you increase the risk that a child will actually experience harm when they hear unkind words. And rare is the child who will get through childhood without ever hearing an unkind word. But if you tell a child that they are strong, that while sticks and stones may break their bones, mere words will never hurt them—then you decrease the risk that a child will experience real, lasting harm when they hear unkind words.

Once again: I am not condoning unkind words. On the contrary, I often work with schools to share what I have learned about bullying-prevention strategies that actually work and how best to create a school community where all are welcome. Nor am I suggesting that students should *ignore* unkind words. I think it's important for students to keep teachers and administrators in the loop so that the grown-ups know what's really happening. That's especially important with girls, because girls' unkindness can be harder to detect.

I learned a good tip along these lines when I visited Carman Trails Elementary School, a public school in St. Louis. Cindy Rudman, who teaches second grade at Carman Trails, shared with me her little trick for encouraging her students to share their secrets with her. She calls it "the tattle box." Other teachers have told me about this approach as well. You can use a little lockbox with a slit on top, like the wooden suggestion boxes you can pick up at an office supply store. Ms. Rudman explains to the students that if there's anything they want her to know, but they don't feel comfortable coming directly to her to talk about it, they can write it on a slip of paper and put it in the tattle box. "I've never actually seen any girl put anything in the tattle box," Cindy told me. "But somehow they manage to do it when nobody's looking. At the end of the week, there's always a few notes in there." She reads every one. Sometimes a girl will use the tattle box to tell the teacher about how one girl is bullying another. I think this method, or something like it, is a good way to ensure that their students can share with them what's really happening in their lives. If unkind words are being spoken, the grown-ups need to know. Ms. Rudman's tattle box is a good way to find out what's happening and, if necessary, correct the bully, without telling students that they are fragile and will be permanently harmed by an unkind word. Ms. Rudman told me that she also has a second box, for students who want to give other students secret compliments. At the end of the week the compliment box is always full, while there are usually only a few notes in the tattle box.

Ms. Rudman's tattle box is a great strategy for kids in elementary school. For older kids, I have found schools having success with programs such as SchoolMessenger's Quick Tip program. SchoolMessenger provides a free app for students to use on their phones or online. The student can provide as much or as little information as they like about their concern: bullying, drugs, weapons, anything. The tip is submitted anonymously. Again, the idea is to give the student *agency*—the knowledge that they are not helpless, the recognition that they can make a difference—without making them feel *fragile*.

Respect your daughter's feelings. But teach her that she must govern her feelings rather than allow herself to be governed by them.

self-control

Learning self-control is central to becoming a happy and fulfilled adult. Earning good grades is not. When I speak to parents, I sometimes ask for a show of hands: Which characteristic in a child best predicts health, wealth, and happiness in adulthood? Is it grades at school? Nobody raises their hand. They know, in their heads, that grades at school are not the most important thing, according to the research. They are not terribly surprised when I report that *self-control* in childhood is a far better predictor of success—health, wealth, and happiness in adulthood—than are grades at school.

They know that. But they don't act that way. I find that many American parents *act as if* grades at school are the most important thing. If their daughter starts getting Bs instead of As, it's a major catastrophe. They ask me, "Do you think she has

ADHD? Should we try a medication?" I assure those parents that getting a B instead of an A is not a catastrophe. Researchers have followed kids from childhood, through adolescence, and into adulthood, and they consistently find that whether you earned Bs instead of As in middle school and high school does not predict whether you will be healthy and happy twenty years down the road. But self-control at, say, age eleven *does* predict health, wealth, and happiness twenty years later.[9] One group of investigators who did such a study, conducted over decades, concluded that "childhood self-control strongly predicts adult success, in people of high or low intelligence, in rich or poor, and does so throughout the entire population, with a step change in health, wealth, and social success at every level of self-control."[10]

There is tension between self-control, governing yourself, versus giving in to your feelings. Giving in to your feelings, and acting accordingly, is often the very opposite of self-control. Yet a pervasive and harmful message in American popular culture right now is to "trust your feelings." What should you do if someone makes a comment that you feel is biased? The University of Michigan–Ann Arbor, one of our nation's leading public universities, has officially advised students that "the most important indication of bias is your own feelings."[11] If you feel that someone is biased against you, that's proof that they *are* biased against you—according to those guidelines. But those guidelines are not based in evidence. A mature adult listens to her feelings but is also prepared to question and challenge those feelings. *Govern* your feelings, gather more information, and be charitable toward others. Being charitable toward others means that your default response should be to assume the best intentions in the actions of others rather than the worst intentions.

How do you help your daughter develop self-control? You begin by saying, "No dessert until you eat your vegetables." You say, "No TV or internet or video games until after you've done your homework."

If you want your daughter to develop better self-control, then sit down with her and say so. Parents who explicitly announce that "things are changing as of today" and then enforce the new rules and are not cowed when their child yells, "You are totally ruining my life! I hate you!" are often surprised by how dramatic the change is. Not in one day. Not in one week. But after six weeks of consistent enforcement of the rules, your daughter will have better self-control. And most likely, both of you will be enjoying life more as well.

Your daughter's self-control is not hardwired. It is not determined at birth. It is something you can teach. It is something she can, and must, learn.[12]

nice girls

The short story "Cat Person," published in *The New Yorker*, became a viral hit shortly after its publication, with millions of reads.[13] In the story, a twenty-year-old student named Margot stumbles into a relationship with a thirty-four-year-old man. On their first and only date, she is "wildly uncomfortable." Their first kiss was "a terrible kiss, shockingly bad; Margot had trouble believing that a grown man could possibly be so bad at kissing." He "practically poured his tongue down her throat." When he undressed and she saw "his belly thick and soft and covered with hair, Margot recoiled. But the thought of what it would take to stop what she had set in motion was overwhelming." So she drank some of his whiskey in order "to bludgeon her resistance into submission." The sex was awful. "She imagined herself from above, naked and spread-eagled with this fat old man's finger inside her, and her revulsion turned to self-disgust and a humiliation that was a kind of perverse cousin to arousal." He flipped her around like "a doll made of rubber, flexible and resilient, a prop for the [porn] movie that was playing in his head." The next day, she hopes "that he would disappear without her having to do anything," but of course he doesn't. He wants to do it again. When he texts her, she feels "overwhelmed with a skin-crawling loathing that felt vastly disproportionate to anything he had actually done." The story concludes with his increasingly rude, profane, and hostile texts. The End.[14]

This story is important, not just because of its honesty in portraying a hook-up with a near stranger as the dismal misery that it so often is, but also because of the story's massive and immediate popularity. It hit a nerve. Many, many women recognized themselves in Margot. Maureen Dowd, a regular columnist for the *New York Times*, commenting on the story, asked, "Why would a woman go home with a man, decide she's not attracted to him but have sex with him anyway?" Dowd noted how weird it is that so many young women today can Lean In in the boardroom, but they can't Walk Out of the bedroom.[15] Katherine Kersten, commenting on Margot and other young women like her, wrote that "they lack both a sense of their own dignity and the qualities of character necessary to preserve it, including prudence, wisdom, courage, and self-reliance."[16]

In Chapter 3, I talked about the danger of being a "nice girl." Nice girls don't make a fuss. They get in the car with a drunk boyfriend rather than refusing. Likewise, a nice girl who has made the choice of going to a man's home at the end of the evening may feel obligated—in today's hook-up culture—to have sex with him. But self-control and agency mean standing up for what you want and need. It means having the courage to walk out.

We must recognize that girls and young women today are immersed in a toxic culture, a culture that undermines self-control and devalues dignity, a culture that encourages women to think of themselves as victims rather than as agents in control of their destiny. When your daughter finds herself in a bad situation, you don't want her to think of herself as a victim, helpless to change her course. You want her to have the courage to break the expectations of others. We have to work harder to empower our daughters to become strong women who can walk out rather than "nice girls" who do whatever is expected of nice girls. And maybe, just maybe, that empowerment might begin by letting them climb trees, and whittle wood with sharp knives, at five years of age.

chapter 6

body

*If you intended for a girl to suffer a major injury, you would take
away all her other sports before puberty, make her play her one
sport all year round . . . and then you would just wait.*

MICHAEL SOKOLOVE[1]

Which is better, hopscotch or baseball? Jump rope or soccer?
Better for whom? Better for what?

Physical education for elementary school kids in North
America usually includes instruction in baseball: learning how
to swing a bat to hit the ball, run the bases, and so forth. It's
much less common for kids to receive formal instruction in
hopscotch. We encourage kids to play competitive soccer far
more often than we encourage them to play competitive jump
rope. How come?

Eight-year-old boys are, on average, better than girls at
tasks that require targeting a moving object in space[2]—which
means boys are likely to have an edge in games that involve
swinging a bat to hit a pitched ball or kicking a moving soccer ball into a goal. Eight-year-old girls are, on average, better
than boys at tasks that require balance[3]—which means girls
will have the edge in games such as hopscotch or jump rope.

Our physical education programs for children usually promote sports where boys have the advantage while deemphasizing or ignoring sports where girls have the advantage.

When surveyed, girls typically think boys are better athletes than girls.[4] One reason may be that our physical education programs emphasize sports such as baseball, football, and soccer, in which boys enjoy advantages, while devaluing or ignoring activities where girls enjoy the advantage, such as the balance beam, hopscotch, or jump rope.

Ignoring gender puts girls at a disadvantage. In the gym, as in the classroom, we teach girls pretty much the same way we teach boys simply because there hasn't been much serious consideration that maybe what works best for boys might not always work best for girls. I still encounter suspicion when I suggest that girls should be taught differently, either in the classroom or on the playing field. Whenever I make such a suggestion, I often get the response "Are you suggesting that girls can't do what the boys can do?" But ignoring differences between girls and boys doesn't provide a level playing field. As we will see, it often puts girls at a disadvantage and at risk.

A second reason that so many girls believe that boys are better athletes is probably because the boys tell them so, beginning in elementary school. Many boys boast about their athletic prowess. As one team of investigators reported, "Girls are more realistic about their competencies while boys overestimate their physical competence, especially in the early years."[5] Most adult women, and many teenage girls, have figured out that boys often exaggerate their athletic skills. But most eight-year-old girls haven't yet discovered that boys are not trustworthy regarding their self-assessment of their own athletic ability.

What's the point of physical education? Why bother? Is it about the joy of sports? But the sports that bring joy to a child may be different for girls compared with boys. And the best way to engage girls in sport is often different from the best way to engage boys. Men may be less likely to understand how to engage girls in sport than women are.

If that's true, it would be helpful to have women coaching girls. But the majority of coaches for most team sports are men; in fact, the proportion of coaches who are women has actually declined significantly over the years. In 1972, 90 percent of coaches of women's teams at American colleges and universities were women. By 2006, the proportion of women coaches among coaches of women's sports had dropped to 42 percent.[6] The latest survey shows that proportion to have dropped further, slightly, to 41 percent.[7]

We have more girls and young women playing sports today but proportionately fewer women coaching them. That's true at every level, from beginner leagues for seven-year-olds right up through college. As Michael Sokolove writes in his book about girls in sport, "The unspoken feeling in many settings is that men know sports—they've been at it longer—so if you want your daughter's travel team to succeed and the girls to get scholarships, you'd better have a male coach."[8] Among parents who have kids playing competitive sports, more than 27 percent of fathers coach their child's sport team; less than 4 percent of the mothers are coaches.[9] That imbalance leads to a third reason why so many girls assume that sports are, fundamentally, male territory: the experts—the coaches—are overwhelmingly male. The fact that so many girls think that males are better at sports may also explain why most girls attach more weight to their father's opinion about their own athletic ability than they do to their mother's opinion.[10]

Gym teachers matter. Coaches matter. The style of the coach or the PE teacher may have a big influence on how your daughter views sports and her own ability to play. Some coaches have a relentless focus on playing to win. That's not helpful for most kids, both girls and boys, but it's particularly harmful for many girls. The research consistently shows that girls are more likely to be engaged in sports when coaches focus on helping kids master skills, praising good performance and offering encouragement and supportive criticism when girls make mistakes.[11] Coaches or gym teachers who make fun of the klutzy kids, or coaches who ignore kids who aren't athletically talented, will not make good coaches for most girls. We also know that coaches who play favorites can turn girls off a sport very quickly.[12] If girls believe that the coach has favorites, then the unfavored girls may quit.

Girls should be active and as athletic as they can be, within healthy limits (we discussed some of the limits and warning signs in Chapter 3). As a parent, you can help your daughter choose the sports and physical activities she most enjoys and where she can fulfill her athletic potential with the greatest benefits and lowest risks.

All sports carry some degree of risk, of course. You must understand the risks and balance them against the benefit. In helping your daughter choose a sport, the first question you need to answer is this:

which are the most dangerous sports?

Ashley Marie Burns was just a few weeks away from starting ninth grade. She was one of twelve incoming freshmen girls chosen for the cheerleading team at Medford High School in Massachusetts.[13] She and three other girls were rehearsing a stunt called an arabesque double down. The three other girls were to throw Ashley in the air and then catch her. Ashley had previously executed the stunt without a problem; indeed, she was renowned as one of the best "fliers" on the squad.[14]

At 4:51 p.m., the girls tried the stunt. Ashley came down wrong, landing in the other girls' arms with her chest down instead of on her back.[15] She didn't appear to be injured—nothing was broken or dislocated—but she complained of feeling short of breath. The coach told her "to stretch her hands over her head, and then sent her to the bathroom to splash cold water on her face."[16] Ashley still didn't feel right, but nobody called 911 until she passed out half an hour later. She never regained consciousness. She was pronounced dead at the hospital at 6:00 p.m. An autopsy revealed that she had lacerated her spleen when she fell. She died of massive internal bleeding.

Unfortunately Ashley's story is not unique, nor was her injury an incredibly rare accident. Girls' cheerleading is by some measures the most dangerous sport kids do today—more dangerous even than football or ice hockey if the measure of danger is the number of serious injuries per thousand athletes. The National Center for Catastrophic Sports Injury Research (NCCSI) publishes an annual report chronicling deaths and serious injuries sustained by high school and college athletes. Over twenty-five years, the NCCSI documented a total

Figure 7: Which sport is the most likely to cause catastrophic injury? Football? Ice hockey? No, it's cheerleading. Like most cheerleading squads at basketball games, this squad is executing a gymnastics stunt over a bare wooden floor. *Photo courtesy of Andres Valenzuela, www.andresvalenzuelablog.com.*

of 156 serious injuries* or deaths among high school girls and college women. Of those, 97 occurred in cheerleading—that's more than in *all* other girls' sports *combined.*[17]

Dr. Robert Cantu, a professor of neurosurgery at Boston University School of Medicine and a coauthor of the NCCSI report, says, "What's staggering, really, is that the single most

---

* A "serious injury" in this report is an injury with the potential of causing permanent disability of life-changing significance, such as a fractured cervical vertebra leading to paralysis. A broken ankle or ruptured ACL does not count as a "serious injury" in the NCCSI report.

dangerous activity in sports in schools is to be a flier in cheer-leading," he says. "The chance for catastrophic injury is exponentially higher than for any other sports activity."[18]

Cheerleading epitomizes some of the worst aspects of sports for girls. To begin with, there is a major emphasis on how you *look*. If you are playing volleyball, the coach isn't going to care (and shouldn't care) whether your socks match or whether your gym shorts have a smudge of dirt on them. But in cheerleading and related sports like drill team and dance team, you not only have to execute the stunt—you also have to look pretty and smile while you do it.

In most jurisdictions, cheerleading is organized as an "activity" rather than a bona fide sport. That means that the safety requirements for the cheerleading squad are no different from the requirements for the chess team or the debate team. The chess team isn't required to have a certified athletic trainer in attendance. Neither are the cheerleaders. The coach of the debate team isn't required to be certified in injury assessment. Neither is the coach of the cheer squad. Ashley's life might have been saved if the adults in attendance had understood the risks of splenic injury after a fall and had called 911 immediately rather than waiting until Ashley lost consciousness.

Cheerleading has changed dramatically over the past four decades. Thirty years ago, cheerleaders were usually girls who jumped up and down on the sidelines, leading cheers. Nowadays the emphasis, beginning around age ten, is on high-flying stunts. Today, "cheerleading most closely resembles the sport of gymnastics, only without the mat and safety regulations," says former Massachusetts state representative Peter

Koutoujian, who is trying to make cheerleading safer. Kimberly Archie, founder of the National Cheer Safety Foundation, says that the emphasis is on "death-defying, gravity-defying stunts. That's a long way from shaking pom-poms on the sidelines like I did in the '80s."[19]

If your daughter is five or six years old, you may think that this advice doesn't apply. Nobody is going to ask your daughter to do an airborne somersault anytime soon. But there are long-term consequences to the choices that young girls make about which activities and sports they will participate in. Ask any girl over eight years of age which sports she likes the most, and the answer will almost invariably be whatever sports her friends do. If she joins Midget Poms at age six, she will probably want to carry on with her friends to Junior Cheer. At age ten, when she's been with the same girls for four years and the coach is beginning to teach them some airborne stunts, it may be difficult for you to suggest that she switch to a safer sport. She will say, "But all my friends are on the cheer squad!"—and she may be right. It's much easier to steer your six-year-old daughter in a healthy direction than it is to ask your ten-year-old daughter to change her sport and her friends.

Encourage your daughter to choose sports in which the emphasis is on what she *does* on the field of play, not on how she *looks* while she's doing it. Archery, badminton, field hockey, soccer, softball, swimming, tennis, track, and volleyball are all good choices by that criterion. Cheerleading, dance team, and gymnastics may not be good choices. The risks in cheerleading, dance team, and gymnastics often outweigh the benefits of exercise; the focus on appearance, on looking cute, is often relentless.

Don't allow your daughter to specialize too early. Specializing in a sport before the onset of puberty appears to increase the risk of physical injury and mental burnout. According to an official policy paper from the American Academy of Pediatrics (AAP), "Those who participate in a variety of sports and specialize *only after reaching the age of puberty* tend to be more consistent performers, have fewer injuries, and adhere to sports play longer than those who specialize early."[20] A second AAP committee, examining the same question, came to the same conclusion: "Young athletes who participate in a variety of sports have fewer injuries and play sports longer than those who specialize before puberty."[21] The National Athletic Trainers Association recently issued similar guidelines: kids should take at least two days a week off from their sport, should not specialize in one sport year-round, and should postpone specializing in one sport as long as possible.[22] In his book about girls who get hurt playing sports, Michael Sokolove writes that "nearly every injured athlete I met in the course of researching this book played one sport exclusively, beginning at age ten or younger."[23]

Don't allow your daughter to compete in the same sport year-round. In the 1980s it wasn't possible to play the same sport year-round. There was soccer or field hockey in the fall, basketball in winter, and lacrosse or track or tennis in the spring. But beginning in the early 1990s, club teams and travel teams began to grow in popularity. Now it's common to find girls playing on a club team all year long. But the evidence strongly suggests that specializing in one sport, and competing in that sport year-round, greatly increases the risk of injury. Each sport uses a particular group of muscles. Overdeveloping one set of muscles, while neglecting the others, throws the body out of alignment.

There's a second reason, aside from the risk of injury, why your daughter should not compete in the same sport year-round: if she's playing the same sport winter, spring, summer, and fall, she's likely going to be with the same group of girls for a great deal of time. Being respected and liked by those particular girls may become the highest priority in her life. If she sustains a minor injury, she will be less likely to mention her injury to anyone for fear that the doctor might restrict her participation. Her enthusiasm for the sport itself may wane, but she won't consider quitting the team, because that's where her friends are. The time commitment may be causing her grades to suffer, but she doesn't want to let her friends down.

It's all about balance. Sports are great, but when a particular sport becomes an obsession, it's time for you to step in. You and your daughter have to find a sensible balance between risk and benefits. As Sokolove observes, "We can't prevent every injury, but what we are currently doing is manufacturing them. If you *intended* for a girl to suffer a major injury, you would take away all her other sports before puberty, make her play her one sport all year round . . . and then you would just wait."[24]

The earlier you make your intervention, the easier it will be. Too many parents today go with the flow until it's too late. We all want to be supportive of our daughter's interests. What could be healthier than sports? Sokolove describes parents of highly motivated girls, parents who are supportive of their daughters but bewildered by the culture. "The children, as often as not, are the ones leading the way," Sokolove found. "They do not so much put pressure on themselves as they absorb it from the youth sports culture. The parents get subsumed in ways they never anticipated. 'We had no idea what we were getting into,' says one parent. 'You just feel your way as you go.'"[25] Don't be that parent. Know what your daughter is getting into before it's too late. Don't be intimidated by the coach or by the culture. You know better than the coach what is best for your daughter. Your coach has a different agenda. He[†] is concerned about winning. If your daughter is injured, emotionally or physically, it's not his problem. It's not going to keep him awake at night. There are other girls who can take her place.

In the name of safety, don't allow your daughter to focus only on sports that involve the same muscle groups. A girl who plays soccer in the fall and runs track in the winter and spring is running all the time. Swimming would be a better winter sport for her, because swimming exercises different muscle groups, complementary to those used in running.

Many parents, especially in the United States, assume that early specialization in a particular sport will give their daughter a competitive advantage. The evidence doesn't support that notion. Colleen Hacker, who has served as a psychologist for US Women's Soccer for more than twenty years, told Sokolove, "The big misconception is thinking that there is a linear connection between the development of a young athlete and the time spent being coached, attending organized practices, and playing organized games. There's no support for that. There may be belief and a hope, but not evidence." The most successful athletes, the ones who make it to the Olympics, usually have a history of playing many sports, specializing only once they

---

[†] I have noted earlier in this chapter that most coaches of girls' sports are, unfortunately, men.

reach their teens. Diversity of experience—cross-training—
makes the body stronger, better coordinated, and less prone
to injury. Dr. Hacker expresses frustration that so many parents don't understand this basic reality about the developing
human body. "This message [about the importance of athletic
diversity] is not getting across," she says. "We need to encourage parents, coaches, sports leagues, [and] the culture itself to
go back to multiple sports participation. And there needs to be
real off-seasons with unstructured play. No adults. No rules.
No leagues. No registration cards. One of the best sentences
a parent can utter is 'Go outside and play.' One of the worst is,
'It's 9 a.m. Get in the car, we're going to practice.'"[26]

Not all girls care about team sports. Some girls do care pas-
sionately about team competition, about victory and defeat.
For those girls, the traditional sports of soccer, basketball, and
baseball/softball may be a good match. But many girls are not
particularly motivated by the opportunity to bash the other
team. If you have the sense that your daughter might be such
a girl, try to expose her to a wide range of activities, including
those that don't necessarily involve team competition: mar-
tial arts, fencing, and archery, to name three. (Some of these
sports *can* be done in a team-competitive way, but they don't
have to be, and often are not.)

a girl's knee is not a boy's knee

The most popular team sports, such as soccer, baseball, and
basketball, were developed mainly by men to be played by men
and boys. In the past fifty years, girls have begun playing these
sports in record numbers. For the most part they are playing

boys' sports according to boys' rules, and they are usually coached by men. Few people have asked whether these sports should be modified to make them safe for girls. Many people bristle when this question is raised. "Are you suggesting that girls are not as tough as boys?" one parent asked me.

On the contrary, girls seem to be tougher, if the criterion of toughness is how severe an injury is needed to knock the athlete out of the game. Girls and young women appear to be more willing to play while injured compared to same-age boys.[27]

But girls are different. When researchers tested girls and boys at eight years of age, they found that girls' quadriceps were very strong relative to their hamstrings, while boys had more of a balance between their hamstrings and quadriceps.[28] (In case you're a bit weak on anatomy: the quadriceps is the four-headed muscle on top of your thigh bone that straightens your leg; the hamstrings are the muscles in the back of your thigh that bend your leg.)

Puberty exacerbates these differences. As a girl's hips widen, her "Q angle" increases. The Q angle is the angle formed by the femur (the thigh bone) in relation to the vertical. The widening of the pelvis that is a normal part of puberty in girls leads to a larger Q angle for young women. As a result, activities that involve the quadriceps—activities such as running, jumping, or kicking a ball—create a more severe torque on the anterior cruciate ligament (ACL) in girls than in boys.

Fatigue stresses the female knee differently, and more severely, compared with the male knee.[29] A girl's leg responds differently to a "run and cut" maneuver compared with a boy's executing the same maneuver.[30] As a result, girl gymnasts are more than *five* times as likely to injure their knees compared to boy gymnasts; girls playing basketball are more than twice as likely to rupture their ACL than boys playing basketball.[31] College women are four to six times more likely to injure their ACLs than men playing the same sport at the same level of competition.[32]

The consequences of knee injuries can be significant and long-lasting. If your daughter experiences an ACL injury, there is more than a fifty-fifty chance that she will develop significant arthritis in that knee within seven to twenty years after the injury.[33] She may need a knee replacement by the time she's in her thirties.

Girls who are injured are more likely to be reinjured, compared with boys who suffer the same injury playing the same sport.[34] This is not because girls are more fragile than boys but because the entire culture of sport has developed around what works for boys, not what works for girls. For example, consider how coaches usually warm up their players before a game. Generations of men have prepared boys before a game by having the boys run a few laps around the track or do some jumping jacks or simple stretching exercises. That may be fine for boys, but it's not helpful for girls. Orthopedic specialists designed a completely different warm-up routine based on girl/boy differences in anatomy. The girls' warm-up routine should involve, among other things, running *backward* as well as prone hamstring flexion exercises. It doesn't cost any more money or time than the boys' routine. It doesn't require any special equipment. But it's different. When girls do these girl-specific routines before practice and competition, the risk of ACL injury is reduced by an astonishing 88 percent compared with girls on comparable teams doing the traditional warm-up.[35]

Ask the coaches of your daughter's team whether they are aware of this girl-specific warm-up and its proven benefits. If they aren't, make sure they learn.

a girl's head is not a boy's head

Samantha Firstenberg was a top-ranked high school lacrosse player. She was sprinting with the ball toward the opposing goal in a high school game. Three girls defending the goal tried to stop her. At least one girl whacked her in the head with a lacrosse stick. Samantha never lost consciousness, but she didn't feel right. She sat out of the game for a few minutes. Then she went back in.

Samantha had suffered a concussion. For several days, she was nauseated, felt dizzy, and had difficulty thinking clearly. Her parents took her to see a specialist at Children's Hospital in Washington, DC. When her symptoms persisted, Samantha and her parents traveled to consult another specialist at the University of Pittsburgh. Even three weeks later, her symptoms were nearly as bad as they had been the day after the game. She couldn't focus for more than ten or fifteen minutes at a time. It took months for her to recover fully.

More than a year later, Samantha sustained a second concussion during a lacrosse match. But she wouldn't give up the sport. She was recruited by Colgate to play NCAA Division I lacrosse. However, just a few days before she was to leave for Colgate, she bumped her head while tubing on a lake. The headaches and dizziness returned. After consulting with specialists, Samantha decided to leave the team and end her career as a competitive lacrosse player. The risks were too great. "Over the next few months, I struggled to define myself without lacrosse shaping who I was and what I did," she told me. She decided to transfer from Colgate to Georgetown, and she took up long-distance running. One year later, she ran the Marine Corps Marathon for the Make-A-Wish Foundation. "But I definitely miss playing lacrosse," she told me at the time.[36]

Most team sports are played by the same rules for girls and for boys at the high school and college level. Lacrosse is a notable exception. Boys are required to wear helmets while playing lacrosse; girls aren't. The reason given is that boys' lacrosse is a contact sport. Boys are allowed to make physical contact with other boys. Girls' lacrosse is supposedly a noncontact sport, because girls are not supposed to make intentional physical contact with other girls.

For most of the past century, research on sports-related head injuries meant research on sports-related head injuries *for boys and men*. Even though girls and women have been playing competitive sports for decades, the first attempt at a thorough investigation of the risk for girls, compared to boys, wasn't published until 2007. That study, undertaken by the NCAA in association with Ohio State University and based on data from 100 high schools and 180 universities across the United States, demonstrated that girls playing high school soccer have a risk of concussion 60 percent higher than boys; girls playing high school basketball have a risk of concussion 300 percent higher than boys.[37]

Which NCAA sport has the highest concussion rate, measured as number of concussions per time played? If you said "football," you'd be wrong. The college sport that carries the highest risk of concussion is women's ice hockey. Women playing ice hockey have more than double the risk of concussion than men playing college football.[38] In every sport played by both girls and boys—basketball, soccer, ice hockey, lacrosse—girls' risk of concussion is significantly higher than the risk for boys.

One can imagine several possible explanations. However, the most plausible explanation is that girls' heads are built differently from boys' heads. Consider the lateral ventricles, which are basically big holes in the brain that contain nothing but cerebrospinal fluid, the watery liquid that encases and insulates the brain. These fluid-filled holes in the brain are significantly bigger in boys than in girls, even after adjusting for any differences in overall body size.[39] The lateral ventricles act as fluid-filled hydraulic shock absorbers. If a boy's head collides with a soccer ball, the odds of damage are lower than if a girl's head collides with the same soccer ball.[40] That makes sense if the boy's lateral ventricles are bigger than the girl's: he has more empty space in his head to absorb the blow.

Some have suggested that maybe the reason that girls have a greater risk of concussion is merely because girls are, on average, smaller than boys. That hypothesis doesn't fit the facts. Girls are more likely to have a concussion compared with boys of the same size, and girls are more likely to suffer lasting cognitive deficits after concussion than boys are. These sex differences are not attributable to differences in overall size or body mass, according to researchers who have carefully controlled for these variables.[41]

Dr. Joseph Bleiberg is a clinical neuropsychologist with a particular interest in head injuries. He says that comparing the male and female skull and brain is "like comparing an SUV and a VW Bug. The same level of impact is probably not going to cause the same level of damage."[42]

What should we, as parents, do to minimize the risk of our daughters suffering a significant head injury?

First: I think it's wise to try to steer your daughter away from the highest-risk sports such as ice hockey, figure skating, and gymnastics.

Second: If your daughter is going to play an intermediate-risk sport such as soccer or lacrosse or basketball, I think you should insist that she wear the new headband-style protective gear. These devices look like overgrown headbands, but they act like helmets. One example is the Full 90, www.full90.com, which comes complete with an opening for your daughter's ponytail in the back. Just make sure that she doesn't regard the helmet as a license to kill.

Third: Insist that the coach and staff have appropriate training in recognizing the signs of concussion, including sex differences in the presentation of concussion. Male coaches whose experience has been mostly with boys may not be aware that girls are at higher risk for concussion. They may not be as thorough in assessing a girl for concussion after she has been knocked in the head but hasn't lost consciousness.

I spoke with Samantha again in November 2019, ten years after our previous conversation. What had happened in the years since? Samantha explained that her doctors advised her against returning to lacrosse or any sport with a high risk of head injury: the danger of another concussion, and lasting disability, was just too great. Instead, she plunged into endurance sports. And I use the word "plunge" literally. In addition to running marathons, Samantha has completed three full

Ironman competitions. The Ironman competition begins with a 2.4-mile swim, followed by a 112-mile bike race, followed by a 26.2-mile marathon. She now ranks in the top 5 percent of Ironman athletes worldwide. She has also completed several half-Ironman competitions and a number of marathons, and she has coached girls' high school lacrosse.

Samantha graduated from Georgetown with a double major in math and psychology. She then went on to the Harvard Graduate School of Education, where she earned a master's degree. After three years teaching sixth-grade math, she returned to graduate school to earn a second master's degree, this one in educational innovation, simultaneously with an MBA, both at the University of Virginia. She hopes someday to launch her own K-12 school.

In her TEDx talk, Samantha is frank about how she felt when she realized she would never play lacrosse again. She felt that she had failed. "Nothing brought me joy," she said. Competing in marathons and Ironman events helped her to overcome that low.

I asked Samantha what advice she would have for other girls struggling to recover after concussion. "Listen to your doctor," she said. "If they tell you to take a week off of school, do it. Try to find someone else who has gone through it. And remember: this too shall pass."

a girl's bones are not a boy's bones

When I was a medical student at the University of Pennsylvania back in the 1980s, we were taught that osteoporosis—brittle bones—is something that happens mostly to older women. Today doctors recognize that although osteoporosis usually *manifests* in women over sixty years of age, it is best understood as a disease that begins in *childhood*, caused by the failure to build sufficient bone in childhood and adolescence. A girl makes most of her bone between six and seventeen years of age. By the time she's seventeen, a young woman has acquired more than 90 percent of all the bone mineral she will ever have. After about age twenty-four, it's mostly downhill.[43]

I'm not saying that women in their forties can't do anything about their bone density, but if your bones are strong at age twenty, you're in good shape. If your bone density is significantly below average at age twenty, it's going to be a real struggle to make up the difference when you're in your forties or fifties. It's much easier for women over age thirty to *maintain* their bone density than to try to *build* bone they should have built when they were younger. So your daughter needs to exercise right, and she needs to eat right.

Researchers at Oregon State University randomly assigned children six to eight years old either to jumping or stretching exercise. The jumpers were asked to jump off a two-foot box one hundred times, three days a week, for seven months. The stretchers did stretching exercises for an equivalent length of time. There were no differences in bone density between the two groups of kids when they enrolled in the study, but at the end of the seven months, the kids who had been assigned to the jumping exercise had significantly stronger bones than the kids who were assigned to the stretching exercise. Even more important, significant improvements in bone density, relative to the control group, were still in evidence seven *years* after the intervention ended—for girls as well as for boys.[44]

In a separate study by Canadian researchers, ten-year-old girls were randomly assigned either to high-impact exercise (lots of jumping) for ten minutes at a time, three times a week, or to regular physical education for the same amount of time. After two years, the girls who had been assigned to be jumpers had stronger bones than the girls who had been assigned to regular PE, even though there was no difference in bone density at the beginning of the study.[45]

Every able-bodied girl can do jumping exercises. It doesn't require any special athletic talent, or any special training for staff, or any expensive equipment.

So your daughter needs to exercise—and so do you. You have to practice what you preach. It's great if your school's PE instructor is familiar with this research, but you can do these exercises with her yourself. Don't rely on your daughter's school, or the coach of her team, to make sure she gets enough exercise. It's *your* responsibility to get her out of the house, jumping up and down in the field or at the park or wherever. The earlier you start, the better. By eight years of age, girls who are more active have significantly stronger bones than girls who are less active.[46]

As with every other aspect of development we've considered here, the rule is this: everything in moderation. Girls who *over*exercise and get too skinny put themselves at risk for stress fractures; that's especially true for girls in track, gymnastics, and cheerleading.[47] Too much of one kind of exercise, without cross-training, is not a good thing.

As for eating right, forget everything you've learned from studies of boys or men. Diet doesn't seem to matter as much in building boys' bones, compared to girls'.[48] Girls, for starters, must drink plenty of milk and avoid cola beverages. Consumption of cola beverages is linked to lower bone density and fractures in girls.[49] (This appears to be true of older women as well.[50]) Drinking soft drinks is associated with brittle bones in teenage girls but not in teenage boys.[51] Girls who drink plenty of milk have stronger bones compared with girls who are equally well nourished but who don't drink much milk; other sources of calcium in the diet do *not* appear to be able to compensate for not drinking milk.[52] There may be more to the story than just calcium; recent research suggests that there are some as-yet-unknown factors in milk that help to build strong bones, especially in girls.[53]

Soy milk, rice milk, and almond milk are increasingly popular. While some dairy farms are closing due to lack of demand for cow's milk, manufacturers of plant-based alternatives report difficulty keeping up with the surging appetite for their product.[54] I encounter parents who believe that these alternatives deliver nutritional benefits comparable to real milk. Those parents are mistaken. One team of pediatricians reported cases of toddlers right here in the United States who showed signs of advanced malnutrition—kwashiorkor and rickets—normally encountered only among severely impoverished families in the Third World. The parents were well educated and caring. They thought they were doing the best thing for their child by giving their child soy milk or rice milk rather than actual milk. The authors note that it is misleading to use the term "milk" for these beverages. They prefer the term "soy beverage" rather than "soy milk."‡ These authors note that

---

‡ In the European Union, the term "milk" is reserved by law for the product of a lactating mammal; see, for example, https://brooklynworks.brooklaw.edu

the parents of one toddler "assumed that they were providing their toddler with superior nutrition, because of the fortified status and relatively high cost of the beverage." But the beverage in question—like many rice, soy, and almond "milks"—provided less than one-tenth the protein found in cow's milk, 1.7 grams of protein per liter, compared with 33 grams of protein per liter in cow's milk.[55]

Your daughter needs to drink milk. Milk from a cow. Or a goat. Soy milk doesn't count. Almond milk doesn't count. If necessary, you can let her drink flavored milk. Girls who drink flavored milk do not become fatter than girls who drink unflavored milk.[56] Girls who are lactose-intolerant need to take special measures.[57]

So give your five-year-old daughter her very own little bottle of strawberry-flavored milk. Don't wait until puberty. In one study, investigators measured bone density in eight-year-olds, then followed the children until they were sixteen years old. Girls who had brittle bones at age eight were significantly more likely to break their bones by the age of sixteen, compared with girls who had strong bones at age eight.[58]

the promise and perils of exercise

The evidence suggests that girls who are involved in sports are more likely to remain active through adolescence, when other girls generally become less active.[59] Girls who are involved in vigorous physical activities, including but not limited to

---

/cgi/viewcontent.cgi?article=2202&context=blr. The beverage sold in the USA as "soy milk" is sold in the EU as "soy mylk" or "soy beverage."

organized sports, also appear to be at lower risk for becoming depressed—and that protective effect holds true regardless of body mass index or even fitness. In other words, an overweight girl who exercises regularly is less likely to become depressed than an equally heavy girl who doesn't exercise.[60] And girls who exercise regularly are less likely to feel tired.[61] Exercise has all sorts of benefits that have nothing to do with how much you weigh or how you look.

But some girls exercise too vigorously or for the wrong reasons. One study of girls age nine to sixteen years found that 46 percent of girls want to look like a female celebrity, and that's part of the reason why they exercise.[62] That's not a healthy motivation. It's *other*-referenced rather than *self*-referenced. The goal should be "to help girls have realistic and healthy body images and recognize the importance of physical activity for overall health and well-being—not just for appearance-focused reasons."[63]

Lauren Fleshman is a veteran of collegiate sports. As an undergraduate at Stanford, she won five NCAA titles in track and field and was a fifteen-time All-American. She observed firsthand other female athletes who were starving themselves. She blames that "on a sports system built by and for men."[64] I certainly agree that when young women are coached by men who have had no training in the gender-specific strategies that work best for girls and women, and who may have inaccurate, stereotyped beliefs about female athletes—such as the mistaken belief that female athletes must be rail thin in order to win—then bad things often happen.

Many girls are on the edge of an unhealthy obsession when it comes to exercise. Some girls fall over that edge. Obsessive exercise can be hazardous to your health. Researchers at San Diego State University interviewed girls at six different California high schools and found that 18 percent of girls playing interscholastic sports reported disordered eating attitudes or behaviors.[65] Almost one in four (23.5 percent) had irregular menstrual periods; almost as many girls (21.8 percent) had low bone density. In another study, young women who participated in sports where leanness is desirable—sports such as gymnastics—were almost twice as likely to have irregular menstrual periods compared to young women participating at the same level of competition in sports such as softball, where leanness is not essential (24.8 percent of girls in "lean" sports compared with 13.1 percent of girls in other sports).[66] We discussed the "athletic triad"—the association of excessive exercise with brittle bones, disordered eating, and loss of the menstrual period—back in Chapter 3.

On the one hand, you don't want your daughter to obsess about her weight. On the other hand, girls who are out of shape are at greater risk not only for overweight and obesity but also for depression and fatigue. How can you encourage the right kind of healthy exercise without pushing your daughter over the edge? In order to answer those questions, we need to understand the role that culture plays, and the role played by something psychologists call *social contrast effects*.

what do girls in chicago have in common with hopi girls in arizona?

Carol Cronin Weisfeld and her colleagues wanted to understand how much of the difference in girls' and boys' interest in sports is due to culture and how much might be due to other factors—perhaps psychological rather than cultural. They decided to watch girls in Chicago playing dodgeball, first girls against girls, then girls and boys together. Then they did the same thing with Native American children on a Hopi reservation in Arizona.

When Chicago girls played against other Chicago girls, there was lots of variation in the style and quality of play. Some of the girls were really serious about the game: as soon as play began, those girls would adopt what coaches call the "athletic stance," knees bent, arms flexed, eyes focused, ready to jump for the ball. When play got underway, these girls were real competitors: they would jump for the ball, grab it, sometimes even wrestling the ball away from another girl. The girls who were most engaged were, not surprisingly, the highest-skilled girls at playing the game. Other girls were not particularly excited about the game and certainly were not jumping and grabbing for the ball; again, not surprisingly, these girls were less skilled. Weisfeld and colleagues found the same variation in engagement and skill among the Native American girls in Arizona.

When boys were brought into the gym so that there were an equal number of girls and boys playing, the picture changed dramatically. The Hopi girls still participated in the game, but the high-skill girls no longer demonstrated their skill. They didn't want to fight the boys for the ball. When the boys were playing, the high-skill Hopi girls looked very much like the low-skill girls. Most of the high-skill Chicago girls didn't even hang around for the game when boys were playing. Instead, they left the playing area altogether and went off in little groups to dance with one another or to snack on potato chips. Most of these kids, girls and boys, were twelve years old. In this study, the average girl in Chicago and in Arizona was bigger and taller than the average boy in Chicago and in Arizona, respectively—which is not surprising, because twelve-year-old girls are often bigger and taller than twelve-year-old boys. Nevertheless, the high-skill girls seemed to lose much of their enthusiasm for the game when boys came on the court.

In a peculiar twist, the investigators—who had previously rated the skill of each girl and each boy in single-sex competition—arranged a game in which high-skill girls played against low-skill boys. The girls didn't do well. They didn't try hard. Only one Chicago girl and only one Hopi girl seemed to be comfortable fighting the boys for the ball.

This study illustrates what psychologists call *group contrast effects*.[67] When members of two different groups are present, members of each group tend to exaggerate the differences between the two groups. Boys and girls categorize themselves as "boys" and "girls," respectively, and will be more likely to behave according to the prevailing cultural stereotype. When girls are around, boys are less willing to exhibit any behavior that might be considered feminine; when boys are around, girls are reluctant to exhibit behaviors that might be considered boyish. I've seen this phenomenon myself while visiting coed schools and single-sex schools with regard to displays of affection for the teacher, for example. At coed elementary and middle schools, it's common to find girls giving the teacher hugs, but you won't find many boys hugging the teacher. At coed schools, hugging the teacher is something girls do. But if that school adopts the single-sex format, with boys in all-boys classrooms, all of a sudden you will find boys hugging the teacher as though it's the most natural thing in the world for a boy to do—which of course it is, as long as there aren't any girls around.[68]

Likewise in the study of Hopi girls and Chicago girls. If grabbing the ball out of somebody else's hands is perceived as "something boys do," then girls will be less likely to do that if boys are present. When the girls are by themselves, you see a wider range of individual differences, from the competitive athlete to the disengaged girl. When boys are added into the mix, group contrast effects kick in, and many of the girls act more "girly"—less competitive, more talkative. The coed format, especially in sports, has the effect of homogenizing the girls: variations among the girls diminish, and differences between the sexes are exaggerated.

And here's what I found strangest of all about the Chicago/Arizona study: when the investigators asked the girls which format they preferred, all-girls or coed, the girls in both locations overwhelmingly said that they preferred the coed format, even though the video showed clearly that the girls were less engaged and did much less well when the boys were playing.[69]

That's important. *Asking* girls which format they prefer isn't a reliable indicator of which format is actually best for them in terms of athletic engagement. What girls say they prefer may not always be what is best for them. Nowadays it wouldn't be cool for most girls to say, "No, I would prefer to do my physical exercise just with other girls, no boys." Such a comment might make a girl vulnerable to the charge of being, God forbid, a prude.

But there's good reason to believe that for most girls, particularly after the onset of puberty, the all-girls format is usually preferable for physical activity. Part of this has to do with the "swimsuit becomes you" phenomenon we considered in Chapter 1. When the boys are around, "you can feel them looking at you," one girl said.[70] Some girls might worry about how they look in the eyes of the boys; other girls are simply annoyed by the way boys rate girls' bodies, as some boys do. There is some evidence that girls from kindergarten through high school are more likely to exercise when offered a single-sex gym class rather than a coed class.[71]

Before 1980 it was common for girls and boys to take their physical education classes separately, even if all other classes were mixed. Today, most coed schools in the United States have coed PE classes. There are many other reasons why this may not be such a good idea beyond the changes just discussed. The best way to provide instruction in physical education may be different for girls than it is for boys. For example, one strategy that is often effective for girls is to have one girl, more experienced in the sport, teach the sport to a novice girl. The more experienced girl is more likely to be sensitive to the needs of the less experienced girl and more interested in really helping her to learn the sport. Girls seem more interested in sharing their knowledge for the sake of sharing, whereas boys are generally more interested in showing off, so this strategy—pairing older kids one-on-one with younger kids—works less well for boys.[72]

The reasons kids play sports are often different for girls than boys. For many boys, the thrill of victory and the agony of defeat is what sports are all about. But "many girls may be more interested in developing their personal capacities through sport than they are in establishing personal superiority over others," according to a report from researchers at the University of Minnesota.[73] Many boys engage in sports because they want to win. The best way to get them engaged in a PE class is to have a real game with clearly defined winners and losers. Though some girls have that same competitive drive, for other girls a win-at-all-costs mentality may be less appealing—and may even push them away from sports. Girls are, on average, more likely to enjoy sports when the emphasis is on having fun and getting in shape rather than on beating the other team.[74]

You can begin to appreciate how a physical education program with girls and boys in the same gym class might result in zero-sum choices for the instructor. If you, the instructor, organize a winner-takes-all competition, then you may engage many of the boys but you risk disengaging many of the girls. But if you structure the class along the lines of "everybody gets a trophy, everybody's a winner," then you may lose at least some of the boys.

The single-sex format can broaden horizons for boys as well as for girls. Again, group contrast effects may be part of the explanation. Several years ago I was interviewing a boy at an all-boys school in Perth, Western Australia. I asked him whether he saw any advantages to attending a boys' school. Was he doing anything at the boys' school that he wouldn't be doing at a comparable coed school?

"Ballet," he responded without hesitation. This young man was the top football player at the school (we're talking Australian rules football, of course). He was tall and muscular. "But there's no way I'd do it if the class were mixed." He explained that when it's just guys in the ballet studio, and some of those guys are his teammates, then it's OK to work on balance and poise and fourth position. "If girls were around, you wouldn't feel as comfortable doing a deep plié?" I asked.

He shook his head. "I just wouldn't be there," he said.

I have found that parents are often receptive to the idea of single-sex physical education for teenagers, provided that the same facilities and resources are available to the girls and boys. That willingness seems to arise in part because so many parents are concerned about the sexual overtones that might kick in when teenage girls and boys engage in strenuous physical activity in close proximity. Too much heavy breathing.

But many parents balk at the idea of single-sex physical education for younger kids. "I don't see the point of separating girls and boys for gym class in second grade," one parent told me. "Seven-year-olds don't have a sexual agenda at that age, do they?" she asked. Seven-year-olds hopefully do not have a sexual agenda, but they certainly do have gendered notions about physical activity. As I noted earlier, seven-year-old boys are more likely to boast about their (imaginary) physical prowess, and seven-year-old girls may believe them, so girls may get the notion very early that the gym and the playing field are the boys' domain. An all-girls physical education program, beginning in kindergarten, might enable more girls to take ownership of the whole domain of physical activity.

We need to help our daughters take that ownership, to feel comfortable on the playing field. By the time kids reach adolescence, "boys are much more comfortable than girls in basketball courts, playing fields, streets, local parks, and other public spaces conducive to physical activity," according to researcher Dr. Kandy James. "Girls often see these places as belonging to boys, and they fear being teased, excluded, or hurt if they try to join in. Instead they sit on the periphery as passive spectators or avoid these active spaces altogether." Many of the girls surveyed by Dr. James said they would use their school basketball courts if the courts were located where boys could not watch them.[75]

Work with your school to ensure that all-girls athletic options and all-girls physical education are available. But the all-girls format won't be so great if you have a male instructor screaming at the girls. We parents need to insist that the instructors who are teaching our daughters understand and respect gender differences in order to help each girl to fulfill her physical potential.

In her book *Perfect Girls, Starving Daughters*, Courtney Martin describes her own years-long struggle to accept her body, to move beyond her obsession with what she ate and how she looked. Her body was her enemy. She began to glimpse a resolution to her struggle one day while taking a yoga class. The instructor told her to "meet your body where it is." This was a new concept for her. *Meet your body where it is.* Be comfortable in your body. Work on your fitness, but be at home in your own body.[76]

Psychotherapist Madeline Levine writes that many communities "overvalue a very narrow range of academic and extracurricular accomplishments."[77] Many parents sign their daughters up for soccer or basketball without investigating whether those sports are really the best choice for their daughter. For some girls, yoga or aerobics might be a better way of connecting with their own bodies. Or maybe canoeing.

I recall Shannon, a teenage girl from my own practice, who discovered on her own at the age of thirteen that she had a passion for canoeing and kayaking. Her father asked if she wanted to join a kayaking club so that she could compete against other teenagers. She had no interest in competing. She didn't want to beat anybody. She just enjoyed the feeling of being on the river, gliding along the water on her own power.

During the summer between tenth grade and eleventh grade, Shannon spent two weeks canoeing the Snake River in the Yukon Territory (Canada) with a group of other girls. She told me later how much she valued that experience. "We spent all day every day either canoeing or portaging our canoe. By the time it was evening and time to make camp, I was *so* hungry. You can't believe how good fresh river trout tastes after you've spent six hours canoeing and two hours portaging your canoe and your gear."

Then after a pause, she said, "It's the most spiritual thing I've ever done. Out there in the wilderness, on the river, where there's no trace of anything human—it's so easy to believe in something more. Paddling on the river became a kind of prayer for me, you know?"

I nodded, because that's what doctors do, but I wasn't sure I understood.

"The physical . . . becomes spiritual," Shannon said and then shook her head as though she had said something wrong, or as though she were on the brink of tears.

chapter 7

_____

spirit

What good is it for someone to gain the whole world,
yet forfeit their soul?

MARK 8:36 (NIV)

Up to this point, we have addressed areas where I think and hope we can all be in agreement. Every girl should use her mind to be in control of her emotions rather than her emotions controlling her. Every girl should strive to be physically fit, within healthy limits. While we may not always agree about the best strategies to achieve these objectives, we all agree on the objectives: for every girl to fulfill her physical and intellectual potential.

But when we turn to matters of the spirit, some parents are uncomfortable. When I'm speaking to parents and I say something like, "For some girls, life is about more than just mind and body; the core of their identity is all about the *spiritual* journey," I see some parents grow visibly restless. It's easy to understand why. Ten or twenty or thirty years ago, some of these parents were themselves teenagers who rebelled against their own parents' attempts to indoctrinate them into a particular religion. Often they don't see the point of religious involvement, or even spiritual engagement, in the twenty-first century.

Your daughter is not your clone. Nowhere is this more true than in matters of the spirit. I spoke with one father who takes pride in having broken free of the strict religion that his parents observed. He believes that most organized religions are sexist, patriarchal, and out-of-date. So this father was baffled when his fourteen-year-old daughter, Zoe, told him that she had become an evangelical Christian. He thought at first that her religious devotion must be her form of rebellion against his parental authority, just as he had rebelled against his own parents. That might be true for some girls, but in Zoe's case teen rebellion just wasn't part of the story.

Other parents say, "My daughter simply has no interest in spiritual or religious matters." Maybe she doesn't. But if your daughter is younger than fourteen years of age, you don't really know yet who she is going to become on this dimension. I don't think anybody can reliably tell what the spiritual or religious proclivities of a girl will be, prior to the completion of puberty.

Age matters. Girls on average are more concerned with pleasing their parents than boys are,[1] so a young girl will often follow in her parents' footsteps, particularly in areas where Mom and Dad are in agreement. If Mom and Dad are both devoutly religious, then their eight-year-old daughter is likely to appear devout. If Mom and Dad both think religion is an antiquated relic of a bygone era, then their eight-year-old daughter is not likely to be interested in religion or spirituality, except maybe as it affects her peer relationships: "Lori and Jessica are going to Vacation Bible School. How come I don't get to go?"

A girl's willingness to follow in her parents' footsteps may change during puberty, when girls often question the spiritual foundations of their lives. For some girls, those are the years of spiritual awakening.[2] That's when they struggle to figure out what matters most to them.

Contemporary American culture assumes that what matters most, or what should matter most for adolescents, is doing well in school, getting accepted to a good university, and getting a good job. Adolescents often question that script, as they should. "Isn't life about more than having a good job?" they may ask—and they are right to ask. Adolescence is the time of life when you need to figure out what you really care about and what will truly make you happy. If you don't figure that out in adolescence, you are setting yourself up to be miserable in adulthood, working hard at a job you don't like, in pursuit of goals that are not meaningful to you.

Puberty is often disorienting for girls and for their parents. So much is changing at once. The girl who used to enjoy going to church services and Sunday school now stubbornly refuses. Or, as in Zoe's case, the girl who never wanted to go to church during the first thirteen years of her life now insists on going every Sunday—and on Wednesday evenings for Bible study, and most Saturday evenings, too, for the youth prayer meeting.

Mix sexuality into the brew, and everybody's confused. Once Dad accepted that Zoe's religiosity was not a form of rebellion against him personally, he seized on the idea that she must have a crush—probably on Luke, a fifteen-year-old boy in the church youth group. Luke's parents were driving Zoe to church for the Saturday-evening prayer service—with Luke in the car, of course. And maybe Zoe did have a bit of a crush on Luke. She certainly blushed when I asked her about it. Maybe Zoe herself wasn't sure how much of her zeal for the Saturday-evening prayer service was due to religious fervor and how much was due to Luke fervor. It's easy for fourteen-year-old girls (and boys too) to confuse the sexual or romantic realm with the religious or spiritual domain.

I think it's important to support and nurture our daughters' spirituality, even if it's not easy. It's especially difficult if your daughter wants to go in a spiritual direction different from your own. It can feel like a personal rejection if, like Zoe's dad, you have no interest in the spiritual life, and your daughter does. Don't take it personally.

Because parents do matter. Researchers have consistently found that the greatest single influence on children's spiritual development is their parents. "Contrary to popular misguided cultural stereotypes and frequent parental misperceptions," wrote the authors of a large nationwide survey, "the evidence clearly shows that the single most important social influence on the religious and spiritual lives of adolescents is their parents." To be sure, teens often deny outright any possibility that their uncool parents could influence them in any way, and particularly in regard to religion and spirituality. But the teens are mistaken. Parents are the most important determinants of their children's spiritual life—or lack thereof.[3]

If you fail to nurture your daughter's budding spirituality, it may be extinguished. And if that happens, then your daughter will be at risk for the all-too-common substitution of sexuality in place of spirituality. The spiritual and the sexual are often tightly linked, especially for teenagers and young adults.

Some girls will try to find the deepest meaning of their lives in a romantic or sexual relationship. It's one of the charms of adolescence that they do so. But it can be dangerous, because no boy can fill the niche in the heart that belongs only to the spirit. Many girls don't know that. In the thrill of sexual awakening, they may plunge into sex and romance with the zeal of a religious convert.

Those girls are in jeopardy of falling into the wrong kind of relationship, one in which a girl gives her boyfriend a kind of spiritual authority over her soul, surrendering her own voice to his. And some boys are all too willing to take that authority. Heather Norris was seventeen years old when she started dating Joshua Bean. It wasn't long before her mom became concerned. "When he would call or text her, she had to answer right away or there was trouble," Ms. Norris said. "She became quiet and withdrawn around him, and that wasn't like her." After three years, Heather tried to break off the relationship and escape from Joshua. He stabbed her to death, dismembered her body, and stuffed the pieces into garbage bags, which he deposited in various dumpsters.[4]

Heather's horrific death was a rare tragedy. But the underlying dynamic is all too common. Stephanie Berry, director of the Behavioral Health Collaborative at Indiana University, reports seeing similar cases frequently. They rarely end in violent death, but the destruction done to a girl's spirit is still devastating. As Berry explains, teenage girls often "see the jealousy and protectiveness as 'Oh, he loves me so much.' Girls make excuses for it and don't realize it's not about love, but it's about controlling you as a possession." Dr. William Pollack, a psychologist who directs the Centers for Men and Young Men at McLean Hospital in Belmont, Massachusetts, sees it too. "Usually when adolescent boys get involved with girls, they fall into the societal model which we call 'macho,' where they need to show they are the ones in control. Actions like nonstop texting or phoning often are efforts to gain control back," said Dr. Pollack.[5]

Robert Bly, a poet who happened to be male, joined together with Dr. Marion Woodman, a psychoanalyst who happened to be female, to try to understand the relationship between femininity, masculinity, and spirituality. They believed that our modern culture leads young people to what they called "the ready-made masculine and the ready-made feminine,"[6] by which they meant the caricatures of masculinity and femininity presented in so many movies, on television, and online. Bly and Woodman believed that each girl must work out for herself what "feminine" will mean for her, what kind of woman she will be; and likewise, each boy must discover and create what "masculine" will mean for him.

Most enduring cultures of which we have any record have taken this process—the transition from childhood through adolescence to a *gendered* adulthood—very seriously. We ignore it. American parents seldom speak to their children at all about "what it means to be a woman" or "what it means to be a man" as opposed to generic, ungendered adulthood. Many parents today don't know what to say.

But girls still want to know: What does it mean to be a woman? Boys still want to know: What does it mean to be a man? Because parents don't tell them, social media fill the vacuum, providing templates for "the ready-made masculine

and the ready-made feminine" that are unrealistic caricatures. But young people don't recognize them as caricatures,
because they have received no guidance; or sometimes, watching a teenager doing an exaggerated, affected makeup tutorial
on YouTube, they *do* recognize those performances as caricatures, but they still have no idea what the real thing looks like.

I think Bly and Woodman identified a major reason why
a growing proportion of girls are anxious, depressed, and
tired; why there are so many girls who can tell you a great deal
about what they *do* but not so much about who they *are*. Part
of a girl's identity as she makes the transition to womanhood
is what kind of a woman she will be, how she will express her
feminine side—and her masculine side.

All of us, as human beings, have both feminine and masculine dimensions. Fifty years ago, the conventional wisdom was
that masculine and feminine are opposites. In popular culture,
on social media and on YouTube, that notion is still prevalent.
According to that notion, the more feminine you are, the less
masculine you are. It's a one-dimensional either/or:

Feminine ◄———————► MASCULINE

If you don't fit in that one-dimensional construct, then
you are "genderqueer" or "genderfluid"—or so you might
think, if all you know is YouTube and social media. But in
reality, if you don't fit in that one-dimensional construct, that
doesn't mean that you are "genderqueer" or "genderfluid"—it
just means that you are human. Very few of us fit into that one-
dimensional construct.

We now have a more informed understanding of the way
we construct gender. For more than four decades now,

scholars in the field of gender studies have recognized that masculine and feminine are two independent dimensions.[7] Any individual may be very feminine; or very masculine; or both feminine and masculine, *androgynous*; or neither feminine nor masculine, *undifferentiated*. It's a two-dimensional both/and. Masculine and feminine are not exclusive.

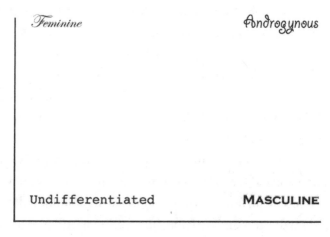

"You should become who you are" is good advice for any teenager.[8] We should help our daughters to understand who they are and who they want to become, regardless of the pressures from the popular culture to conform to a "ready-made" caricature of the feminine.

Bly and Woodman argued that we have neglected the importance of each individual discovering for herself the right balance of feminine and masculine. The right balance for Emily, who loves fashion design and makeup, will not be the right balance for Melissa, whose favorite pastime is corralling hogs at her uncle's farm—and still different from Sonia, who enjoys both working with farm animals and looking at prom dresses; or from Vanessa, who doesn't enjoy either farm work or prom dresses but would rather do crossword puzzles or play Scrabble.

Figuring out how to express your inner masculine in the right balance with your inner feminine is an essential part of the transition to full adulthood, Bly and Woodman believed. And the way you balance the masculine and feminine within you comes very close to the core of who you are. It's a spiritual journey. "In our essence, the opposites are not in opposition," wrote Bly and Woodman[9]—because masculine and feminine are not opposites at all; they are simply different, nonexclusive ways of being human. My wife hates grocery shopping; she always has and probably always will. She would rather mow the lawn. In our marriage, I do the grocery shopping, and she mows the lawn. I can imagine a woman who might enjoy both mowing the lawn and shopping for groceries, but that woman is not my wife.

People are complicated. We shouldn't pretend otherwise. We should celebrate the complexity of the human experience, which includes the complexity of how we map our gender on that infinite two-dimensional space. Bly and Woodman believed that one aspect of a fully developed sense of self has to do with how you work out within yourself the balance of your inner masculine and your inner feminine.

Some girls are spiritual by nature. They yearn for spiritual fulfillment, but they find no satisfaction of that yearning in twenty-first-century popular culture, in the performative culture of social media. When they try to find that fulfillment in sex or in romance, wrote Bly and Woodman, "the result is that the American adolescent tries to receive from sexuality the marvelous ecstasy. . . . But the ecstasy doesn't come. What arrives is disappointment. The adolescent feels horrific despair when the sexual chakra does not deliver the ecstasy that he or she believes will come. Sex is brief and flat. No one can overestimate how huge this Disappointment is."[10] Bly and Woodman observed that some girls then try "to fill the emptiness with alcohol, sexual conquests, clothes, designer drugs, rudeness, flights from home, breakings of the law, self-pity, spiky hair, pregnancy, [or] agreeing to be no one."[11]

That observation is echoed by Courtney Martin, who is herself a young woman chronicling her own struggles and those of her friends. Like Bly and Woodman, Martin has found that much of the obsessive activity of young women today results from an unsatisfied appetite for the spiritual:

> Some of us, for lack of a "capital G" God, have searched out little gods. We worship technology, celebrities, basketball players, rock stars, supermodels, video games. . . . These empty substitute rituals, this misguided worship, intellectualization, addiction to moving fast has led my generation to a dark and lonely place. In the inevitable stillness that frightens the hell out of a perfect girl, she must ask herself not *What is the size of my stomach?* but *What is the quality of my soul? What do I believe in? What is my purpose? Is there a black hole where my core should be?*[12]

Two centuries ago, Western culture tried to sublimate the sexual urge into religious practice. The result was a lot of sexually repressed teenagers and young adults. Today, our culture pushes girls to divert their spiritual impulse into a romantic or sexual channel. The result is a growing proportion of young women who are disillusioned with sex. After a few years of hooking up, they wonder, "Is that all there is?"[13]

The sexual is good. The spiritual is good. But they are not the same thing.

the great disappointment

Bly and Woodman described the spiritual condition of the child before the onset of puberty as characterized by the feeling that "something marvelous is going to happen." Then sometime after the onset of puberty, navigating through adolescence, the teenager "is hit with the awareness that something marvelous is *not* going to happen. That's the moment of The Great Disappointment."[14] In our culture, that moment is sometimes postponed until young adulthood, when the twentysomething finally realizes that she isn't ever going to compete in the Olympics or have a million followers on social media or make a million dollars off her YouTube channel. Technology writer Amelia Tait recently noted that "for every mega-famous YouTube superstar, there are millions struggling for a taste of the big time."[15]

Adolescence should be the time when kids learn about their own limits. In a world that contains more than seven billion people, 99.999 percent of us are going to have to get used to the idea that we are not anybody special. Becoming a mature adult means reconciling yourself to the fact that you're not going to be a movie star, you're not going to be on the cover of *People* magazine, you're not going to be famous.

Our culture today does a terrible job of preparing kids for this moment and helping them to make the transition to mature adulthood. One reason our culture is so lacking in this regard is that we don't understand one key element in this transition: kids don't want to be generic "adults"; rather, girls want to become *women* just as boys want to become *men*.[16] But instead of providing girls with a rich and multidimensional understanding of the feminine and masculine within them, we parents today mostly ignore the topic. We pretend that gender doesn't matter. The consequences of our neglect can be severe.

When boys encounter the Great Disappointment, many of them find solace in the world of video games. If you're a boy or a young man and you invest twenty hours or more each week playing *Red Dead Redemption 2*, you can indeed become master of that universe. And for many boys, that is satisfaction enough. In *Boys Adrift*, I described how easily these boys can become addicted to video games. The games fill the spiritual void. There are a growing number of boys and young men who are finding their spiritual fulfillment, their ultimate meaning of life, playing video games. If you don't think that's possible, you haven't experienced the power of the newest generation of video games, which are—at least for some boys—wholly immersive, well designed, with compelling stories and realistic video. I'm thinking of games such as *Red Dead Redemption 2* and *Call of Duty: Modern Warfare*.

Girls are less likely than their brothers to find satisfaction for their spiritual hunger in the fantasy world of video games, shooting imaginary enemies in an imaginary world. Girls are more likely to plunge into a real-world obsession—which might be an obsession with athletics, thinness, alcohol, cutting, and/or social media. But none of these obsessions will satisfy. It's like drinking water when you're hungry for food.

ivy league student athlete

Madison Holleran had a dream. It seemed like a good dream: to be a student athlete at an Ivy League school. Then something terrible happened. Her dream came true.

Madison was the top scorer on her girls' high school soccer team. She led her team to the New Jersey state championship in her junior year—and then, unbelievably, in her senior year as well. State champions two years in a row. To stay in shape in the off-season, she started running track—and she turned out to be great at track as well. She won the state championship in the eight-hundred-meter. She was named Female Athlete of the Year by the local newspaper, the Bergen County *Record*.

She had lots of friends. She was doing well in school. She had a loving mother and father. Lehigh College offered her a scholarship to play soccer. Then the University of Pennsylvania, an Ivy League school, recruited her to run track.

She had to make a choice: play soccer at Lehigh, which is a small school and not highly selective—or run track at Penn, a highly selective Ivy League school. No-brainer, right? She chose Penn. That was her dream: to be a student athlete at an Ivy League school. Her dream had come true. She was giddy with excitement in the weeks before she enrolled.

But within days of her arrival on campus, her mood began to change. She hadn't realized how much of her enjoyment of soccer and of track at her high school had come from the comradery of being with the other girls, some of whom she had known since kindergarten. They knew each other well; they enjoyed playing soccer together and running together and spending time together. Running track at Penn, she soon realized, would have none of that comradery: instead, she would be doing endless circuits around the track, competing against her own times but having little interaction with the other athletes, every one of whom was a stranger to her. Team sports like soccer have comradery practically baked in: you connect with your teammates at every practice and in every game. But running track is essentially an individual endeavor.

Madison had been a track star in high school almost without breaking a sweat. But the same time that would have earned her a first-place finish in Bergen County was now only an average time at an NCAA Division I track meet. "[Madison] wasn't okay with being good—ever," said her mother, Stacy. "Good was not good enough."[17]

Academics were also, suddenly, a challenge. Madison had been a top student at her high school without too much effort. At Penn, the courses were harder, and Madison felt that she was struggling just to earn a passing mark. And she didn't have enough time to study; track practice consumed every spare moment.

Madison had no history of any kind of psychiatric disorder prior to enrolling at Penn. On the contrary, she had always been bubbly, smiling and laughing, and others laughed with her. She had many friends and admirers, again without seeming to try too hard.

No one seems to have been more surprised than Madison by the depression that hit her shortly after the start of her freshman year. In November, she made an appointment to see a counselor on campus, who asked her about homesickness and counseled her to eat three meals a day. She felt that visit was a total waste of time.

Over the winter break, Madison texted her high school friend Emma to say how much she missed being on a soccer team, having friends on a team. She had looked at Clara's Facebook page—Clara was a high school friend who had gone to Lehigh, the college Madison almost attended—and Lehigh looked like fun. Emma suggested that Madison might transfer, if not to Lehigh, then maybe somewhere else, maybe Vanderbilt. "I wanna!!!!!" Madison texted back.

But the very next day, on January 3, 2014, Madison texted her Penn track teammate Ashley Montgomery to say that she didn't want to transfer, at least not yet. "I don't WANT to transfer. I'm gonna see how this semester turns out ya know? I wanna love penn! Like we always said."

Madison appears to have been haunted by her own dream. On her desk at college was a small sign with the words "Dream Big." Her dream had been to be an Ivy League student athlete. And her dream had come true. How could she walk away from that?

But she had to do something. Quitting track seemed to be the best answer. That would take off the pressure and give her more time: time to do her homework, time to just have fun instead of always feeling stressed and overwhelmed. She arranged to meet with her coach.

She prepared for the meeting carefully. First, she wrote out notes to herself, including "transferring is not an option." Then she wrote two pages, single spaced, that she would read to the coach to explain her decision to quit. She revised it and revised it again. "I never thought it was possible to sink so low, so drastically," she wrote. "Before coming to Penn I was confident, focused, motivated, silly and mainly just a happy girl."

On January 13, 2014, Madison met with her coach. Coach Dolan opened the meeting by congratulating Madison on her success. She was one of the top five fastest women on Penn's cross-country team, despite never having run cross-country in high school. She also had the fifth-highest semester GPA on the entire track team. From Coach Dolan's perspective, Madison was excelling.

Then it was Madison's turn. She took out the two pages she had printed and began to read.

> For as long as I can remember sports have defined me, but now I think it's time for another path. Now I think it's time to define myself. Thank you for giving me the opportunity to compete for Penn and be a part of Penn track, but right now, I'm really not ready to compete. I don't know what is the right choice for me here at Penn, how to be "happy" again, but I know something needs to change . . . the only thing I really want is a break. Maybe taking this semester off will make me realize I want to be on the team again and compete next year, but as of right now I strongly believe that isn't the right choice for me.

Coach Dolan suggested a different path. Instead of staying on the team or quitting, he offered another option: don't quit entirely. Madison could choose what events she would compete in, or stop competing and just practice with the team. Madison's mother, Stacy, who was present throughout the meeting, says that Coach Dolan was "just so sweet and accommodating." But Kate Fagan, Madison's biographer, writes, "Maddy may not have felt empowered; she may only have felt the walls of the cage taking a new shape around her."[18]

"OK, I'll try," Madison said at the end of the meeting.

As I mentioned earlier, I have visited a great many schools over the past twenty years. Often I have seen posters in school hallways that say "Dream Big—Never Quit" or some variation on that theme. But listening to girls, I have begun to understand the dark side of "Dream Big—Never Quit." What if your dream has led you to a dark place? How can you wake up when the dream becomes a nightmare?

On January 14, the day after her meeting with the coach, Madison texted a friend: "I don't think things are gonna change. I just don't know how to express that to [Coach Dolan] without feeling guilty or like a disappointment to him." Shortly before midnight, she texted another friend to say that Coach Dolan "is so friggin nice and awesome and a genuinely good person and I feel like it'd be a huge disappointment to him if I quit . . . I just honestly feel like I'd be letting him down. And my parents."

The morning of January 17, 2014, she made her bed in her dorm room. She scribbled a note: "I don't know who I am anymore. Trying. Trying. Trying. I'm sorry. I love you . . . sorry again . . . sorry again . . . sorry again . . . How did this happen?" Then she bought presents for her family: Godiva chocolates for her father, a necklace for her mom, and gingersnaps for her grandparents, their favorite cookie. She put the items in a shopping bag, along with a photo of herself, smiling and holding a tennis racket, taken when she was a little girl. Next she went to Rittenhouse Square in Center City, a neighborhood in Philadelphia. She took a photograph of the square, edited it to make it more beautiful, and posted the photo to her Instagram. Without a caption.

Then she went to the top of the parking garage at the corner of Spruce and Fifteenth Street. The very top floor. She set the shopping bag with the presents on the ground, with a note explaining which gift was for whom. She also wrote, "I love you all . . . I'm sorry. I love you."

Then she jumped off the roof to her death. Her biographer, Kate Fagan, wrote, "She landed in the bike lane some distance from the side of the building, which seems to suggest a momentum that could not have been gained from standing on the edge, looking down, and dropping. If she'd taken a running leap, then Maddy never had to stare at the ground, truly contemplate it, before choosing to let go."[19]

The first edition of *Girls on the Edge* was published in 2010, three years before Madison Holleran enrolled at Penn. In the weeks and months after Madison's suicide, friends and acquaintances emailed me to ask, "Have you heard what happened to a girl named Madison Holleran?" I received even more emails after Kate Fagan, a writer for ESPN, published a lengthy account of Madison's story in May 2015.[20] After two more years of research, interviewing every one of Madison's friends and family members, Fagan published a book-length account titled *What Made Maddy Run*. My friends recognized at once that Madison's story illustrated in heartbreaking fashion the message I was trying to communicate in *Girls on the Edge*: namely, that the dream can become a nightmare; that the unending pressure to excel can trap even a girl with every possible advantage, a bright, beautiful, athletic girl, in a labyrinth from which she sees no way out. That a girl can look great on the outside and yet be on the edge, on the very brink, about to jump.

Who or what is to blame for the death of Madison Holleran? That's a question I have been asked when I have shared Madison's story in my presentations to parents, to teachers, to coaches, and to clergy. I answer that some of the blame has to be assigned to our culture of "Dream Big—Never Quit." American culture now attaches great importance to going for it all and winning. Never giving up. "Winners Never Quit and Quitters

Never Win" is another poster I see in American schools. "Grit" has become almost a fetish.

Thanks to the cooperation of Madison's friends and family, and the diligence of biographer Kate Fagan, the last weeks and months of Madison's life are remarkably well documented. Fagan reviewed every text message Madison sent, every email she wrote, every photo she posted on Instagram. Madison had no history of depression before she arrived at Penn. The evidence strongly suggests that she came to regret her decision to run track at Penn. Yet she couldn't bring herself to quit. She did try. But when her coach made what seemed like a reasonable accommodation, offering her a lighter schedule, she wasn't able to respond, "No. I want to quit. I have to quit." Because that would mean that she was a quitter. Winners never quit. And quitters never win.

How often do we counsel kids that sometimes it's OK to quit? We don't say it as often as we should. We need to tell kids that sometimes you have to walk away, for your own sanity, for your own survival. Sometimes you have to give up the dream, find a different dream. Yes, it's important for kids to persevere, but they also need to know that there comes a time to walk away and that there is no shame in walking away.

buckle your seatbelt, don't smoke cigarettes, and go to church

Girls who are actively engaged in religious and/or spiritual life are healthier than girls who aren't. That was the conclusion of a years-long survey of more than three thousand American teenagers, from every region of the country, representing a wide variety of religions. The researchers found that teens who are actively engaged and committed to their religious community "are much less likely to smoke cigarettes regularly, drink alcohol weekly or more often, and get drunk.... [They] are also more likely to not drink alcohol and not smoke marijuana."[21] The size of the protective effect is startling. For example, only 1 percent of religiously devoted teens smoke marijuana regularly or occasionally, compared with 21 percent of disengaged teens. These differences remain statistically significant even after controlling for teens' age, race, region of residence, parental marital status, parental education, and family income.[22]

The differences in attitude toward sex were particularly dramatic. Only 3 percent of religiously devoted teens think it's OK to have sex "when you're ready for it emotionally," compared with 56 percent of disengaged teens. In other words, disengaged teens were almost twenty times more likely to say that you can have sex whenever you feel ready for it—and in a culture that prizes risk-taking, the pressure is on to say that you're ready even when you may not be.[23]

Religious involvement seems to work as an antidote or as protection against preoccupation with physical appearance and unrealistic standards of thinness. In the survey, 54 percent of religiously engaged teens say they are "very happy" about their own body and physical appearance, compared with 29 percent of disengaged teens. Only 1 percent of teens who are involved in religion are very unhappy about their body or physical appearance, compared with 7 percent of disengaged teens.[24] Surprisingly, nonreligious teens are more likely than religious teens to say that they "feel guilty about things in life fairly often or very often."[25]

Whereas our twenty-first-century culture often pushes girls to *act* sexual before they *feel* sexual, a religious community can provide an alternative perspective. The survey researchers spoke with Catholic girls at a religious retreat who "seemed exhilarated by the idea that they might actually take charge of their romantic relationships and may not have to barter their bodies simply to get boys' attention."[26] The fact that religious communities often bridge generations, bringing young people together with adults of different ages in many kinds of sharing and social interchange, may be part of the reason why participation in such communities can empower girls to define themselves spiritually rather than sexually. As the researchers point out, "American religion is one of the few major American social institutions that is not rigidly age-stratified and emphasizes personal interactions over time, thus providing youth with personal access to other adult members in their religious communities."[27]

Girls who are fully engaged in the spiritual life are less likely to be depressed than girls from the same demographic who are disengaged from spirituality. The antidepressant effect of being involved in the spiritual or religious life gets bigger, but *only for girls*, after the onset of puberty. In one major study, researchers interviewed 3,356 adolescent girls to understand their degree of religious involvement and the extent to which they were experiencing depression or depressive symptoms. They found that religious involvement protects girls against depression, but the degree of protection appears to be a function of physical maturity (rather than age per se). Girls who have not yet experienced the onset of puberty, or who have just begun the process of puberty, are about 20 percent less likely to be depressed if they are religiously involved. But for girls who are further along in the process of puberty, or who have completed puberty, the benefit roughly doubles; among the more physically mature girls, those involved in religion are 40 percent less likely than nonreligious girls to become depressed.[28]

Sociologists have recognized since the 1990s that religious or spiritual involvement has benefits for girls and women that it doesn't have for boys and men—particularly with regard to preventing depression.[29] For example, Shirley Feldman and her colleagues interviewed girls and boys between thirteen and eighteen years of age about how they cope with stress. Then the researchers came back six years later and interviewed the same people, who were now young women and men. They found that girls who prayed regularly, or who talked to a pastor or other clergy about their problems, were more likely to be doing well and coping better than nonreligious girls. But the reverse was true for boys; boys who "turned to religion" to help deal with stress were actually doing worse than other boys.[30]

In another study, Columbia University researchers Alethea Desrosiers and Lisa Miller suggest that "spirituality experienced in a personal way through a relationship to God may be uniquely protective against depression in girls and women."[31] They interviewed 615 adolescents: girls and boys; Christian and Jewish and Muslim and Buddhist; Asian and black and Hispanic and white. They found that measures of "relational spirituality"—such as praying daily to a God who answers and/or turning to clergy for help with problems—were associated with a significant protective effect against depression in girls from every demographic group. But this protection was seen only in girls, not in boys, regardless of race or religion. These researchers believe that the growing "epidemic" (their word) of depression among girls and young women may be due in part to "broad cultural lack of support or validation of relational spirituality during individuation in girls." That's a fancy way of saying that our culture no longer encourages girls to pray every day, and one result, according to these researchers, is that a lot more girls are depressed.

Girls who are especially inclined toward spirituality, but who find no healthy expression for their spirituality, may be particularly at risk. "A psychological propensity may be either cultivated into a source of resilience, or if left uncultivated, pose risk for pathology," these researchers suggest. A girl who is by nature spiritual might harness that spirituality "through prayer to deepen spiritual connection, but if left 'willy-nilly' might account for the previously established increased depressogenic sensitivity to life events."[32] In other words, a spiritually inclined girl who doesn't find a suitable outlet for her spirituality might actually be *more* likely than average to become depressed, whereas if that same girl becomes integrated into a religious or spiritual community and practices daily devotions, then she will be *less* likely than average to become depressed.

Some people don't want to hear this. I have heard from proud atheists who say, "So you're telling me I should indoctrinate my daughter into some religion I don't believe in, or some spiritual incense-burning and navel-gazing, just because teaching her the mumbo-jumbo *might* decrease her risk of drug use and depression?"

Religious people are sometimes equally annoyed by any mention of the mental-health benefits of religion. As one pastor said to me, "Religion should not be promoted as a form of public health. Faith is not like a flu shot you can get at the mall. I want people to believe that Jesus Christ is their Lord and Savior because it's true, not because it will make them happy or keep them off antidepressant medication."

To the devout pastor I say, "OK, but it's important that you understand the gender differences in what works for tweens and teenagers. Otherwise you may have boys who think that your church is for girls, and girls who are left cold by your services and your youth programs."

To the free-thinking parent I say, "If you want to try to raise your daughter to follow your beliefs, that's your right as a parent. But don't deny *spirituality* just because you can't believe in any *religion*. Commune with nature if you like. Or meditate in the dark with a candle. But you have to help your daughter see that there is more to life than school and extracurriculars and her circle of friends. There is more to life than performance, more to life than achievement. You have to help her to develop all aspects of herself—and that has to include her spirit, not just her mind and her body."

In Chapter 4, while discussing puberty in girls, I mentioned Lyra Belacqua, the heroine of the children's fantasy books *The Golden Compass*, *The Subtle Knife*, and *The Amber Spyglass*. One of the wacky ideas that give these books their unique flavor is that in Lyra's world, everyone's soul is visible in the form of some animal who always stays near the person to whom the soul belongs. In the first book, depending on Lyra's mood, her soul, Pantalaimon, is variously a mouse, a hare, a fox, or a badger. In the course of puberty, each child's soul becomes fixed as one particular animal. There is no more shape-changing once puberty is underway.

The dramatic tension in these scary fantasy books is provided by evil grown-ups who seek to excise the soul from children prior to the onset of puberty. The most haunting images are the children whose souls have been excised. Their minds are intact, their bodies are intact, they don't look any different, but they are missing that special thing that animates them. They are dull and listless.

I see such kids. Often.

the dark night of the soul

Why is the spiritual journey so important? Because life doesn't go as planned. Because death and loss happen. Because disappointment hurts. Even if a girl has a brilliant mind and has earned top marks in every subject, and she is in great physical shape, those achievements of mind and body will count for nothing when the crisis hits. She will then discover that she has been living on the edge of the abyss. It may not take much to push her over that edge. Achievements in academics and athletics won't get you through the dark night of the soul. If her life is just mind and body, then she may feel her life falling apart. She may experience an awful disorientation as she wonders whether anything is worthwhile, whether life is worth living. Maybe it's not. Maybe (she thinks) she would be better off dead. Recall the story of Madison Holleran.

But if she has nurtured her spirit, nurtured it because you have taught her to cherish it, then she can endure through that dark night. It still won't be easy, but it won't poison her as it might if she were not spiritually centered.

Rabbi Sandy Eisenberg Sasso explains why parents—even parents without a strong sense of spirituality themselves—should make this effort. "We want our children to be more than consumers and competitors. We want something much more," she says. "We want them to have courage in difficult times. We want them to have a sense of joy and purpose. That's what it means to nurture their spiritual life."[33]

OK, but how do you do that, exactly?

One place to start, Rabbi Sasso suggests, is with prayer. Maybe you don't believe in a God who answers prayers. Maybe the very idea seems childish to you. Maybe it conjures up an image of an overworked bureaucrat trying to answer too many emails. Try it anyhow. As Rabbi Sasso observes, "Our children are so bombarded with noise and activity, there is very little time for silence and reflection." A quiet time for prayer or meditation is a good antidote to all the noise.

This exercise is not about you. It's about your daughter. If nothing else, you may find that your daughter is able to say things to God, out loud with you listening, that she would never say directly to you.

Here's what you do. You sit down with your daughter, perhaps in the evening, or perhaps during a rainy indoor afternoon. You take her hands in yours, and you are silent with her for a moment. Then you pray. You first, then her. You pray out loud.

How are you supposed to do that if you aren't a religious person? Rabbi Sasso makes these suggestions for a do-it-yourself prayer—and remember to say it out loud, so your daughter can hear.

1. Name some of the things you are grateful for.
2. Then name some of the things you hope for.
3. Then ask for protection from some of the things you fear.
4. Then say Amen.
5. Then tell her it's her turn.

You may be surprised at what happens. As Rabbi Sasso says, "If you can take the hand of your child on that journey, you not only enrich his or her life, you enrich your own. [Children] open part of our lives that maybe has been dormant for a long time." Once that door is opened, there's no telling where it may lead. If nothing else, you are creating new channels for communication with your daughter.*

"i believe there is a god and stuff"[34]

You may start with a prayer, but you have to do more. Ideally you want to help your daughter to figure out what she believes about spirituality; that's part of what it means to honor and

---

* Rabbi Sasso has written a series of picture books, intended to be read out loud to children, specifically to facilitate this conversation. Two of my favorites are *In God's Name* and *But God Remembered: Stories of Women from Creation to the Promised Land.*

cherish the spirit. The survey researchers found that most American teens, even religiously involved teens, are remarkably inarticulate on this point. "For many of the teens we interviewed, *our interview was the first time that any adult had ever asked them what they believed and how it mattered in their life.* Very many seemed caught off-balance by our simple questions, uncertain about what we were asking, at a loss to know how to respond."[35]

Here's a verbatim transcript of one of their interviews:

INTERVIEWER: Where do you get your ideas about God?
TEEN: The Bible, my mom, church. Experience.
I: What kind of experience?
T: He's just done a lot of good in my life, so.
I: Like, what are examples of that?
T: I don't know.
I: Well, I'd love to hear. What good has God done in your life?
T: I, well, I have a house, parents, I have the internet, I have a phone, I have cable.[36]

This could almost be an interview with one of the zombie-like victims in Pullman's dark fantasy. This is what a child disconnected from her own spirit sounds like.

If you want your daughter to develop a strong and healthy spirit, you should do the same as you do to help her develop a strong and healthy body: you should help her to exercise it. Ask her questions. Do you believe in God? How come? Does

God have anything to do with you? Are prayers ever answered? If so, why are some prayers answered and others are not? Of course, these questions should be asked in an age-appropriate way. The conversation with your sixteen-year-old will be different from the conversation with your five-year-old. But you need to have the conversation.

Many adults today are uncomfortable discussing such questions with their children. Try to overcome your reluctance. We adults don't hesitate to teach our kids about school or sports.[37] If you know something about the life of the spirit—even if it's just something about deep breathing that you learned in yoga class—share it. If you don't know anything about the spiritual life, then find someone who does to teach your daughter. And maybe you should go to the classes with her.

You don't learn physics by watching the instructor do physics problems. You have to work out the problems yourself, perhaps with some help from the instructor. You don't learn soccer by watching the coach play. You have to get out on the field and play yourself. Likewise, you can't learn religion or spirituality by watching the pastor pray or the monk meditate. In matters of the spirit, as with the mind or the body, we learn by doing.

Lauriston is a girls' school in a suburb of Melbourne, Australia. For Year Nine (i.e., ninth grade), Lauriston girls don't go to the main Lauriston campus. Every girl in Year Nine spends the academic year at the school's satellite facility, a three-hour drive northeast, deep in the forested hills between Mansfield and Mount Butler. There you will find a collection of cabins set back in the woods.

Cell phones are not permitted. There's no ready access to any kind of shopping, not even for snacks. You eat what the school provides in the cafeteria. If you want candy or chocolate or an espresso, you're out of luck. The girls live in simple wooden cabins with no internet access. More than a few Lauriston girls dread Year Nine, and some of them freak out when they arrive. "My first thought was, 'How am I going to survive without being able to text my friends on my mobile?'" one girl told me when I visited the compound. "And I had no idea what I would do on the weekends. I was so used to going to Chapel Street to shop almost every Saturday. I couldn't imagine what I would do stuck in the middle of nowhere, which is what it seemed like to me."

Slowly, and with some guidance from the staff, the girls start to discover the rhythms of a simpler life. That involves hard work. Manual labor. The cabins are heated by wood stoves; the girls must carry the wood and prepare the fire. Within a few weeks, the hysterics have subsided and the girls are starting to appreciate the experience.

Every girl must do a solitary overnight campout. They are provided with the necessary training over the first few months. The area where the campout takes place is secured and patrolled by adults from the school, so the girl's safety is never in doubt, and she knows this. For many of these girls, however, such an experience is completely unprecedented: alone, outdoors, responsible for making your own campfire, cooking your own meal, pitching your own tent, no electricity, no adults to help (except in case of emergency).

"I was really dreading it," one girl told me. "But when the time finally came, I really enjoyed it. I loved the quiet. It felt *sacred*—more sacred than being in church."

Another girl told me how she started getting up early with her friend to go for a morning run and watch the sun come up over the mountain:

> I was one of those girls who really complained about having to do this whole year out in the bush.[†] And the first few weeks I really hated it. I missed my mobile and shopping and the internet. I really considered those things to be necessities, and I couldn't imagine not having them. But after about two months, I didn't miss them so much. And then one day, while I was sitting and watching the sunrise, it suddenly occurred to me: the mobile and the shopping and the internet—those things are not *necessary* for happiness, they actually *get in the way* of being happy. It was an epiphany.

The girls at Lauriston come mostly from either middle-class or affluent families. They have all sorts of material advantages. Not all girls are so lucky.

I visited the PACE Center in Orlando, Florida. The PACE Centers for Girls comprise twenty-one centers across the state of Florida, serving girls at risk (www.pacecenter.org). Each center includes an all-girls public school, but each center is more than a school. "We're not [just] a school," Jill Gentry, director of the PACE Center in Orlando, told me. "We are a

---

[†] "The bush" is Australian English for "the forest"—not to be confused with "the outback," which is the term used by Australians for the desert areas of their country.

comprehensive center for girls." Roughly half of PACE's services don't fall within the traditional school model. Every girl has a counselor who meets with her frequently, one-on-one; there's also an extensive network of social workers and other social service providers at each center. Most of the girls are from low-income households. Some of the girls are in foster placement.

The motto of the PACE Center in Orlando is "Honor the female spirit." I asked Jill Gentry what that means.

"The female spirit might mean something different for each girl here," she told me. "But there's one thing we're sure of: 'honoring the female spirit' means not letting someone else define you: not the media, not a boy, not even the other girls."

She told me about a recent graduate from the school, a girl named Carmen. Carmen has only vague memories of her mother, a drug addict who died when Carmen was young. Carmen was placed in foster care. By age eleven she was using drugs herself. By age thirteen she was in state-sponsored drug rehab. From rehab she went to living in a residential group facility for teens. That's when she came to the PACE Center in Orlando.

At the center, for the first time in her life, Carmen was welcomed into a community of women who were looking out for her. "If you're one of our girls, we're going to watch over you," Ms. Gentry told me. "If there's a man waiting for you in the parking lot, we're going to ask you: Who's that man? What are you doing with him? What does he expect you to do for him? If a girl comes to school with a bruise on her face, we are going to find out how she got that bruise."

To me it sounded intrusive, but Carmen, and many of the girls, seem to thrive on it. The staff told me that for many of these girls, this was the first time that any adult had cared enough to ask such questions. Carmen started arriving at school early, earlier than most of the staff. She would pack her breakfast in a bag and eat it at school. "She felt safe here," Gentry told me.

In her second year at the PACE Center, Carmen told the staff that she wanted to have a funeral service for her mother at the cemetery where her mother is buried. The staff helped her plan the service, and six of them attended. Afterward, Carmen acted as though a weight had been lifted off her chest. She set to work on her academics with renewed energy, she graduated on time, and she went on to earn a degree from the local community college.

The PACE Centers are strict. Girls must surrender their purses and cell phones each day when they arrive at school. Some girls try to conceal their cell phones. Gentry told me the story of one girl who hid her phone in a place people used to refer to as "décolletage." Then her phone rang. The girl looked around as if to say, "Anybody hear something? I don't hear anything. Do you hear anything?" The teacher walked over to her, said, "Excuse me. Your boobs are ringing," and held out her hand for the phone. The girl meekly reached in, pulled out the phone, and handed it over.

The teachers eat their lunch with the students. That's unusual in public schools, but Gentry told me that it's vital. When women of all different ages eat lunch with teenage girls, there's a community being formed.

Gentry told me about another girl, Alejandra, who was "almost invisible" when she came to the school. Alejandra was cutting herself. She seldom made eye contact—not with teachers, not with the other girls. And she never spoke. After a few weeks at the school, she started to make connections, both with the other students and with the teachers and the counseling staff. A few months later, the cutting stopped.

After two years at the school, Alejandra was a shining star: she was doing well academically and had developed a nourishing circle of friends. She spoke to more than three hundred adults at a fundraiser for the school—and she spoke from the heart. The fundraiser was a big success. "Once a girl at this school finds her voice, she will not lose it," Gentry told me.

The stories of these girls are different, just as the girls themselves are different, but they have one important element in common: each girl was part of a close-knit community of girls and women.

a community of girls and women

Community matters. The kind of community in which your daughter engages will shape the person she becomes. In Chapter 2, I described how a girl growing up forty or fifty years ago was more likely to be involved in communities that included adult women, whether at church, in her extended family, in a sewing circle, or just sitting on her neighbor's front porch. Today, a girl's community is more likely to consist primarily of other girls her own age.[38]

That means girls talking mostly with other girls. But girl talk can be toxic to girls, even when they don't mean it to be.

When girls talk with one another, the most popular topics tend to include their own personal problems. That's as true of nine-year-old girls as it is of nineteen-year-old women. All too often, the sharing and self-disclosure can spin into an obsessive rehash of negative emotion. As the old saying goes, rolling in the mud is not the best way of getting clean. "When girls are talking about these problems, it probably feels good to get that level of support and validation," says Amanda Rose, professor of psychology at the University of Missouri. "But they are not putting two and two together, that actually this excessive talking can make them feel worse."[39]

Dr. Rose and her colleagues call this phenomenon *co-rumination*. It seems to be increasingly common among girls today but remains rare among boys. The essence of co-rumination is that talking with same-age peers about personal problems makes girls more anxious. Tessa Lee-Thomas, thirteen years old, gave a reporter an example of how it can happen. "Sometimes we get into disagreements. And we have to settle them. My friends think that my other friend did something wrong, but she didn't do something wrong. Sometimes it makes the situation worse than where we were when we began. It spiraled into something bigger than it was."[40]

That's what can happen when girls counsel other girls, because girls providing counsel to same-age girls isn't the right kind of community. The right kind of community bridges the generations, connecting girls with women. The right kind of community involves girls learning from women their mother's age and their grandmother's age. Older women can provide your daughter with mature context and perspective. Girls who are the same age as your daughter can't do that.

It doesn't have to be anything formal or structured. Sophia was a high school girl working part-time as a receptionist at a medical clinic when she told me how much she valued the opinions and support provided by her coworkers at the clinic, all of whom are adult women. She had a huge crush on a guy at her high school, and he was taking advantage of her. The other girls at the high school saw nothing wrong with what was going on. In fact, they envied her because he was popular and athletic, and he wasn't being physically intimate with anybody else. But he wasn't making any promises to her either.

When she told the older women in her office about it, they offered a different perspective.

"If you act like a doormat, don't be surprised when he steps all over you," one of them told her.

"If you let him treat you like a piece of meat, don't be surprised if he chews you up and spits you out," said another older woman.

Sophia broke off the relationship—if you could call a series of late-night booty calls a relationship. "He wasn't fazed at all. He was like, 'OK. Whatever. I was getting tired of it anyhow.' I think he said that just to be mean, but it proves that the women at work were right. He wasn't serious about us, about having a relationship. He was just using me."

How does a girl become a woman? What does it mean to be a "real" woman?

These are questions that almost every enduring culture has answered by providing a community of women to show girls the way. I'm not talking only about mothers teaching their daughters but about a community of women teaching the girls. We used to have many such communities in the United States, formal and informal: quilting circles, sewing circles, all-female

Bible study groups, all-female book clubs, Girl Scout troops, the variety of women's clubs that operated in association with the General Federation of Women's Clubs, and so forth.[41] Remnants of such groups still exist, but girls today are much more likely to hang out with other girls their age than they are to mix socially with women their parents' age.

Girls teaching same-age girls what it means to be a woman is a new phenomenon in human history. It's equivalent to the blind leading the blind. Teenage girls don't have the wisdom, experience, and perspective that a thirty-five-year-old woman or a sixty-five-year-old woman can provide.

Many cultures have rituals to mark a girl's passage into womanhood: the quinceañera in many Spanish-speaking cultures, the relatively recent emergence of the bat mitzvah in many Jewish communities today, and *kinaaldá* among the Navajo are three examples. But as the demise of the early twentieth-century debutante ball illustrates, these coming-of-age rituals for girls can be empty or even counterproductive if the focus shifts from identity to surface, from a focus on who you *are* to a focus on how you *look*. And even with the best of intentions, a one-day ritual like a bat mitzvah or quinceañera isn't enough. One day or one week isn't enough. Girls need a community that lasts.

Some girls' schools understand this. A girls' school can easily provide an authentic community of girls and women— as long as the leadership of the school understands the reality that the school's mission must go beyond academics. Men may be fine for teaching girls English or Spanish or mathematics or social studies. Indeed, some of the most effective and most popular teachers I have met at girls' schools have been men.

But only a woman can teach girls what it means to be a woman: how each girl must figure out for herself how she will express and balance her inner feminine and her inner masculine. I have visited a number of girls' schools—such as Lauriston in Australia, Oakcrest School in Virginia, and the PACE Center in Orlando—that consciously, thoughtfully, and intentionally provide that community of women for girls.

But the great majority of girls attend a coed school. You can't expect most coed schools to have much interest in creating all-female communities. You may have to take the lead yourself. You need to create an alternative counterculture in which it's cool for girls to spend time in a community of women. If your daughter attends a coed school, then you might look to your church or synagogue or mosque to provide that community. If you don't belong to a local church or synagogue or mosque, consider joining one—not for your sake but for your daughter's.

If your church or synagogue or mosque doesn't offer an all-female religious retreat, try to organize one. Remind the leaders of your congregation that Christianity, Judaism, and Islam each have long traditions of celebrating all-female religious communions and community. No men allowed.

Most churches and synagogues and mosques in North America offer youth groups for children and teenagers. These groups are usually coed and stratified by age. A typical youth group activity nowadays is a pizza party, or an outing to the bowling alley, for all the ninth-grade girls and boys together. But everything we've learned suggests that a better approach might be to offer a single-sex group, not stratified by age. In fact, it might be time to rethink the whole idea of the church youth group or synagogue youth group or Muslim youth group. These groups should not be about teens hanging out with teens. If teens want to hang out with teens, most of them don't need any help from the church or the synagogue or the mosque. The church or synagogue or mosque should offer opportunities for activities that the kids can't easily arrange by themselves: for example, an all-female hiking trip along a stretch of the Appalachian Trail or an all-female canoe trip, with girls from age eleven on up to grandmothers.

You don't have to tie into an established organization or religious group to do this. Organize a get-together with half a dozen girls and at least two adult women. You might create a sewing circle, if you or a friend of yours knows how to sew. You could organize a once-a-month cooking or baking club, with the club meeting at a different girl's house each month. In December you make holiday treats, in the summer you make slushies and smoothies—something different each season.

My wife, my daughter, and I recently visited my brother's family in Shaker Heights, Ohio. When my brother's wife, Lynda, heard that my daughter, Sarah, likes to knit, Lynda invited Sarah to come with her to a little shop in Shaker called Around the Table Yarns. When Sarah entered the shop, she encountered a single large table, with women of all different ages, including one other teenage girl, seated around the table. One grandmother was knitting an elephant for her grandchild. The room was lined with cubbyholes filled with skeins of yarn for sale, from inexpensive cotton thread to luxurious cashmere. But you don't have to pay anything or buy anything in order to sit at the table and knit. Anybody is welcome to come in and sit down—as long as you want to knit! The two owners,

Pam and Beth, will be happy to help you with any problems you're having with your knitting project. No charge.

Lynda told me later, "I've made so many friends there. I meet someone new almost every time I go. You can talk about your kids, your family, your vacation plans. Nobody looks at their phones. We're really just enjoying each other. At Starbucks, everybody is looking at their phone, or they're talking to the one person they brought with them. At this shop, people are sitting around the table and talking. With everybody. That's what the place is for." Sometimes people bring in home-baked cookies to share. It's a relaxed place to create bonds across generations, where a thirteen-year-old girl like my daughter can easily strike up a conversation with a seventy-four-year-old grandmother, and everybody's having a good time.

If sewing, knitting, and baking seem gender-stereotyped to you, then come up with something else, maybe a backcountry hiking or fishing trip. It's not about the activity. The sewing, the knitting, and the baking are only an excuse to get women and girls together, to create an opportunity for connection.

Your group should bridge the generations. That means ideally involving not just other parents but also grandparents. Encourage your daughter to develop friendships with women your age and your mother's age.

Sometimes we may just need to rediscover old ways of connecting girls with women. Sewing circles were never primarily about sewing; they were about women and girls helping each other, which included helping girls to negotiate the transitions through adolescence and into womanhood. The challenges are different today, of course, but the value of a mature adult perspective hasn't changed.

Your daughter may know more than you do about how to upload videos from a cell phone to a YouTube channel, but you know more than she does about how alcohol affects the behavior of teenage boys. She needs your perspective and the perspective of other adults your age and older.

Don't let your daughter fall into the trap of thinking that her *knowledge* is a substitute for your *wisdom*. As Bly and Woodman observed, the average twelve-year-old girl today knows more about the varieties of human sexual experience than the average sixty-year-old knew in 1890—for example, regarding oral sex and anal intercourse.[42] But knowledge is not the same thing as wisdom. Most girls today don't fully understand the harm that sex can do to a girl, to her spirit, if it's sex at the wrong time in her life or sex with the wrong person. That understanding is not a matter of knowledge. It's a matter of wisdom. Very few twelve-year-old girls (or boys) have that wisdom, and it can't easily be taught in a sex education class. That's why they need you and other adults your age.

I was discussing this topic with Reverend Alan James, who has hosted me on several speaking engagements in Minnesota. When Reverend James was pastor of the small Presbyterian church in Maple Plain, Minnesota, he helped to organize summer canoeing trips: girls with women, and separate trips for boys and men. In a typical trip, eight girls and eight women would gather at the headwaters of the Namekagon (NAM-uh-KAG-in) River in Wisconsin. They would canoe down the Namekagon to the St. Croix River, which divides Wisconsin from Minnesota. That canoe ride is on the St. Croix National Scenic Riverway, managed by the National Park Service, and the Park Service maintains many beautiful campsites accessible only from the river. A typical trip begins with one girl paired with one woman, and together they canoe to the first stop, about two hours downriver. They pull the canoe off the river at the designated campsite and wait for the other pairs to join them. They all make lunch together. Then the girl gets back in the canoe, with a different woman, for another two-hour trip downriver. They pull off the river at the next campsite, where they gather brush and prepare a campfire. All the girls and women then cook supper together. They sit around the campfire, tell stories, sing songs. Then they go to sleep in their tents. Three days and two nights. Each two-hour trek downriver, the girl is paired with a different woman. Two hours in a canoe on a quiet, beautiful river is a great opportunity for a girl to talk to a woman, to listen to a woman, and to learn from a woman.

Reverend James told me that the river excursions were very popular in his day but that his former church no longer offers them. He isn't sure why.

I think I know why. Parents today are less likely than parents in previous generations to *tell* their daughter what the daughter will be doing this summer. Instead, today's parents are more likely to *ask* the daughter what the daughter wants to do. And very few girls today will answer, "Well, what I'd really like to do is to spend three days canoeing down the Namekagon River with some random group of women from the church who I don't even know." Instead, the girl says, "I'd like to do the summer session at Stanford University, for top high school students—I think that would look great on my college application." Or she says, "I'd like to go to the summer intensive field hockey program—I think it would improve my chances of getting a scholarship at an NCAA Division 1 program. I'm thinking UConn." Or she says, "I want to work on my YouTube channel. I want to be the next JoJo Siwa." (If you don't know who JoJo Siwa is, you might start by watching her YouTube video "Boomerang," which she made at twelve years of age and which has had over 840 million views on YouTube.) These experiences—at Stanford, or at the field hockey camp, or in the bedroom making a YouTube video—are very different from one another. What they have in common is an emphasis on *performance*, on impressing other people with how amazing you are. None of them invites, or requires, a spiritual journey. None of them will nurture your girl's core sense of identity, her sense of who she *is* as something separate from what she *does*.

Contemporary North American popular culture does not value bonds across generations. There are very few shows on broadcast or cable TV, very few popular videos on YouTube, that portray their value and significance. That means you can't wait for your daughter to ask for an activity that nurtures and promotes intergenerational bonds. You have to find such an activity, creating it from scratch if necessary, and then offer it to her.

That's what Yollanda Zhang did. She created a program called Girl. Strong. specifically to grow these bonds across generations (www.wearegirlstrong.com). Her program has five components, or pillars. One of the five pillars is a weekend overnight mother-daughter retreat at Albion Hills Conservation Park, about an hour's drive northwest of Toronto. The weekend includes a ropes course, where girls have to work as a team with their moms to walk along ropes suspended mid-air; building shelter and starting a fire using materials nearby;

using a rope swing to get from one platform to another; and so forth.

Parents are enthusiastic about Zhang's program. One mother described how the program has "done wonders for my daughter . . . her teachers at school have all remarked at how much she is coming out of her shell." Another mom reports how her daughter, since participating in the mother-daughter weekend, now amazes her "with her ability to speak confidently in front of strangers."[43]

One weekend won't change everything, but it's a start. And not every parent can be a Yollanda Zhang. But you must try to find a program like hers for your daughter.

"If we choose, we can accept our unique place in history," wrote Bly and Woodman.[44] For the first time in history, there is a general international consensus among educated people that girls and women have a fundamental right to equal opportunity. For the past three decades, most of us have assumed that the best way to ensure equal opportunity is to pretend that girls and women are more or less the same as boys and men, that we should instruct them in the same sports in the same way, and that they have the same spiritual needs.

That assumption hasn't worked very well. In matters of the spirit, as in athletics, simply lifting the strategies that have been used for boys and applying them to girls, in gender-blind fashion, doesn't work well for many girls. We have to recognize that girls need girl-specific interventions. Sewing circles might not be the best way to engage boys in a community of men, but I'm hearing about some communities where it seems to be a great idea for girls.

If girls are not healthy spiritually, they may find themselves not so much *living* as *performing*. I discussed in Chapter 2 how easily this can happen in the era of social media. The technology of social networking sites and texting makes it easy for girls to think they are living their own lives, when in fact they are really putting on a show for their peers. Even back in the 1990s, years before modern social media even existed, Marion Woodman wrote that most girls "have been performing since they were tiny children. They don't know there's any other way to live except for the voice inside that's saying, 'If this is it, it's not worth living.'"[45] Today that problem is more severe.

In Chapter 3, I shared my encounter with an anorexic girl whom I called Lauren. Lauren seemed to be perfectly at peace. In the context of this chapter, one might say that she had connected with her own spirituality and she was comfortable with it. But it was the wrong kind of spirituality, one based on asceticism and self-deprivation devoid of any larger spiritual context, a spirituality divorced from any purpose or perspective outside of the self.

But I have found other girls who manifest the same peace and contentment Lauren has. Carmen, the girl who graduated from the PACE Center in Orlando, has it. Emily, the girl I mentioned in Chapter 3 who dropped out of college to work at the animal shelter, also radiates that same peace and contentment. It wasn't easy for Emily to get to that quiet place, because her parents wanted her to keep on pretending to be somebody she wasn't. They wanted her to keep on *performing* while she wanted to start *living*. In Emily's spiritual quest, she explored Roman Catholicism before deciding not to convert;

she read the works of Thomas Merton, St. Francis of Assisi, and the Buddhist monk Thich Nhat Hanh. Emily herself believes that her devotional reading *and* her conversations at the coffeehouse with Rachel and Carol—two women her mother's age—were crucial in enabling her to find her way, to connect to her true self.

In Chapter 4, I mentioned Michael Pollan's book *In Defense of Food*. I noted there that Mr. Pollan summarizes his book in three short sentences:

> *Eat food.*
> *Not too much.*
> *Mostly plants.*

By *food* he means real food, honest-to-goodness food like asparagus and salmon and carrots and oranges, not factory-manufactured food-like stuff such as Twinkies and Cheez Whiz.

I think I can summarize some of the most important advice this book has to offer to girls in three equally short sentences:

> *Have friends.*
> *Not too many.*
> *Mostly females.*

Have friends. Not too many. As I described in Chapter 2, many girls today are concerned with their six hundred followers on social media, not the one or two real friends who matter. A follower on social media is not a real friend any more than Cheez Whiz is real cheese. Girls who are immersed in the world of Instagram and YouTube may be confused about who should matter more: followers on social media or real friends. As a result, they may jeopardize their real friendships, and their connection with their own inner selves, in their frantic quest to entertain hundreds of acquaintances or near strangers on social media.

Mostly females. It's great for your daughter to be friends with boys, and it's wonderful for her to have a close and loving relationship with her father. In Chapter 4, we considered some evidence that a good relationship with her biological dad may have some unexpected and profound benefits. But the core of a girl's emotional life, for most girls, has to be founded on close friendships with other girls and women. Ideally, the girl's mom should be first on that list. A healthy mother-daughter relationship can be an anchor in the storm. Other close female friends might include another blood relative such as an aunt or a cousin, plus one or two girls her own age, and hopefully at least one woman besides Mom who is not her own age, ideally someone Mom's age or older. Those friendships can last for decades, long after the boys are forgotten.

As I said earlier, parenting is an art, not a science. Sometimes you have to push your daughter into unfamiliar territory when she would rather be sheltered at home. Sometimes you have to shelter her at home when she would rather spend spring break with the cool kids getting drunk at the beach. And the right decision this year may be not quite right next year.

When she is young, you may need to challenge her, gently pushing her out of her comfort zone so that she can explore her world. That may be the only way that she can discover her strengths and her weaknesses. Help her to develop that sense of agency, of being able to create, to imagine, to take the initiative.

The onset of puberty is likely to change her. Don't back away even when she tells you to get lost. Speak to her the words of the poet:

Dig into yourself...
... find out how deep is the place from which your life
springs;
at its source you will find the answer to your question.[46]

The job description of a good parent changes as your daughter grows up. When she's four years old, you have to be in charge. As your daughter matures intellectually, physically, and spiritually, your role has to change. You're no longer the captain; you have to help your daughter take the helm, at first perhaps with your hand on the wheel, but then, as the time becomes ripe, you have to step away and let her chart her own course.

Your daughter's journey, becoming the woman she is meant to be, is a journey to an unknown destination. You don't know the woman she is meant to be. Neither does she. You don't know how she might blend her inner feminine and her inner masculine to find the right balance for her unique spirit. As a parent, it's tempting to think that you know where your daughter's destination should lie. You naturally want to guide your daughter to that destination the way a captain guides a ship. Some parents find it hard to let their daughter take the helm. But that approach—continually trying to steer instead of letting your daughter take control—is likely, eventually, to lead to shipwreck.

Ultimately only your daughter can be the captain of her own ship. But you can be the lighthouse, warning of unseen dangers. You can be the shipwright, helping patch holes and make the ship stronger and better. And you can be the safe harbor, welcoming the sailor home before she sets out on her next voyage.

acknowledgments

My first debt is to the girls who came to see me as patients during my eighteen years as a family physician in Montgomery County, Maryland. What I learned from those girls as they progressed through childhood and adolescence and into adulthood became the foundation for everything I have to share in this book. To them, and to their parents, I express my most sincere thanks. I could not have written any sort of book about girls without the firsthand experience I gained as a family doctor serving Barnesville, Beallsville, Darnestown, Dickerson, Poolesville, and Potomac, Maryland.

However, if I had stayed in my own neighborhood, then this book might be only a memoir of life in western Montgomery County, Maryland. And so I am most grateful to the following schools (listed in alphabetical order) that opened their doors to me over the past fifteen years for personal, face-to-face interviews and/or conversations with girls and/or their teachers and/or their parents:

- Abbotsleigh (Wahroonga, Australia)
- Academy of the Holy Names (Tampa, Florida)
- Academy of the Sacred Heart (Bloomfield Hills, Michigan)

- Academy of the Sacred Heart (Grand Coteau, Louisiana)
- Academy of the Sacred Heart (New Orleans, Louisiana)
- Agnes Irwin School (Bryn Mawr, Pennsylvania)
- Ambleside School (McLean, Virginia)
- Ambleside School of Fredericksburg (Fredericksburg, Texas)
- Anne Bailey Elementary School (St. Albans, West Virginia)
- Atlanta Girls' School (Atlanta, Georgia)
- Averroes High School (Fremont, California)
- Bel Air High School (Bel Air, Maryland)
- Bernard Zell Anshe Emet Day School (Chicago, Illinois)
- Beverly Hills Academy (Beverly Hills, Michigan)
- Bishop Ryan Catholic School (Minot, North Dakota)
- Branksome Hall (Toronto, Ontario)
- Brigidine College St. Ives (Sydney, Australia)
- Burlington Central High School (Burlington, Ontario)
- Caddo Heights Elementary School (Shreveport, Louisiana)
- Canberra Girls Grammar School (Canberra, Australia)
- Canterbury School (Greensboro, North Carolina)
- Carman Trails Elementary School (St. Louis, Missouri)
- Carrington Elementary School (Carrington, North Dakota)
- Carter County High School (Ekalaka, Montana)
- Chatham Hall (Chatham, Virginia)
- Cheyenne High School (Las Vegas, Nevada)
- Cimarron Middle School (Parker, Colorado)
- City of London School for Girls (London, England)
- Clear Water Academy (Calgary, Alberta)

- Colorado Rocky Mountain School (Carbondale, Colorado)
- Columbus School for Girls (Columbus, Ohio)
- Cunningham Elementary School (Waterloo, Iowa)
- Cypress Heights Academy (Baton Rouge, Louisiana)
- Deerfield Academy (Deerfield, Massachusetts)
- Dent Middle School (Columbia, South Carolina)
- Derby Academy (Hingham, Massachusetts)
- Duchesne Academy of the Sacred Heart (Houston, Texas)
- Ellis School (Pittsburgh, Pennsylvania)
- Episcopal School of Dallas (Dallas, Texas)
- Epsom Girls' Grammar (Auckland, New Zealand)
- Everest Academy (Clarkston, Michigan)
- Faith Academy (Mobile, Alabama)
- Faith Christian School (Lafayette, Indiana)
- Foley Intermediate School (Foley, Alabama)
- Gateway Academy (Chesterfield, Missouri)
- Girls Preparatory School (Chattanooga, Tennessee)
- Glenelg Country School (Ellicott City, Maryland)
- Grace Church School (New York, New York)
- Greenwich Academy (Greenwich, Connecticut)
- Hampton Roads Academy (Newport News, Virginia)
- Hastings Girls' High School (Hastings, New Zealand)
- Hathaway Brown (Shaker Heights, Ohio)
- Helen Keller Middle School (Easton, Connecticut)
- Hendrix College (Conway, Arkansas)
- Hewitt School (New York, New York)
- The Highland School (Warrenton, Virginia)
- The Highlands School (Irving, Texas)

- Hillcrest Academy (Cincinnati, Ohio)
- Immaculate Heart Academy (Township of Washington, New Jersey)
- Independence Middle School (Coal City, West Virginia)
- Irma Lerma Rangel School (Dallas, Texas)
- Jefferson Middle School (Springfield, Illinois)
- Jefferson Montessori School (Gaithersburg, Maryland)
- The Joy School (Houston, Texas)
- JSerra Catholic High School (San Juan Capistrano, California)
- Kambala (Sydney, Australia)
- Katherine Delmar Burke School (San Francisco, California)
- Kilgraston School (Perthshire, Scotland)
- Kirk Christian Day School (Town and Country, Missouri)
- Korowa Anglican Girls' School (Melbourne, Australia)
- Lake Forest Country Day School (Lake Forest, Illinois)
- Langston Charter Middle School (Greenville, South Carolina)
- Laurel (Shaker Heights, Ohio)
- Lauriston (Melbourne, Australia)
- L'École Notre Dame des Victoires (San Francisco, California)
- Liceo Monterrey (Monterrey, Mexico)
- Linden Hall (Lititz, Pennsylvania)
- Logos Preparatory Academy (Sugar Land, Texas)
- Lorien Wood School (Vienna, Virginia)
- Madeira School (McLean, Virginia)

- Mary Institute and Country Day School (St. Louis, Missouri)
- McLain High School (Tulsa, Oklahoma)
- Mercy Academy (Louisville, Kentucky)
- Mercy Montessori School (Cincinnati, Ohio)
- Merion Mercy Academy (Merion Station, Pennsylvania)
- Michigan Islamic Academy (Ann Arbor, Michigan)
- MLC School (Perth, Australia)
- MLC School (Sydney, Australia)
- Montrose School (Medfield, Massachusetts)
- Moravian Academy (Bethlehem, Pennsylvania)
- Mother Teresa High School (Ottawa, Ontario)
- Mountain View High School (Los Altos, California)
- Muslim Community School (Potomac, Maryland)
- Nativity of Our Lord School (Broomfield, Colorado)
- North Shore Country Day School (Winnetka, Illinois)
- Oak Grove School (Green Oaks, Illinois)
- Oakcrest School (Vienna, Virginia)
- PACE Center of Orlando (Orlando, Florida)
- Peck School (Morristown, New Jersey)
- Penrhos College (Perth, Australia)
- Pinecrest Academy (Cumming, Georgia)
- Plevna Public School (Plevna, Montana)
- Porter-Gaud School (Charleston, South Carolina)
- Potomac School (McLean, Virginia)
- Providence High School (San Antonio, Texas)
- Punahou School (Honolulu, Hawaii)
- Purnell School (Pottersville, New Jersey)
- Randle Highlands Elementary School (Washington, DC)

- Redlands Christian Schools (Redlands, California)
- Regents School of Austin (Austin, Texas)
- Rippowam Cisqua School (Mount Kisco, New York)
- River Oaks Baptist School (Houston, Texas)
- Riverview High School (Sydney, Nova Scotia)
- Robert Frost Middle School (Hazel Crest, Illinois)
- Rocky Heights Middle School (Lone Tree, Colorado)
- Rocky Mount Preparatory School (Rocky Mount, North Carolina)
- Ross School (East Hampton, New York)
- Royal Palm Academy (Naples, Florida)
- Sacred Heart Greenwich (Greenwich, Connecticut)
- Santa Catalina School (Monterey, California)
- Seymour College (Adelaide, Australia)
- St. Aidan's Anglican Girls' School (Brisbane, Australia)
- St. Andrew's Schools (Honolulu, Hawaii)
- St. Anthony's School (West Vancouver, British Columbia)
- St. Bernard Academy (Nashville, Tennessee)
- St. Brigid of Kildare School (Dublin, Ohio)
- St. Catherine's School (Richmond, Virginia)
- St. Clement's School (Toronto, Ontario)
- St. Cuthbert's College (Auckland, New Zealand)
- St. George's School for Girls (Edinburgh, Scotland)
- St. Helena Montessori School (Saint Helena, California)
- St. James Academy (Monkton, Maryland)
- St. Mary's Anglican Girls' School (Karrinyup [Perth], Australia)
- St. Mary's Episcopal School (Memphis, Tennessee)
- St. Michael's Catholic School (Houston, Texas)

- St. Michael's Collegiate School (Sandy Bay, Tasmania)
- St. Paul's Episcopal Day School (Kansas City, Missouri)
- Stonewall Jackson Middle School (Charleston, West Virginia)
- The Temple—Ohabai Sholom (Nashville, Tennessee)
- Thomas Jefferson Preparatory School (Darnestown, Maryland)
- Trinity Episcopal School (Galveston, Texas)
- Valley School of Ligonier (Rector, Pennsylvania)
- Village School (Pacific Palisades, California)
- Visitation Academy (St. Louis, Missouri)
- West Windsor—Plainsboro High School South (Princeton Junction, New Jersey)
- Wingham School (Elm Creek, Manitoba)
- Woodbridge Middle School (Woodbridge, Virginia)
- Woodford House (Havelock North, New Zealand)
- Woodlands Academy of the Sacred Heart (Lake Forest, Illinois)
- Woodward Avenue Elementary School (Deland, Florida)
- Yakutat School (Yakutat, Alaska)

At several points in this book, I place considerable weight on comments by author Courtney Martin and on the insights of Rabbi Sandy Eisenberg Sasso. I would like to thank both these women for reading relevant portions of the manuscript and, when necessary, correcting or clarifying the text. Any remaining errors are of course solely my responsibility. I also thank Jill Gentry for reading and correcting my retelling of some of the stories I heard during my visit to her school. I am also indebted to Dr. Bonnie Ellinger for double-checking my translation of the key line from Shir HaShirim (Song of Songs). And of course I am grateful to Samantha Firstenberg for sharing her story, for her thoughtful comments regarding girls' risk of concussion, and for updating me in 2019 and 2020 to give her follow-up, ten years later.

I am grateful to Professor Jean Twenge for reading and offering feedback on my discussion of her work, and to Reverend Alan James for sharing his account of the canoe trips down the Namekagon River, and also to Yollanda Zhang for describing her Girl. Strong. program to me. I would like to thank Martina Maderspacher, director of the *Waldkindergarten* in Oberammergau, for allowing me to visit her outdoor kindergarten and to talk with the children there. And my thanks to Dr. Tom Hall for sharing his story of "Sara."

I would also like to thank my agent, Felicia Eth, as well as the team at Basic Books: Amanda Moon, who guided the development of the first edition of this book in its early stages; Whitney Casser, who handled all the necessary editing chores with aplomb; and John Sherer, the publisher of the first edition, for his personal support of the project. Thanks also to Liz Stein, who provided a line-by-line critique of the first edition. I am also grateful to Lara Heimert, publisher of the second edition, for suggesting a second edition. I am especially grateful to Eric Henney, my editor for the second edition, for dragging me into the modern world and for a detailed critique of the text, and to Megan Schindele, who offered many helpful suggestions during the final review of the manuscript. Once again, any errors that remain are my responsibility.

It takes a bit of chutzpah for a middle-aged man, however well-informed, to write a book about girls. My wife, Katie, encouraged me at every step of the way and provided helpful feedback on each chapter. She also helped immensely with all the traveling chores. My hosts were often amazed by my fashionable dress. *"Du seist auch noch so ferne, du bist mir nah."*

And finally, thanks to my daughter, Sarah, who gave me the most important motivation to write this book: the hope that what I have learned will make me a better dad. She was a preschooler when I wrote the first edition. Now she's a teenager. My fingers are crossed. I'm saying prayers. And she still asks me to read to her, every night.

permission credits

The following images have been reproduced with permission of the copyright holder:

Figure 1 is reprinted with permission of the American Psychological Association from the article by Brooke E. Wells and Jean M. Twenge, "Changes in Young People's Sexual Behavior and Attitudes, 1943–1999: a Cross-Temporal Meta-Analysis," *Review of General Psychology*, volume 9, number 3 (2005), p. 254.

Figure 2 is reprinted with permission of the American Psychological Association from the article by Barbara L. Fredrickson, Tomi-Ann Roberts, Stephanie M. Noll, Diane M. Quinn, and Jean M. Twenge, "That Swimsuit Becomes You: Sex Differences in Self-Objectification, Restrained Eating, and Math Performance," *Journal of Personality and Social Psychology*, volume 75, number 1 (1998), p. 279.

Figure 3 is reprinted with permission of Springer Nature, *Psychiatric Quarterly*, Jean M. Twenge and W. Keith Campbell, "Media Use Is Linked to Lower Psychological Well-Being: Evidence from Three Datasets," volume 90, number 1 (2019).

Figure 4 is reprinted by permission of Oxford University Press from the article by Jennifer Ahern, Sandro Galea, Alan Hubbard, Lorraine Midanik, and S. Leonard Syme, entitled "'Culture of Drinking' and Individual Problems with Alcohol Use," *American Journal of Epidemiology*, volume 167, number 9 (2008), p. 1046.

Figure 5 is in the public domain.

Figure 6 is a registered trademark of the Playtex Marketing Corporation.

Figure 7. The photograph of the cheerleaders in Chapter 6 is courtesy of Andres Valenzuela. All Rights Reserved. For more information, please go to www.andresvalenzuelablog.com.

The figure on p. 209 with the words "dream big, never quit" is reproduced with permission of Vector Stock.

The figure on p. 211 with the words "Winners never quit and quitters never win" is reproduced with permission of Shutterstock.

The following lyrics have been reproduced with permission of the copyright holder:

"Paradise by the Dashboard Light,"
written by Jim Steinman; used by permission of
Edward B. Marks Music Company.

notes

Epigraph: Rainer Maria Rilke, "Letters to a Young Poet" (*Briefe an einen jungen Dichter*, Franz Xaver Kappus), letter 1, written February 17, 1903. The original German reads: *"Graben Sie in sich . . .die Tiefen zu prüfen, in denen Ihr Leben entspringt; an seiner Quelle werden Sie die Antwort auf die Frage finden . . ."* The translation is my own.

introduction

1   Except where indicated, the names of the girls have been changed, and certain details have been changed to protect each girl's anonymity. For example, "Emily" was in fact rejected from both Harvard and Princeton, and she did in fact matriculate at a highly selective university, but it wasn't the University of Pennsylvania.

2   These two quotes are from Dr. Meeker's book *Raising a Strong Daughter in a Toxic Culture* (Washington, DC: Regnery, 2020), p. 16.

3   National Institute of Mental Health, "Major Depression," February 2019, https://www.nimh.nih.gov/health/statistics/major-depression.shtml. My figures are drawn from Figure 4, "Past Year Prevalence of Major Depressive Disorder among US Adolescents."

4   For a comprehensive and ongoing scholarly review of studies showing a continuing and rapid rise in the rate of depression among American and British adolescents, see Jonathan Haidt and Jean Twenge, "Is There an Increase in Adolescent Mood Disorders, Self-Harm and Suicide Since 2010 in the USA and UK? A Review," https://tinyurl.com/TeenMental HealthReview.

5   Sally Curtin and Melonie Heron, "Death Rates Due to Suicide and Homicide among Persons Aged 10–24: United States, 2000–2017." NCHS Data Brief, number 352, October 2019, https://www.cdc.gov/nchs/data/data briefs/db352-h.pdf.

6   Donna Ruch and colleagues, "Trends in Suicide among Youth Aged 10 to 19 Years in the United States, 1975 to 2016." *JAMA Network Open*, May 17, 2019, doi:10.1001/jamanetworkopen.2019.3886.

7   Melonie Heron, "Deaths: Leading Causes for 2017," *National Vital Statistics Reports*, volume 68, number 6, June 24, 2019, https://www.cdc.gov/nchs/data/nvsr/nvsr68/nvsr68_06-508.pdf. See Table 1.

8   I have found evidence for a similar phenomenon in Europe, which I presented—using data from Germany—in my book *Jungs im Abseits*, published by Koesel/Bertelsmann in 2009, and also in my book *Pourquoi les garçons perdent pied, et les filles se mettent en danger*—using data from France, published by JC Lattès in 2014.

chapter 1

1   Ariel Levy, *Female Chauvinist Pigs: Women and the Rise of Raunch Culture* (New York: Free Press, 2005), p. 34.

2   These words are spoken by Pamela Josse, a precocious twelve-year-old girl in Muriel Barbery's novel *The Elegance of the Hedgehog*, translated by Alison Anderson (New York: Europa Editions, 2008), p. 192.

3   Stephen Hinshaw and Rachel Kranz, *The Triple Bind: Saving Our Teenage Girls from Today's Pressures* (New York: Ballantine, 2009), p. 112.

4   American Psychological Association, Task Force on the Sexualization of Girls, *Report of the APA Task Force on the Sexualization of Girls* (Washington, DC: American Psychological Association, 2007).

5   See previous reference, p. 3, emphasis added.

6   Streaming video of the routine, along with discussion on *The Early Show*, is available at this link: http://www.washingtonpost.com/wp-dyn/content/video/2010/05/14/VI2010051402601.html?sid=ST2010051404337&noredirect=on.

7   "Grammar School Single Ladies Cause Uproar," *Inside Edition*, May 13, 2010, transcript and streaming video online at https://www.insideedition.com/headlines/638-grammar-school-single-ladies-cause-uproar.

8   See, for example, https://www.pinterest.com/calinemr/dare-to-bare/.

9   Margaret Mead's book *Coming of Age in Samoa* was a best seller when it was first published back in 1928, and it had tremendous influence on American popular culture for decades thereafter. Mead claimed to have found a society where uninhibited girls and boys engaged in unconstrained sexual intimacy beginning at the onset of puberty. Six decades later, a series of investigative reports demonstrated that Mead had gotten the story completely wrong. She had not lived with the islanders but only interviewed a handful of them. Her primary informant, a twenty-four-year-old woman named Fa'apua'a Fa'amu, invented an outrageous story about mixed-sex sleepovers and free sex among young teenagers. Fa'apua'a Fa'amu was a virgin at the time. Sixty years later, she recanted on camera and in a sworn

legal affidavit, explaining that she had told the story to Mead as a joke, not dreaming that anyone would take it seriously. The reality turns out to be almost the opposite of what Mead reported: Samoan culture, like most other traditional cultures, has strict rules prohibiting sex until marriage, with severe punishments for transgressors. See, for example, Derek Freeman, *The Fateful Hoaxing of Margaret Mead: A Historical Analysis of Her Samoan Research* (New York: Basic Books, 1998).

10   Germaine Greer, *The Female Eunuch* (New York: McGraw-Hill, 1970), p. 4, emphasis in original.

11   Ariel Levy in her book *Female Chauvinist Pigs* (New York: Free Press, 2005), and Pamela Paul in her book *Pornified* (New York: Times Books, 2005) both call attention to the irony of these supposedly liberated twenty-first-century girls putting themselves on display for the boys and thinking that somehow this display is empowering and liberated.

12   Gail Collins, "Bristol Palin's New Gig," *New York Times*, May 6, 2009, https://www.nytimes.com/2009/05/07/opinion/07collins.html.

13   See, for example, Heather A. Rupp and Kim Wallen, "Sex Differences in Response to Visual Sexual Stimuli: A Review," *Archives of Sexual Behavior*, volume 37 (2008), pp. 206–218; and Amy D. Lykins, Marta Meana, and Gregory P. Strauss, "Sex Differences in Visual Attention to Erotic and Non-Erotic Stimuli," *Archives of Sexual Behavior*, volume 37 (2008), pp. 219–228.

14   Please see Chapter 6 of the second edition of my book *Why Gender Matters* (New York: Harmony, 2017) for more evidence supporting this assertion.

15   Laura Kipnis, "Harvey Weinstein Is Monster of the Moment, but the Whole System Is Rigged," *New York Times*, January 6, 2020, https://www.nytimes.com/2020/01/06/opinion/weinstein-trial-metoo.html.

16   Hinshaw and Kranz, *The Triple Bind*, p. 105.

17   Marc Hollender, "The Need or Wish to Be Held," *Archives of General Psychiatry*, volume 22 (1970), pp. 445–453.

18   Courtney Martin, *Perfect Girls, Starving Daughters: The Frightening New Normalcy of Hating Your Body* (New York: Free Press, 2007), p. 54.

19   Jessica Bennett, "Are We Turning Tweens into 'Generation Diva'?," *Newsweek*, March 30, 2009, https://www.newsweek.com/are-we-turning-tweens-generation-diva-76425. The subtitle of Bennett's article is "how our obsession with beauty is changing our kids." I don't think that's quite right. Bennett mentions a few maniacal parents, such as some of the mothers on the TLC reality show *Toddlers & Tiaras*, who sit their young daughters down at the vanity and prod them to apply blush and lipstick. But in most families in which a preteen girl is obsessed with beauty products, it's the girl, not the parents, who are pushing for it.

20   Sofia Perpetua and Ashley Maas, "Celebrating at the Spa" (video), *New York Times*, January 2, 2015, https://www.nytimes.com/video/us /100000003303817/a-glamorous-spa-day-for-little-girls.html.

21   From "The Fashion Runway Part," Sweet & Sassy, accessed April 25, 2020, https://www.sweetandsassy.com/parties/fashion-runway/.

22   Maree Thyne and colleagues, "'It Is Amazing How Complete Is the Delusion That Beauty Is Goodness': Expectancies Associated with Tween Makeup Ownership," *International Journal of Consumer Studies*, volume 40 (2016), pp. 543–551.

23   Brooke Wells and Jean Twenge, "Changes in Young People's Sexual Behavior and Attitudes, 1943–1999: A Cross-Temporal Meta-Analysis," *Review of General Psychology*, volume 9 (2005), pp. 249–261.

24   Carolyn Tucker Halpern and Abigail Haydon, "Sexual Timetables for Oral-Genital, Vaginal, and Anal Intercourse: Sociodemographic Comparisons in a Nationally Representative Sample of Adolescents," *American Journal of Public Health*, volume 102 (2012), pp. 1221–1228.

25   I still find people who are not aware that Margaret Mead was the victim of a hoax when she wrote that girls in Samoa enjoy years of unconstrained sexual activity prior to marriage. See my note 9, above.

26   Wells and Twenge, "Changes in Young People's Sexual Behavior and Attitudes, 1943–1999," Figure 1, p. 254.

27   For a thorough and scholarly reflection on the replacement of dating culture by hookup culture, see Kathleen Bogle, *Hooking Up: Sex, Dating, and Relationships on Campus* (New York: NYU Press, 2008). Bogle's book addresses only the college and university experience; we don't yet have a comparable *scholarly* book addressing the contemporary sexual experience of girls in middle school and high school.

28   Levy, *Female Chauvinist Pigs*, p. 93.

29   I'm referring to the November 2009 issue of *Cosmopolitan*.

30   Meg Meeker, *Strong Fathers, Strong Daughters: 10 Secrets Every Father Should Know* (New York: Ballantine, 2007), pp. 104–105.

31   Denise D. Hallfors and associates, "Which Comes First in Adolescence— Sex and Drugs or Depression?," *American Journal of Preventive Medicine*, volume 29 (2005), pp. 163–170.

32   Laura Sessions Stepp, "Hot Fun (or Not Fun) in the Summertime," *Washington Post*, July 22, 2006, p. C1.

33   Leonard Sax, "'Twilight' Sinks Its Teeth into Feminism," *Washington Post*, August 17, 2008.

34   Although this blog is hosted by *Education Week*, the blog itself is anonymous. Here's the link: http://blogs.edweek.org/edweek/eduwonkette /2008/08/leonard_sax_girl_whisperer_or.html.

35   Barbara Fredrickson and associates, "That Swimsuit Becomes You: Sex
      Differences in Self-Objectification, Restrained Eating, and Math Perfor-
      mance," *Journal of Personality and Social Psychology*, volume 75 (1998),
      pp. 269–284. Fredrickson and her team replicated this finding in a more
      recent paper (lead author Diane Quinn, but only with women subjects),
      "The Disruptive Effect of Self-Objectification on Performance," *Psychology
      of Women Quarterly*, volume 30 (2006), pp. 59–64. I do not attach much
      significance to the finding that boys did better while wearing swim trunks
      compared with boys wearing sweaters. In a replication, the boys wearing
      swim trunks did less well than boys wearing sweaters; see Michelle Hebl,
      Eden King, and Jean Lin, "The Swimsuit Becomes Us All: Ethnicity, Gen-
      der, and Vulnerability to Self-Objectification," *Personality and Social Psy-
      chology Bulletin*, volume 30 (2004), pp. 1322–1331. Our culture does not
      expect boys to wear revealing clothes to school. Boys don't have to worry
      about whether their tummy is a "muffin top," and I haven't seen many
      boys wearing midriff shirts to school. So even if boys and girls are equally
      vulnerable to self-objectification while wearing swimsuits, it's still the girls
      who are at greater risk, because we don't expect boys to wear swimsuits
      (or their equivalent) to social gatherings or to school.

36   You can read Megan Fox's June 2009 interview for *Esquire* magazine, in
      which she said, "I think people are born bisexual," at https://www.esquire
      .com/entertainment/interviews/a5874/megan-fox-pics-0609/.

37   Researchers at Cornell University, examining data collected from a rep-
      resentative sampling of young Americans that included more than twenty
      thousand individuals across the United States, found that 14.5 percent
      of the women were categorized as lesbian, bisexual, or "bisexual leaning
      heterosexual." Among young men, 5.6 percent were categorized as gay,
      bisexual, or "bisexual leaning heterosexual." See Ritch Savin-Williams and
      Geoffrey L. Ream, "Prevalence and Stability of Sexual Orientation Com-
      ponents during Adolescence and Young Adulthood," *Archives of Sexual
      Behavior*, volume 36 (2007), pp. 385–394. The proportions in the United
      States might even be lower than in some European countries. For exam-
      ple, in Norway, more than 20 percent of girls and young women were
      categorized as lesbian or bisexual: see L. Wichstrøm and K. Hegna, "Sex-
      ual Orientation and Suicide Attempt: A Longitudinal Study of the Gen-
      eral Norwegian Adolescent Population," *Journal of Abnormal Psychology*,
      volume 112 (2003), pp. 144–151. In another study, 23 percent of girls and
      young women in New Zealand—nearly one in four—were sexually attracted
      to other girls and young women: see N. Dickson and colleagues, "Same-Sex
      Attraction in a Birth Cohort: Prevalence and Persistence in Early Adult-
      hood," *Social Science and Medicine*, volume 56 (2003), pp. 1607–1615.

38　See, for example, Roy Baumeister, "Gender Differences in Erotic Plasticity: The Female Sex Drive as Socially Flexible and Responsive," *Psychological Bulletin*, volume 126 (2000), pp. 347–374.

39　See, for example, Lisa Diamond, "The Evolution of Plasticity in Female-Female Desire," *Journal of Psychology and Human Sexuality*, volume 18 (2006), pp. 245–274.

40　The number one hit song I am thinking of is "I Kissed a Girl," sung by Katy Perry:

I kissed a girl and I liked it
The taste of her cherry chap stick
I kissed a girl just to try it
I hope my boyfriend don't mind it
It felt so wrong
It felt so right

This song reached number one on Billboard—the number one hit song for Katy Perry—and remained in the number one slot on Billboard for seven weeks. https://www.billboard.com/music/katy-perry/chart-history/HDS /song/568259.

41　Jude Dry, "First Same Sex Couple in 'Bachelor' History Hailed as 'Groundbreaking' and 'Vital,'" *IndieWire*, August 21, 2019, https://www .indiewire.com/2019/08/bachelor-in-paradise-lesbian-lgbt-demi-burnett -1202167604/.

42　Levy, *Female Chauvinist Pigs*, p. 150.

43　Stephen Martino and associates, "Exposure to Degrading Versus Nonde-grading Music Lyrics and Sexual Behavior among Youth," *Pediatrics*, volume 118 (2006), pp. e430–e441.

44　American Psychological Association, *APA Task Force on the Sexualization of Girls*, p. 7.

45　See, for example, the opening sequence in the popular teen movie *Superbad*, in which the two main characters debate the pros and cons of various online porn sites. This movie was among the top-grossing teen movies for 2007. Such a sequence—with characters casually discussing different genres of pornography—would have been unthinkable in a movie for teens thirty years ago.

46　Erik Hedegaard, "The Dirty Mind and Lonely Heart of John Mayer," *Rolling Stone*, February 4, 2010, pp. 38–45, 68.

47　This verse occurs three times in Song of Songs: chapter 2, verse 7; chapter 3, verse 5; and chapter 8, verse 4. Here is chapter 8, verse 4 in the original Hebrew:

הִשְׁבַּעְתִּי אֶתְכֶם בְּנוֹת יְרוּשָׁלָיִם:　מַה-תָּעִירוּ וּמַה-תְּעֹרְרוּ אֶת-הָאַהֲבָה עַד שֶׁתֶּחְפָּץ:

The literal translation would be "I charge you, daughters of Jerusalem: Do not arouse and do not awaken love until she desires." The repetition of ideas—do not arouse, do not awaken—is a common usage in biblical Hebrew to express emphasis. The writer of this verse recognizes that while it is possible to arouse and awaken love before "she desires," it is not a good idea to do so—hence my translation, "Do not awaken love before its time." My translation is very similar to that found in the New American Bible: "Do not arouse, do not stir up love, before its own time."

chapter 2

1 Author Jeffrey Eugenides made this comment in a commentary for National Public Radio's *All Things Considered*, "Head in a Fog? Reach for *Herzog*," May 18, 2009, https://www.npr.org/2009/05/18/103846270/head -in-a-fog-reach-for-herzog.

2 This quote was the lead heading in an article in *USA Today*, written by Maria Puente, entitled "Relationships in a Twist over Twitter," April 15, 2009. The online version of the article did not include this quote.

3 I have updated the story from the original. When this girl told me this story more than ten years ago, it was all about Facebook. I have replaced the word "Facebook" with "Instagram," but I have made no other changes.

4 These paragraphs are excerpted from Clara Dollar's essay "My So-Called (Instagram) Life," *New York Times*, May 5, 2017, https://www.nytimes.com /2017/05/05/style/modern-love-my-so-called-instagram-life.html.

5 This paragraph comes from Clara Dollar's follow-up essay, "My Modern Love Essay about Instagram Went Viral. So Why Did Everyone Call Me Brave?," Thrive Global, July 19, 2017, https://thriveglobal.com /stories/my-modern-love-essay-about-instagram-went-viral-so-why-did -everyone-call-me-brave/.

6 See, for example, Jacqueline Nesi and Mitchell Prinstein, "Using Social Media for Social Comparison and Feedback-Seeking: Gender and Popularity Moderate Associations with Depressive Symptoms," *Journal of Abnormal Child Psychology*, volume 43 (2015), pp. 1427–1438. See especially Figure 1. For a continuously updated review of similar articles, see the online Google Doc edited by Jonathan Haidt and Jean Twenge, "Social Media Use and Mental Health," https://tinyurl.com/SocialMediaMental HealthReview.

7 This paragraph is adapted from an article I wrote for the *New York Times*, "Why Do Girls Tend to Have More Anxiety Than Boys?," April 21, 2016, https://well.blogs.nytimes.com/2016/04/21/why-do-girls-have-more -anxiety-than-boys/.

8 Robert W. Fairlie, "Do Boys and Girls Use Computers Differently, and Does It Contribute to Why Boys Do Worse in School Than Girls?," CESifo Working Paper Series number 5496, 2015, https://papers.ssrn.com/sol3/papers .cfm?abstract_id=2664007.

9   Victoria Rideout and Michael Robb, *The Common Sense Census: Media Use by Tweens and Teens, 2019* (San Francisco: Common Sense Media), "Section 8, "Boys and Girls Have Vastly Different Tastes in Media," Figure H, https://www.commonsensemedia.org/sites/default/files/uploads/research/2019-census-8-to-18-key-findings-updated.pdf.

10   Susan Herring and Sanja Kapidzic, "Teens, Gender, and Self-Presentation in Social Media," in *International Encyclopedia of the Social and Behavioral Sciences*, second edition, ed. J. D. Wright (Oxford: Elsevier, 2015), 24: pp. 146–161.

11   Mark Bauerlein, *The Dumbest Generation: How the Digital Age Stupefies Young Americans and Jeopardizes Our Future* (New York: Tarcher, 2008), p. 132.

12   Bauerlein, *The Dumbest Generation*, pp. 36, 42.

13   Bauerlein, *The Dumbest Generation*, p. 158.

14   Judith Rich Harris, *The Nurture Assumption: Why Children Turn Out the Way They Do*, revised and updated (New York: Free Press, 2009), p. 44.

15   Perri Klass, "Is 'Digital Addiction' a Real Threat to Kids?," *New York Times*, May 20, 2019, https://www.nytimes.com/2019/05/20/well/family/is-digital-addiction-a-real-threat-to-kids.html.

16   Erin Brodwin, "There's No Solid Evidence That People Get Addicted to Social Media—and Using It Could Actually Be Beneficial," *Business Insider*, March 19, 2018, https://www.businessinsider.com/social-media-iphone-facebook-instagram-addiction-2018-3.

17   Jean M. Twenge and W. Keith Campbell, "Media Use Is Linked to Lower Psychological Well-Being: Evidence from Three Datasets," *Psychiatric Quarterly*, volume 90 (2019), pp. 311–331. The graph contrasting the Goldilocks curve with the dose-response curve is Figure 1 from this paper.

18   Nellie Bowles and Michael Keller, "Video Games and Online Chats Are 'Hunting Grounds' for Sexual Predators," *New York Times*, December 7, 2019.

19   Reed Albergotti, "Teens Find Circumventing Apple's Parental Controls Is Child's Play," *Washington Post*, October 15, 2019.

20   I have updated this story from the first edition, changing MySpace to Instagram or to "social media."

21   Donna St. George and Daniel Devise, "Slur-Filled Web Site Hurtful but Not Illegal," *Washington Post*, May 17, 2009.

22   Emily Nussbaum, "Say Everything: Kids, the Internet, and the End of Privacy," *New York* magazine, February 12, 2007.

23   Stephen Hinshaw and Rachel Kranz, *The Triple Bind: Saving Our Teenage Girls from Today's Pressures* (New York: Ballantine, 2009), pp. 130–131.

24   See, for example, BBC (no byline), "Rihanna Says Naked Photos Were 'Humiliating,'" November 26, 2009, http://news.bbc.co.uk/2/hi/entertainment/8380602.stm.

25   Jeff Temple and colleagues, "Teen Sexting and Its Association with Sexual Behaviors," *Archives of Pediatrics and Adolescent Medicine*, volume 166 (2012), pp. 828–833.

26   Joe Palazzolo and Corinne Ramey, "Prosecutors Have Evidence Bezos' Girlfriend Gave Texts to Brother Who Leaked to National Enquirer," *Wall Street Journal*, January 24, 2020, https://www.wsj.com/articles /prosecutors-have-evidence-bezos-girlfriend-gave-texts-to-brother-who -leaked-to-national-enquirer-11579908912.

27   Rebekah Wells, "The Trauma of Revenge Porn," *New York Times*, August 4, 2019, https://www.nytimes.com/2019/08/04/opinion/revenge-porn -privacy.html.

28   Sameer Hinduja, "Revenge Porn Research, Laws, and Help for Victims," no date, https://cyberbullying.org/revenge-porn-research-laws-help-victims.

29   Nussbaum, "Say Everything."

30   Clive Thompson, "Clive Thompson on the Age of Microcelebrity: Why Everyone's a Little Brad Pitt," *Wired* magazine, November 27, 2007.

31   See Clive Thompson's article (previous citation).

32   I am alluding here to Joshua Meyrowitz, *No Sense of Place: The Impact of Electronic Media on Social Behavior* (New York: Oxford University Press, 1985). Meyrowitz was writing primarily about the impact of television in the now-distant world at the very dawn of the Web. His comments apply with much greater force to the modern era.

chapter 3

1   Courtney Martin, *Perfect Girls, Starving Daughters: The Frightening New Normalcy of Hating Your Body* (New York: Free Press, 2008), p. 159.

2   Martin, *Starving Daughters*, pp. 29, 35.

3   See, for example, "Pro-Ana Websites: What You Need to Know," September 4, 2019, https://americanaddictioncenters.org/anorexia-treatment/pro-ana.

4   "Pro-Anorexia Web Sites: The Thin Web Line," WebMD, no date given, https://www.webmd.com/mental-health/eating-disorders/anorexia -nervosa/features/pro-anorexia-web-sites-thin-web-line#1.

5   Kamryn Eddy, David Dorer, Debra Franko, and associates, "Diagnostic Crossover in Anorexia Nervosa and Bulimia Nervosa: Implications for DSM-V," *American Journal of Psychiatry*, volume 165 (2008), pp. 245–250, http://ajp.psychiatryonline.org/cgi/reprint/165/2/245.

6   Martin, *Starving Daughters*, p. 227.

7   Martin, *Starving Daughters*, p. 236.

8   Martin, *Starving Daughters*, p. 303.

9   For an introduction to this topic, see the review by Michelle Warren and Amanda Stiehl, "Exercise and Female Adolescents: Effects on the

Reproductive and Skeletal Systems," *Journal of the American Medical Women's Association*, volume 54 (1999), pp. 115–120.

10   Anna Quindlen, *Being Perfect* (New York: Random House, 2005), pp. 47–48.

11   Madeline Levine, *The Price of Privilege: How Parental Pressure and Material Advantage Are Creating a Generation of Disconnected and Unhappy Kids* (New York: HarperCollins, 2006), p. 11.

12   Sara Rimer, "For Girls, It's Be Yourself, and Be Perfect Too," *New York Times*, April 1, 2007, https://www.nytimes.com/2007/04/01/world/amer icas/01iht-girls.1.5099528.html.

13   Levine, *Privilege*, 180.

14   Levine, *Privilege*, 134.

15   Liz Funk, *Supergirls Speak Out: Inside the Secret Crisis of Overachieving Girls* (New York: Simon & Schuster, 2009), p. 58.

16   Martin, *Starving Daughters*, p. 238.

17   Dafna Kanny, Yong Liu, Robert Brewer, and Paul Eke, "Vital Signs: Binge Drinking Among Women and High School Girls," *Morbidity and Mortality Weekly Report*, volume 62 (2013), pp. 9–13, https://www.ncbi.nlm.nih.gov /pmc/articles/PMC4604923/.

18   Koren Zailckas, *Smashed: Story of a Drunken Girlhood* (New York: Penguin, 2005), p. 22.

19   Zailckas, *Smashed*, pp. 61, 62; emphasis added.

20   Zailckas, *Smashed*, p. 64.

21   Zailckas, *Smashed*, pp. 96, 224.

22   National Center on Addiction and Substance Abuse, "Big Differences in Why Girls and Boys Use Cigarettes, Alcohol, and Drugs," https://www .centeronaddiction.org/newsroom/press-releases/2003-formative-years.

23   See Almila Erol and Victor Karpyak, "Sex and Gender-Related Differences in Alcohol Use and Its Consequences: Contemporary Knowledge and Future Research Considerations," *Drug and Alcohol Dependence*, volume 156 (2015), pp. 1–13. See also Enrique Baraona and colleagues, "Gender Differences in Pharmacokinetics of Alcohol," *Alcoholism: Clinical and Experimental Research*, volume 25 (2001), pp. 502–507; and also the National Institute on Alcohol Abuse and Alcoholism, "Are Women More Vulnerable to Alcohol's Effects?," *Alcohol Alert*, number 46 (1999), http://pubs.niaaa .nih.gov/publications/aa46.htm. For an investigation of similar sex differences in laboratory animals, see Silvia Alfonso-Loeches and colleagues, "Gender Differences in Alcohol-Induced Neurotoxicity and Brain Damage," *Toxicology*, volume 311 (2013), pp. 27–34.

24   See, for example, Krista Medina and colleagues, "Prefrontal Cortex Volumes in Adolescents with Alcohol Use Disorders: Unique Gender Effects," *Alcoholism: Clinical and Experimental Research*, volume 32 (2008),

pp. 386–394. These researchers found that teenage girls (age 15–17) with alcohol-use disorders had a smaller prefrontal cortex compared with girls who didn't drink; but that wasn't true for male adolescents. Among adults, men and women who drink heavily both have a smaller PFC compared with nondrinkers. See also K. Mann and colleagues, "Neuroimaging of Gender Differences in Alcohol Dependence: Are Women More Vulnerable?," *Alcoholism: Clinical and Experimental Research*, volume 29 (2005), pp. 896–901. They concluded that "brain atrophy [caused by alcohol] seems to develop faster in women."

25   This paragraph, and the following paragraph, are drawn from my discussion of the effects of alcohol in Chapter 7 of my book *Why Gender Matters: What Parents and Teachers Need to Know about the Emerging Science of Sex Differences*, second edition (New York: Harmony, 2017).

26   Krista Lisdahl Medina and colleagues, "Prefrontal Cortex Volumes in Adolescents with Alcohol Use Disorders: Unique Gender Effects," *Alcoholism: Clinical and Experimental Research*, volume 32 (2008), pp. 386–394.

27   See Timo Kvamme and colleagues, "Sexually Dimorphic Brain Volume Interaction in College-Aged Binge Drinkers," *NeuroImage: Clinical*, volume 10 (2016), pp. 310–317. Similar dimorphic findings reported by Lindsay Squeglia and colleagues, "Binge Drinking Differentially Affects Adolescent Male and Female Brain Morphometry," *Psychopharmacology*, volume 220 (2012), pp. 529–539. For a review, see Lynda Sharrett-Field, "Sex Differences in Neuroadaptation to Alcohol and Withdrawal Neurotoxicity," *European Journal of Physiology*, volume 465 (2013), pp. 643–654.

28   K. T. Foster and colleagues, "Gender Differences in the Structure of Risk for Alcohol Use Disorder in Adolescence and Young Adulthood," *Psychological Medicine*, volume 45 (2015), pp. 3047–3058.

29   Zailckas, *Smashed*, p. 235.

30   National Center on Addiction and Substance Abuse, *The Formative Years: Pathways to Substance Abuse Among Girls and Young Women Ages 8–22* (New York: Columbia University, 2003), p. 25.

31   Stephen E. Gilman and Henry David Abraham, "A Longitudinal Study of the Order of Onset of Alcohol Dependence and Major Depression," *Drug and Alcohol Dependence*, volume 63 (2001), pp. 277–286.

32   See Beth Steger Moscato, Marcia Russell, Maria Zielezny, and colleagues, "Gender Differences in the Relation between Depressive Symptoms and Alcohol Problems: A Longitudinal Perspective," *American Journal of Epidemiology*, volume 148 (1977), pp. 966–974. See also J. Wang and S. Patten, "A Prospective Study of Sex-Specific Effects of Major Depression on Alcohol Consumption," *Canadian Journal of Psychiatry*, volume 46 (2001), pp. 422–425; Andrea King, Nancy Bernardy, and Katherina Hauner, "Stressful

Events, Personality, and Mood Disturbance: Gender Differences in Alcoholics and Problem Drinkers," *Addictive Behaviors*, volume 28 (2003), pp. 171–187; and J. W. Maag and D. M. Irvin, "Alcohol Use and Depression among African-American and Caucasian Adolescents," *Adolescence*, volume 40 (2005), pp. 87–101. These studies demonstrate that the association between depressed mood and subsequent alcohol abuse is much stronger in women than it is in men. However, this association appears to be much less strong, and the gender valence may be different, when one looks at children rather than teenagers or young adults. In a recent study of nine- to thirteen-year-olds, depressed mood at the first interview (when the subject was between nine and thirteen years of age) was associated with an increased risk of subsequent alcohol abuse only in boys, not in girls. See Rosa Crum and colleagues, "Is Depressed Mood in Childhood Associated with an Increased Risk for Initiation of Alcohol Use during Early Adolescence?," *Addictive Behaviors*, volume 33 (2008), pp. 24–40.

33   Jennifer Ahern and colleagues, "'Culture of Drinking' and Individual Problems with Alcohol Use," *American Journal of Epidemiology*, volume 167 (2008), pp. 1041–1049.

34   Lin Fang and Steven Schinke, "Alcohol Use among Asian American Adolescent Girls: The Impact of Immigrant Generation Status and Family Relationships," *Journal of Ethnicity in Substance Abuse*, volume 10 (2011), pp. 275–294.

35   Zailckas, *Smashed*, pp. 257–258.

36   National Center on Addiction and Substance Abuse, *Women Under the Influence* (Baltimore: Johns Hopkins University Press, 2006), p. 46. See also Vaughn Rickert, Roger Vaughan, and Constance Wiemann, "Adolescent Dating Violence and Date Rape," *Current Opinion in Obstetrics and Gynecology*, volume 14 (2002), pp. 495–500.

37   Zailckas, *Smashed*, p. 290.

38   Zailckas, *Smashed*, p. 335.

39   See, for example, E. M. Pattison and J. Kahan, "The Deliberate Self-Harm Syndrome," *American Journal of Psychiatry*, volume 140 (1983), pp. 867–872; and E. M. Pattison and J. Kahan, "Proposal for a Distinctive Diagnosis: The Deliberate Self-Harm Syndrome, DSH," *Suicide and Life-Threatening Behavior*, volume 14 (1984), pp. 17–35.

40   Patricia Adler and Peter Adler, "The Demedicalization of Self-Injury," *Journal of Contemporary Ethnography*, volume 36 (2007), pp. 537–570.

41   Adler and Adler, "The Demedicalization of Self-Injury," p. 538.

42   Benedict Carey, "Getting a Handle on Self-Harm," *New York Times*, November 12, 2019, https://www.nytimes.com/2019/11/11/health/self-harm-injury-cutting-psychology.html. See also Martin Monto, Nick McRee, and

Rank Deryck, "Nonsuicidal Self-Injury among a Representative Sample of US Adolescents," *American Journal of Public Health*, volume 108 (2018), pp. 1042–1048; and Karen Rodham and Keith Hawton, "Epidemiology and Phenomenology of Nonsuicidal Self-Injury," in *Understanding Nonsuicidal Self-Injury*, ed. Matthew Nock (Washington, DC: American Psychological Association, 2009), pp. 37–62. In a door-to-door survey of girls age ten to fourteen years of age, conducted by researchers at Yale University, 56 percent of girls had engaged in nonsuicidal self-injury at some point in their life; 36 percent of girls had engaged in nonsuicidal self-injury within the past year. See Lori Hilt, Christine Cha, and Susan Nolen-Hoeksema, *Journal of Consulting and Clinical Psychology*, volume 76 (2008), pp. 63–71.

43   See Monto and colleagues, 2018 (previous citation). For a review of fourteen studies that examined gender differences in the propensity to nonsuicidal self-injury, see Rodham and Hawton, "Epidemiology and Phenomenology of Nonsuicidal Self-Injury," especially pp. 49–54 and Table 3.4.

44   For example, in a survey of Canadian youth fourteen to twenty-one years of age, Mary Nixon and colleagues reported an overall prevalence of nonsuicidal self-injury of 17 percent. They didn't even mention, in their summary of their paper, that females were much more likely than males to hurt themselves this way. But their data show that 24 percent of females in their study were cutting themselves or otherwise deliberately harming themselves, compared with 8 percent of the males (there were also more females than males in the study overall, which is why the overall rate was closer to the female rate than a simple average of the two rates). The citation is Nixon and colleagues, "Nonsuicidal Self-Harm in Youth: A Population-Based Survey," *Canadian Medical Association Journal*, volume 178 (2008), pp. 306–312.

45   Levine, *The Price of Privilege*, p. 3.

46   This quote is from Favazza's introduction to Marilee Strong, *A Bright Red Scream: Self-Mutilation and the Language of Pain* (New York: Penguin, 1998), p. xii.

47   For a review of this evidence, see Leo Sher and Barbara Stanley, "Biological Models of Nonsuicidal Self-Injury," in Nock, *Understanding Nonsuicidal Self-Injury*, especially the section entitled "Role of Opioids in Nonsuicidal Self-Injury," pp. 100–103. See Leo Sher and Barbara Stanley, "The Role of Endogenous Opioids in the Pathophysiology of Self-Injurious and Suicidal Behavior," *Archives of Suicide Research*, volume 12 (2008), pp. 299–308. See also Sarah Victor, Catherine Glenn, and Elisha Klonsky, "Is Non-Suicidal Self-Injury an 'Addiction'? A Comparison of Craving in Substance Abuse and Non-Suicidal Self-Injury," *Psychiatry Research*, volume 197 (2012), pp. 73–77.

48   In his introduction in Strong, *A Bright Red Scream*, Dr. Favazza observes that "the normal course [of a girl cutting herself] is ten to fifteen years, during which the self-mutilation is interspersed with periods of total quiescence and with [other] impulsive behaviors such as eating disorders, alcohol and substance abuse, and kleptomania" (p. xii).

49   Shana Ross, Nancy Heath, and Jessica Toste, "Non-Suicidal Self-Injury and Eating Pathology in High School Students," *American Journal of Orthopsychiatry*, volume 79 (2009), pp. 83–92.

50   Mark Taylor, "End the University as We Know It," *New York Times*, April 26, 2009, https://www.nytimes.com/2009/04/27/opinion/27taylor.html.

51   Quoted in Funk, *Supergirls Speak Out*, p. 44.

chapter 4

1   Sandra Steingraber, *The Falling Age of Puberty in U.S. Girls: What We Know, What We Need to Know* (San Francisco: Breast Cancer Fund, 2007) p. 10, https://d124kohvtzl951.cloudfront.net/wp-content/uploads/2017/03/02025347/Report_The-Falling-Age-of-Puberty_August_2007.pdf. If that URL is too hard to type, go to https://www.bcpp.org/science-policy/pub lications/, search for "falling age of puberty," and click on the link.

2   For the original article communicating the current guidelines, see Paul Kaplowitz and Sharon Oberfield, "Reexamination of the Age Limit for Defining When Puberty Is Precocious in Girls in the United States," *Pediatrics*, volume 104 (1999), pp. 936–941. For an overview of the controversy regarding this redefinition of precocious puberty, see Arnold Slyper, "The Pubertal Timing Controversy in the USA, and a Review of Possible Causative Factors for the Advance in Timing of Onset of Puberty," *Clinical Endocrinology*, volume 65 (2006), pp. 1–8.

3   Steingraber, *The Falling Age of Puberty in U.S. Girls*, p. 10.

4   Steingraber, pp. 21, 22.

5   Dennis M. Styne and Melvin M. Grumbach, "Puberty: Ontogeny, Neuroendocrinology, Physiology, and Disorders," in *Williams Textbook of Endocrinology*, 11th edition, eds. Henry Kronenberg and colleagues (Philadelphia: Saunders Elsevier, 2008), pp. 969–974.

6   See, for example, Jacqueline Johnson and Elissa Newport, "Critical Period Effects in Second Language Learning: The Influence of Maturational State on the Acquisition of English as a Second Language," *Cognitive Psychology*, volume 21 (1989), pp. 60–99.

7   See, for example, Eduardo Mercado, "Neural and Cognitive Plasticity: From Maps to Minds," *Psychological Bulletin*, volume 134 (2008), pp. 109–137; and C. S. Green and D. Bavelier, "Exercising Your Brain: A Review of

Human Brain Plasticity and Training-Induced Learning," *Psychology and Aging*, volume 23 (2008), pp. 692–701.

8   Steingraber, *The Falling Age of Puberty in U.S. Girls*, p. 16. For more on the trade-offs of puberty with regard to brain plasticity, see Cheryl Sisk and Julia Zehr, "Pubertal Hormones Organize the Adolescent Brain and Behavior," *Frontiers in Neuroendocrinology*, volume 26 (2005), pp. 163–174; E. I. Ahmed, Julia Zehr, Cheryl Sisk, and colleagues, "Pubertal Hormones Modulate the Addition of New Cells to Sexually Dimorphic Brain Regions," *Nature Neuroscience*, volume 11 (2008), pp. 995–997; and A. Joon Yun, Kimberly A. Bazar, and Patrick Y. Lee, "Pineal Attrition, Loss of Cognitive Plasticity, and Onset of Puberty during the Teen Years: Is It a Modern Maladaptation Exposed by Evolutionary Displacement?," *Medical Hypotheses*, volume 63 (2004), pp. 939–950.

9   Sarah Kate Bearman, Katherine Presnell, Erin Martinez, and Eric Stice, "The Skinny on Body Dissatisfaction: A Longitudinal Study of Adolescent Girls and Boys," *Journal of Youth and Adolescence*, volume 35 (2006), pp. 229–241.

10   Tamara Vallido, Debra Jackson, and Louise O'Brien, "Mad, Sad, and Hormonal: The Gendered Nature of Adolescent Sleep Disturbance," *Journal of Child Health Care*, volume 13 (2009), pp. 7–18.

11   See, for example, Lars Wichstrøm, "The Emergence of Gender Differences in Depressed Mood during Adolescence: The Role of Intensified Gender Socialization," *Developmental Psychology*, volume 35 (1999), pp. 232–245. See also Rachel Salk, Janet Hyde, and Lyn Abramson, "Gender Differences in Depression in Representative National Samples: Meta-Analyses of Diagnoses and Symptoms," *Psychological Bulletin*, volume 143 (2017), pp. 783–822.

12   Julia Graber, John Seeley, Jeanne Brooks-Gunn, and Peter Lewinsohn, "Is Pubertal Timing Associated with Psychopathology in Young Adulthood?," *Journal of the American Academy of Child and Adolescent Psychiatry*, volume 43 (2004), pp. 718–726.

13   Vaughn Rickert and Constance Wiemann, "Date Rape among Adolescents and Young Adults," *Journal of Pediatric and Adolescent Gynecology*, volume 11 (1998), pp. 167–175; Judith Vicary, Linda Klingaman, and William Harkness, "Risk Factors Associated with Date Rape and Sexual Assault of Adolescent Girls," *Journal of Adolescence*, volume 18 (1995), pp. 289–306.

14   Laurie Schwab Zabin, Mark Emerson, and David Rowland, "Childhood Sexual Abuse and Early Menarche: The Direction of Their Relationship and Its Implications," *Journal of Adolescent Health*, volume 36 (2005), pp. 393–400.

15   The seminal study in this regard was published by researchers at Columbia University: Julia Graber and colleagues, "Prediction of Eating

Problems: An 8-Year Study of Adolescent Girls," *Developmental Psychology*, volume 30 (1994), pp. 823–834. A similar pattern has been reported in Israel by Dorit Kaluski, Barnabas Natamba, Rebecca Goldsmith, and colleagues, "Determinants of Disordered Eating Behaviors among Israeli Adolescent Girls," *Eating Disorders*, volume 16 (2008), pp. 146–159; and in Italy by Elena Tenconi, Noemi Lunardi, Tatiana Zanetti, and colleagues, "Predictors of Binge Eating in Restrictive Anorexia Nervosa Patients in Italy," *Journal of Nervous and Mental Disease*, volume 194 (2006), pp. 712–715. However, a study from the University of Texas failed to demonstrate an association between early menarche and increased risk of eating disorders. Erin Stice, Katherine Presnell, and Sarah Kate Bearman, "Relation of Early Menarche to Depression, Eating Disorders, Substance Abuse, and Comorbid Psychopathology among Adolescent Girls," *Developmental Psychology*, volume 37 (2001), pp. 608–619, finds that though early menarche was associated with increased risk of depression and substance abuse, it was not associated with increased risk of eating disorders. These researchers conjecture that earlier studies from the United States showing such a relationship involved girls who were early maturers at a time when early puberty was a kind of "deviance" (p. 616). Now that so many girls are going through puberty early, it's no longer unusual and hence no longer associated with an increased risk of eating disorders—or so these authors assert.

16   The association between early onset of puberty and subsequent risk of smoking and alcohol abuse, for girls, is strong. See, for example (in chronological order, most recent first): Kesley de Azevedo and colleagues, "Pubertal Maturation and Health Risk Behaviors in Adolescents: A Systematic Review," *Epidemiology, Biostatistics and Public Health*, volume 14 (2017), https://ebph.it/article/view/12156/11224; Kristin Hedges and Josephine Korchmaros, "Pubertal Timing and Substance Abuse Treatment Outcomes: An Analysis of Early Menarche on Substance Use Patterns," *Journal of Child & Adolescent Substance Abuse*, volume 25 (2016), pp. 598–605; Maria Jaszyna-Gasior, Jennifer Schroeder, Elissa Thorner, and colleagues, "Age at Menarche and Weight Concerns in Relation to Smoking Trajectory and Dependence among Adolescent Girls," *Addictive Behaviors*, volume 34 (2009), pp. 92–95; Erika Westling, Judy Andrews, Sarah Hampson, and Missy Peterson, "Pubertal Timing and Substance Use: The Effects of Gender, Parental Monitoring and Deviant Peers," *Journal of Adolescent Health*, volume 42 (2008), pp. 555–563; Grete Bratberg, Tom Nilsen, and colleagues, "Sexual Maturation in Early Adolescence and Alcohol Drinking and Cigarette Smoking in Late Adolescence," *European Journal of Pediatrics*, volume 164 (2005), pp. 621–625; Stephanie Lanza and Linda Collins, "Pubertal Timing and the Onset of Substance Use in Females during Early

Adolescence," *Prevention Science*, volume 3 (2002), pp. 69–82; Margit Wiesner and Angela Ittel, "Relations of Pubertal Timing and Depressive Symptoms to Substance Use in Early Adolescence," *Journal of Early Adolescence*, volume 22 (2002), pp. 5–23; and Erin Stice, Katherine Presnell, and Sarah Kate Bearman, "Relation of Early Menarche to Depression, Eating Disorders, Substance Abuse, and Comorbid Psychopathology among Adolescent Girls," *Developmental Psychology*, volume 37 (2001), pp. 608–619.

17   See, for example, Sarah Lynne, Julia Graber, Tracy Nichols, and colleagues, "Links between Pubertal Timing, Peer Influences, and Externalizing Behaviors among Urban Students Followed through Middle School," *Journal of Adolescent Health*, volume 40 (2007), pp. e7–e13; and Maria Celio, Niranjan Karnik, and Hans Steiner, "Early Maturation as a Risk Factor for Aggression and Delinquency in Adolescent Girls: A Review," *International Journal of Clinical Practice*, volume 60 (2006), pp. 1254–1262; and Andrea Waylen and Dieter Wolke, "Sex 'n' Drugs 'n' Rock 'n' Roll: The Meaning and Social Consequences of Pubertal Timing," *European Journal of Endocrinology*, volume 151 (2004), pp. 151–159.

18   Shannon Cavanagh, Catherine Riegle-Crumb, and Robert Crosnoe, "Puberty and the Education of Girls," *Social Psychology Quarterly*, volume 70 (2007), pp. 186–198. See also Andrew Martin and Katharine Steinbeck, "The Role of Puberty in Students' Academic Motivation and Achievement," *Learning and Individual Differences*, volume 53 (2017), pp. 37–46.

19   Karen Remsberg, Ellen Demerath, and colleagues, "Early Menarche and the Development of Cardiovascular Disease Risk Factors in Adolescent Girls: The Fels Longitudinal Study," *Journal of Clinical Endocrinology and Metabolism*, volume 90 (2005), pp. 2718–2724.

20   Many studies have demonstrated that an earlier onset of menarche is associated with an increased risk of breast cancer. See, for example, William Anderson and colleagues, "Estimating Age-Specific Breast Cancer Risks: A Descriptive Tool to Identify Age Interactions," *Cancer Causes and Control*, volume 18 (2007), pp. 439–447; Françoise Clavel-Chapelon and colleagues, "Differential Effects of Reproductive Factors on the Risk of Pre- and Postmenopausal Breast Cancer: Results from a Large Cohort of French Women," *British Journal of Cancer*, volume 86 (2002), pp. 723–727; Motoki Iwasaki and colleagues, "Role and Impact of Menstrual and Reproductive Factors on Breast Cancer Risk in Japan," *European Journal of Cancer Prevention*, volume 16 (2007), pp. 116–123; and Sumitra Shantakumar and colleagues, "Reproductive Factors and Breast Cancer Risk among Older Women," *Breast Cancer Research and Treatment*, volume 102 (2007), pp. 365–374. In addition, the tempo of puberty may be a factor. If a girl begins to develop breasts at age eight but doesn't experience menarche until age twelve, she has created a four-year-wide "estrogen window," which

may predispose her to developing breast cancer as an adult. In one study of twin sisters, investigators found that the twin who began breast development first had a risk of developing breast cancer *five times higher* than the twin who began breast development later. The reference is Ann Hamilton and Thomas Mack, "Puberty and Genetic Susceptibility to Breast Cancer in a Case-Control Study in Twins," *New England Journal of Medicine*, volume 348 (2003), pp. 2313–2322. See also Genevieve Dall and Kara Britt, "Estrogen Effects on the Mammary Gland in Early and Late Life and Breast Cancer Risk," *Frontiers in Oncology*, May 2017, https://www.frontiersin.org/articles/10.3389/fonc.2017.00110/full.

21   Chantal C. Orgéas and colleagues, "The Influence of Menstrual Risk Factors on Tumor Characteristics and Survival in Postmenopausal Breast Cancer," *Breast Cancer Research*, volume 10 (2008), https://breast-cancer-research.biomedcentral.com/track/pdf/10.1186/bcr2212.

22   These figures come from Cheryl Fryar and colleagues, "Prevalence of Obesity among Children and Adolescents: United States, Trends 1963–1965 through 2009–2010," published September 13, 2012, by the Centers for Disease Control and Prevention, full text online at www.cdc.gov/nchs/data/hestat/obesity_child_09_10/obesity_child_09_10.htm. The figure is adapted from "CDC Grand Grounds: Childhood Obesity in the United States," published January 21, 2011, http://www.cdc.gov/mmwr/preview/mmwrhtml/mm6002a2.htm#fig1.

23   Jaime Gahche and colleagues, NCHS Data Brief 153, May 2014, "Cardiorespiratory Fitness Levels among U.S. Youth Aged 12–15 Years: United States, 1999–2004 and 2012," http://www.cdc.gov/nchs/data/databriefs/db153.htm.

24   David Freedman, Laura Kettel Khan, Mary Serdula, and colleagues, "Relation of Age at Menarche to Race, Time Period, and Anthropometric Dimensions: The Bogalusa Heart Study," *Pediatrics*, volume 110 (2002), p. e43.

25   Kirsten Krahnstoever Davison, Elizabeth Susman, and Leann Lipps Birch, "Percent Body Fat at Age 5 Predicts Earlier Pubertal Development among Girls at Age 9," *Pediatrics*, volume 111 (2003), pp. 815–821.

26   Joyce Lee, Danielle Appugliese, Niko Kaciroti, and colleagues, "Weight Status in Young Girls and the Onset of Puberty," *Pediatrics*, volume 119 (2007), pp. e624–e630.

27   Lise Aksglaede, Kaspar Sørensen, Jørgen H. Petersen, Niels E. Skakkebæk, and Anders Juul, "Recent Decline in Age at Breast Development: The Copenhagen Puberty Study," *Pediatrics*, volume 123 (2009), pp. e932–e939. These researchers were careful to ensure that the girls studied in 2006–2008 had the same demographics—racial, ethnic, and socioeconomic status—as the girls in the early 1990s cohort. The quote comes from p. e935.

28   Frank Biro, Maida Galvez, Louise Greenspan, and colleagues, "Pubertal Assessment Method and Baseline Characteristics in a Mixed Longitudinal Study of Girls," *Pediatrics*, volume 126 (2010), pp. e583–590.

29   Arnold Slyper, "The Pubertal Timing Controversy in the USA, and a Review of Possible Causative Factors for the Advance in Timing of Onset of Puberty," *Clinical Endocrinology*, volume 65 (2006), pp. 1–8.

30   Aksglaede and colleagues, "Recent Decline in Age at Breast Development: The Copenhagen Puberty Study," p. e935.

31   To be sure, there are occasional accounts of environmental toxins having masculinizing rather than feminizing effects. See, for example, L. G. Parks, C. S. Lambright, and colleagues, "Masculinization of Female Mosquitofish in Kraft Mill Effluent-Contaminated Fenholloway River Water Is Associated with Androgen Receptor Agonist Activity," *Toxicological Sciences*, volume 62 (2001), pp. 257–267. As the authors of this article observe, reports of masculinizing effects attributable to environmental toxins are much less common than reports of feminizing effects.

32   Miquel Porta, "Persistent Organic Pollutants and the Burden of Diabetes," *Lancet*, volume 368 (2006), pp. 558–599.

33   Felix Grün and Bruce Blumberg, "Endocrine Disrupters as Obesogens," *Molecular and Cellular Endocrinology*, volume 304 (2009), pp. 19–29. See also Leonardo Trasande and Bruce Blumberg, "Endocrine Disruptors as Obesogens," *Pediatric Obesity*, 2017, https://link.springer.com/chapter/10 .1007/978-3-319-68192-4_14.

34   Styne and Grumbach, "Puberty: Ontogeny, Neuroendocrinology, Physiology, and Disorders," p. 973.

35   For an overview of the rules, see this memo from the United States Food and Drug Administration: "Steroid Hormone Implants Used for Growth in Food-Producing Animals," July 23, 2019, https://www.fda.gov/animal -veterinary/product-safety-information/steroid-hormone-implants-used -growth-food-producing-animals.

36   Anne-Simone Parent, Grete Teilmann, and colleagues, "The Timing of Normal Puberty and the Age Limits of Sexual Precocity: Variations around the World, Secular Trends, and Changes after Migration," *Endocrine Reviews*, volume 24 (2003), pp. 668–693. See also Anders Juul and colleagues, "Pubertal Development in Danish Children: Comparison of Recent European and U.S. Data," *International Journal of Andrology*, volume 29 (2005), pp. 247–255.

37   Christine de Ridder and colleagues, "Dietary Habits, Sexual Maturation, and Plasma Hormones in Pubertal Girls: A Longitudinal Study," *American Journal of Clinical Nutrition*, volume 54 (1991), pp. 805–813. See also Malcolm Koo and colleagues, "A Cohort Study of Dietary Fibre Intake and Menarche," *Public Health Nutrition*, volume 5 (2002), pp. 353–360.

38   See, for example, Rachel Tolbert Kimbro, Jeanne Brooks-Gunn, and Sara McLanahan, "Racial and Ethnic Differentials in Overweight and Obesity among 3-Year-Old Children," *American Journal of Public Health*, volume 97 (2007), pp. 298–305. Curiously, these authors found that "having been breast-fed for at least 6 months significantly decreased the odds of overweight or obesity among children of obese mothers but did not significantly affect outcomes among children of nonobese mothers."

39   According to a recent report from UNICEF, 74 percent of mothers in the United States report ever having breastfed their baby, compared with 82 percent in Germany, 89 percent in Canada, 92 percent in Australia, and 98 percent in Sweden. See "Breastfeeding: A Mother's Gift for Every Child," 2018, https://www.unicef.org/publications/files/UNICEF_Breastfeeding _A_Mothers_Gift_for_Every_Child.pdf.

40   Specifically, they found that though BPA can act like a female hormone in concentrations as low as 0.23 parts per *trillion*, it is commonly found in human tissues in concentrations of 0.3 to 4.4 parts per *billion*. See Frederick S. vom Saal and colleagues, "Chapel Hill Bisphenol A Expert Panel Consensus Statement: Integration of Mechanisms, Effects in Animals and Potential to Impact Human Health at Current Levels of Exposure," *Reproductive Toxicology*, volume 24 (2007), pp. 131–138.

41   Antonia Calafat and colleagues, "Exposure of the U.S. Population to Bisphenol A and 4-Tertiary-Octylphenol," *Environmental Health Perspectives*, volume 116 (2008), pp. 39–44.

42   Vom Saal and colleagues, "Chapel Hill Bisphenol A Expert Panel Consensus Statement," p. 137.

43   Environmental Working Group, "Bisphenol A: Toxic Plastics Chemical in Canned Food," March 5, 2007, https://www.ewg.org/research/bisphenol.

44   See, for example, Ivelisse Colón and colleagues, "Identification of Phthalate Esters in the Serum of Young Puerto Rican Girls with Premature Breast Development," *Environmental Health Perspectives*, volume 108 (2000), pp. 895–900. See also Shanna Swan and colleagues, "Decrease in Anogenital Distance among Male Infants with Prenatal Phthalate Exposure," *Environmental Health Perspectives*, volume 113 (2005), pp. 1056–1061; and Felix Grün and Bruce Blumberg, "Endocrine Disruptors as Obesogens," *Molecular and Cellular Endocrinology*, volume 304 (2009), pp. 19–29.

45   Sheela Sathyanarayana, Catherine J. Karr, Paula Lozano, and colleagues, "Baby Care Products: Possible Sources of Infant Phthalate Exposure," *Pediatrics*, volume 121 (2008), pp. e260–e268. The quotations come from the "Conclusions" section on p. e266.

46   Please see my scholarly paper, "Polyethylene Terephthalate May Yield Endocrine Disruptors," *Environmental Health Perspectives* volume 118 (2010), pp. 445–448, www.leonardsax.com/PET.pdf.

47   P. Montuori and colleagues, "Assessing Human Exposure to Phthalic Acid and Phthalate Esters from Mineral Water Stored in Polyethylene Terephthalate and Glass Bottles," *Food Additives and Contaminants, Part A: Chemistry, Analysis, Control, Exposure, and Risk Assessment*, volume 25 (2008), pp. 511–518.

48   Again, please see my paper, "Polyethylene Terephthalate May Yield Endocrine Disruptors," *Environmental Health Perspectives*, for an overview of how temperature affects the leaching of phthalates from PET bottles. See also Mehdi Farhoodi and colleagues, "Effect of Environmental Conditions on the Migration of Di(2-Ethylhexyl)Phthalate from PET bottles into Yogurt Drinks: Influence of Time, Temperature, and Food Simulant," *Arabian Journal for Science and Engineering*, volume 33 (2008), pp. 279–288.

49   Neil Osterwell, "Local and National Legislation Banning Phthalates and Bisphenol A Considered," *Medscape Medical News*, July 7, 2008.

50   Martin Wagner and Jörg Oehlmann, "Endocrine Disruptors in Bottled Mineral Water: Total Estrogenic Burden and Migration from Plastic Bottles," *Environmental Science and Pollution Research*, volume 16 (2009), pp. 278–286. The quotes (including the comment about "the tip of the iceberg") are from p. 284.

51   Michael Pollan, *In Defense of Food: An Eater's Manifesto* (New York: Penguin, 2008).

52   D. A. Pape-Zambito and colleagues, "Concentrations of 17-Estradiol in Holstein Whole Milk," *Journal of Dairy Science*, volume 90 (2007), pp. 3308–3313.

53   Shanthy Bowman, "Beverage Choices of Young Females: Changes and Impact on Nutrient Intakes," *Journal of the American Dietetic Association*, volume 102 (2002), pp. 1234–1239.

54   Roberto Ferdman, "The Mysterious Case of America's Plummeting Milk Consumption," *Washington Post*, June 20, 2014, https://www.washingtonpost.com/news/wonk/wp/2014/06/20/the-mysterious-case-of-americas-plummeting-milk-consumption/.

55   See Robert Matchock and Elizabeth Susman, "Family Composition and Menarcheal Age: Anti-Inbreeding Strategies," *American Journal of Human Biology*, volume 18 (2006), pp. 481–491; Jacqueline Tither and Bruce Ellis, "Impact of Fathers on Daughters' Age at Menarche: A Genetically and Environmentally Controlled Sibling Study," *Developmental Psychology*, volume 44 (2008), pp. 1409–1420; and Jay Belsky and colleagues, "Family Rearing Antecedents of Pubertal Timing," *Child Development*, volume 78 (2007), pp. 1302–1321.

56   David Popenoe, *Life without Father* (Cambridge, MA: Harvard University Press, 1996), p. 3; and United States Census Bureau, "Historical Living

Arrangements for Children," November 2018, https://www.census.gov
/data/tables/time-series/demo/families/children.html.

57   Lawrence Berger and colleagues, "Parenting Practices of Resident Fathers:
The Role of Marital and Biological Ties," *Journal of Marriage and the Family*, volume 70 (2008), pp. 625–639.

58   The first report documenting earlier onset of menarche in girls who grew
up without their father was reported by B. Jones and colleagues, "Factors
Influencing the Age of Menarche in a Lower Socio-Economic Group in
Melbourne," *Medical Journal of Australia*, volume 2 (1972), pp. 533–535.
For an extensive review of this literature, see Bruce Ellis, "Timing of
Pubertal Maturation in Girls," *Psychological Bulletin*, volume 130 (2004),
pp. 920–958.

59   See, for example, Bruce Ellis and colleagues, "Does Father Absence Place
Daughters at Special Risk for Early Sexual Activity and Teenage Pregnancy?," *Child Development*, volume 74 (2003), pp. 801–821.

60   See, for example, Bruce Ellis and Marilyn Essex, "Family Environments,
Adrenarche, and Sexual Maturation: A Longitudinal Test of a Life History Model," *Child Development*, volume 78 (2007), pp. 1799–1817. However, Matchock and Susman found no effect of socioeconomic status in
their retrospective study of roughly two thousand young women, "Family Composition and Menarcheal Age," pp. 481–491. Girls who grow up in
low-income households in the United States typically are heavier than
girls from more affluent households (see, e.g., Kimbro, Brooks-Gunn, and
McLanahan, "Racial and Ethnic Differentials in Overweight and Obesity among 3-Year-Old Children," pp. 298–305). As we have seen, girls
who are overweight are also more likely to go through puberty earlier.
So it's possible that the finding, reported only by some researchers, that
girls from low-income families go through puberty earlier may be confounded by the fact that girls from low-income families are more likely
to be overweight.

61   See, for example, Jacqueline Tither and Bruce Ellis, "Impact of Fathers
on Daughters' Age at Menarche: A Genetically and Environmentally Controlled Sibling Study," pp. 1409–1420.

62   For example, Jay Belsky and colleagues, "Childhood Experience, Interpersonal Development, and Reproductive Strategy," *Child Development*, volume 62 (1991), pp. 647–670, suggested that girls feel more insecure if they
grow up without their fathers and that insecurity leads them to eat more,
which makes them get fat and thereby accelerates puberty (p. 652).

63   For example, Matchock and Susman, "Family Composition and Menarcheal
Age," pp. 481–491, found that "10.3% of the father-absent girls described
themselves as overweight while growing up, which was not significantly

different from the 10.0% of father-present girls who described themselves as overweight" (p. 490).

64   See Bruce Ellis and colleagues, "Quality of Early Family Relationships and Individual Differences in the Timing of Pubertal Maturation in Girls," *Journal of Personality and Social Psychology*, volume 77 (1999), pp. 387–401.

65   Laurie Schwab Zabin, Mark Emerson, and David Rowland, "Childhood Sexual Abuse and Early Menarche: The Direction of Their Relationship and Its Implications," *Journal of Adolescent Health*, volume 36 (2005), pp. 393–400.

66   Jay Belsky and colleagues, "Family Rearing Antecedents of Pubertal Timing," *Child Development*, volume 78 (2007), pp. 1302–1321; see also Tither and Ellis, "Impact of Fathers on Daughters' Age at Menarche"; and also S. R. Jaffee, Avshalom Caspi, and colleagues, "Life with (or without) Father: The Benefits of Living with Two Biological Parents Depend on the Father's Antisocial Behavior," *Child Development*, volume 74 (2003), pp. 109–126.

67   Bruce Ellis and Judy Garber found that the presence of a stepfather was associated with *earlier* puberty in girls. See their paper "Psychosocial Antecedents of Variation in Girls' Pubertal Timing: Maternal Depression, Stepfather Presence, and Marital and Family Stress," *Child Development*, volume 71 (2003), pp. 485–501. However, Anthony Bogaert found no association between stepfather presence and early puberty in his sample of American girls, "Age at Puberty and Father Absence in a National Probability Sample," *Journal of Adolescence*, volume 28 (2005), pp. 541–546. The lack of association in Bogaert's study still demonstrates that the presence of the stepfather is not able to compensate, on this parameter, for the absence of the biological father. Likewise, Matchock and Susman, "Family Composition and Menarcheal Age," also found no association between early puberty in girls and the presence or absence of the stepfather; whereas girls raised without their *biological* father went through puberty earlier than girls raised with their *biological* father, regardless of whether a stepfather was present. Matchock and Susman were expecting to replicate the finding reported by Ellis and Garber; they admit that their actual finding, of no effect of stepfather presence on girls who were raised without a biological father, was "surprising" to them (p. 487).

68   For an entertaining introduction to this literature, see Douglas Field's article, "Sex and the Secret Nerve," *Scientific American Mind*, March 2007, pp. 21–27.

69   For a review of this research, see Mahmood Bhutta, "Sex and the Nose: Human Pheromonal Responses," *Journal of the Royal Society of Medicine*, volume 100 (2007), pp. 268–274.

70   John Vandenbergh and colleagues, "Partial Isolation of a Pheromone Accelerating Puberty in Female Mice," *Journal of Reproductive Fertility*, volume 43 (1975), pp. 515–523. See also J. R. Lombardi and John Vandenbergh, "Pheromonally Induced Sexual Maturation in Females: Regulation by the Social Environment of the Male," *Science*, volume 196 (1977), pp. 545–546.

71   See John Hoogland, "Prairie Dogs Avoid Extreme Inbreeding," *Science*, volume 215 (1982), pp. 1639–1641. A similar phenomenon was reported in marmoset monkeys; see S. Evans and J. Hodges, "Reproductive Status of Adult Daughters in Family Groups of Common Marmosets," *Folia Primatologica*, volume 42 (1984), pp. 127–133.

72   Bhutta, "Sex and the Nose," p. 271.

73   Matchock and Susman, "Family Composition and Menarcheal Age."

74   Quoted in Mairi McLeod, "Her Father's Daughter," *New Scientist*, February 10, 2007.

75   Bettina Pause and colleagues, "The Human Brain Is a Detector of Chemosensorily Transmitted HLA-class I-Similarity in Same- and Opposite-Sex Relations," *Proceedings of the Royal Society*, volume 273 (2006), pp. 471–478.

76   Magda Vandeloo, Liesbeth Bruckers, and Jaak Janssens, "Effects of Lifestyle on the Onset of Puberty as Determinant for Breast Cancer," *European Journal of Cancer Prevention*, volume 16 (2007), pp. 17–25.

77   Steingraber, *The Falling Age of Puberty in U.S. Girls*, p. 48.

78   Styne and Grumbach, "Puberty: Ontogeny, Neuroendocrinology, Physiology, and Disorders," p. 1051.

chapter 5

1   Nassim Nicholas Taleb, *Antifragile: Things That Gain from Disorder* (New York: Random House, 2012), p. 3.

2   Ellen Sandseter and Leif Kennair, "Children's Risky Play from an Evolutionary Perspective: The Anti-Phobic Effects of Thrilling Experiences," *Evolutionary Psychology*, volume 9 (2011), pp. 257–284, https://journals.sagepub.com/doi/pdf/10.1177/147470491100900212.

3   James Byrnes, David Miller, and William Schafer, "Gender Differences in Risk Taking: A Meta-Analysis," *Psychological Bulletin*, volume 125 (1999), pp. 367–383, http://psycnet.apa.org/journals/bul/125/3/367/.

4   Barbara Morrongiello, Corina Midgett, and Kerri-Lynn Stanton, "Gender Biases in Children's Appraisals of Injury Risk and Other Children's Risk-Taking Behaviors," *Journal of Experimental Child Psychology*, volume 77 (2000), pp. 317–336.

5   My discussion in this paragraph is adapted from Chapter 3 of my book *Why Gender Matters: What Parents and Teachers Need to Know about the Emerging Science of Sex Differences* (New York: Harmony, 2017).

6   My discussion of Margrét Pála Ólafsdóttir's "dare training" program is adapted from Chapter 3 of my book *Why Gender Matters* (previous reference).

7   Lisa Feldman Barrett, "When Is Speech Violence?," *New York Times*, July 14, 2017, https://www.nytimes.com/2017/07/14/opinion/sunday/when-is-speech-violence.html.

8   The study that Barrett cites is "Acute Psychosocial Stress Reduces Cell Survival in Adult Hippocampal Neurogenesis without Altering Proliferation," *Journal of Neuroscience*, volume 27 (2007), pp. 2734–2743, https://www.jneurosci.org/content/27/11/2734.

9   These findings are from Terrie Moffitt, Richie Poulton, and Avshalom Caspi, "Lifelong Impact of Early Self-Control: Childhood Self-Discipline Predicts Adult Quality of Life," *American Scientist*, volume 101 (2013), pp. 352–359. The figures are from page 355.

10   Moffitt, Poulton, and Caspi, "Lifelong Impact," p. 353.

11   "A Judicial Primer on Bias Response," *Wall Street Journal*, Editorial Board, September 30, 2019, https://www.wsj.com/articles/a-judicial-primer-on-bias-response-11569786160.

12   My discussion of self-control at the conclusion of this chapter is adapted from Chapter 6 of my book *The Collapse of Parenting* (New York: Basic Books, 2016).

13   Kristen Roupenian, "What It Felt Like When 'Cat Person' Went Viral," *The New Yorker*, January 10, 2019, https://www.newyorker.com/books/page-turner/what-it-felt-like-when-cat-person-went-viral.

14   Kristen Roupenian, "Cat Person," *The New Yorker*, December 4, 2017, https://www.newyorker.com/magazine/2017/12/11/cat-person.

15   Maureen Dowd, "What's Lust Got to Do with It?," *New York Times*, April 7, 2018, https://www.nytimes.com/2018/04/07/opinion/sunday/women-sex-dating-dowd.html.

16   Katherine Kersten, "False Feminism: How We Got from Sexual Liberation to #MeToo," *First Things*, February 2019, https://www.firstthings.com/article/2019/02/false-feminism.

chapter 6

1   Michael Sokolove, *Warrior Girls: Protecting Our Daughters against the Injury Epidemic in Women's Sports* (New York: Simon & Schuster, 2008), p. 281.

2   See, for example, Jérôme Barral and colleagues, "Developmental Changes in Unimanual and Bimanual Aiming Movements," *Developmental Neuropsychology*, volume 29 (2006), pp. 415–429. In 1974, Eleanor Maccoby and Carol Jacklin published an influential book entitled *The Psychology of Sex Differences* (Stanford University Press), in which they asserted that sex differences in spatial ability don't appear until after the onset of puberty. Maccoby and Jacklin suggested that these differences were merely a social construct, reflecting differences in how girls and boys are raised. By the late 1990s, it was clear that the social constructionist theory of Maccoby and Jacklin did not fit the facts: sex differences in performance on spatial tasks are firmly in place by five years and do not appear to be a function of what kind of games kids are playing. Contrary to the predictions of Maccoby and Jacklin, differences in spatial performance between adult women and men are, if anything, *less* pronounced than the differences between eight-year-old girls and eight-year-old boys. For a review of the literature leading to our current understanding of the ontogeny of sex differences in spatial performance, see Susan Levine and colleagues, "Early Sex Differences in Spatial Skill," *Developmental Psychology*, volume 35 (1999), pp. 940–949. See also Professor Levine's follow-up article, which she wrote with four colleagues, "Sex Differences in Spatial Cognition: Advancing the Conversation," *Cognitive Science*, volume 7 (2016), https://onlinelibrary.wiley.com/doi/abs/10.1002/wcs.1380.

3   Inger Holm and Nina Vøllestad, "Significant Effect of Gender on Hamstring-to-Quadriceps Strength Ratio and Static Balance in Prepubescent Children from 7 to 12 Years of Age," *American Journal of Sports Medicine*, volume 36 (2008), pp. 2007–2013.

4   See, for example, Jennifer Fredricks and Jacquelynne Eccles, "Children's Competence and Value Beliefs from Childhood through Adolescence: Growth Trajectories in Two Male-Sex-Typed Domains," *Developmental Psychology*, volume 38 (2002), pp. 519–533.

5   Tucker Center for Research on Girls & Women in Sport, *The 2007 Tucker Center Research Report: Developing Physically Active Girls* (Minneapolis: University of Minnesota, 2007), p. 19.

6   Sokolove, *Warrior Girls*, p. 57.

7   Richard Lapchick, "The 2018 Racial and Gender Report Card: College Sport," *The Institute for Diversity and Ethics in Sport*, https://www.tidesport.org/racial-gender-report-card. The exact figure was 40.8 percent.

8   Sokolove, *Warrior Girls*, p. 57.

9   Tucker Center, *The 2007 Tucker Center Research Report*, p. 9.

10   Jennifer Fredricks and Jacquelynne Eccles, "Children's Competence and Value Beliefs from Childhood through Adolescence: Growth Trajectories in Two Male-Sex-Typed Domains," pp. 519–533.

11   Tucker Center, p. 10.

12   Stacey Smith, Mary Fry, and colleagues, "The Effect of Female Athletes'
      Perceptions of Their Coaches' Behaviors on Their Perceptions of the Moti-
      vational Climate," *Journal of Applied Sport Psychology*, volume 17 (2005),
      pp. 170–177.

13   David Abel and Caroline Louise Cole, "Medford Athlete Dies at Practice,"
      Boston Globe, August 10, 2005.

14   According to a prepared statement from Ashley's cheerleading coaches,
      "At cheerleading camp, Ashley was selected a team all-star for consistently
      completing all the elite stunt sequences taught at the camp." See Megan
      Tench, "Ashley Died in the Pursuit of Excellence," August 16, 2005, *Boston
      Globe*.

15   See Megan Tench's article (previous citation).

16   Kathleen Burge, "After Cheerleader's Death, a Closer Look at the Sport,"
      Boston Globe, April 18, 2009.

17   Frederick Mueller and Robert Cantu, *Catastrophic Sports Injury Research:
      Twenty-sixth Annual Report* (Chapel Hill: University of North Carolina,
      2008).

18   Burge, "After Cheerleader's Death, a Closer Look at the Sport."

19   Both quotes in this paragraph come from Burge's article "After Cheerlead-
      er's Death."

20   Committee on Sports Medicine and Fitness, American Academy of Pedi-
      atrics, "Intensive Training and Sports Specialization in Young Athletes,"
      Pediatrics, volume 106 (2000), pp. 154–157 (emphasis added).

21   Council on Sports Medicine and Fitness, American Academy of Pediatrics,
      "Overuse Injuries, Overtraining, and Burnout in Child and Adolescent Ath-
      letes," *Pediatrics*, volume 119 (2007), pp. 1242–1245.

22   Roni Rabin, "Parents Should Limit Sports Participation for Children,
      Trainers Say," *New York Times*, October 17, 2019, https://www.nytimes.com
      /2019/10/17/health/children-sports-injuries.html.

23   Sokolove, *Warrior Girls*, p. 277.

24   Sokolove, p. 281. Emphasis in original.

25   Sokolove, p. 234.

26   Sokolove, p. 211.

27   Likewise, Sokolove, *Warrior Girls* (p. 84), observes that it appears to take
      a more serious injury to drive women out of military service, compared
      with men.

28   Holm and Vøllestad, "Significant Effect of Gender on Hamstring-to-
      Quadriceps Strength Ratio."

29   Thomas Kernozek and colleagues, "Gender Differences in Lower Extremity
      Landing Mechanics Caused by Neuromuscular Fatigue," *American Journal
      of Sports Medicine*, volume 36 (2008), pp. 554–565.

30   Scott Landry, Kelly McKean, and colleagues, "Neuromuscular and Lower Limb Biomechanical Differences Exist between Male and Female Elite Adolescent Soccer Players during an Unanticipated Run and Crosscut Maneuver," *American Journal of Sports Medicine*, volume 35 (2007), pp. 1901–1911.

31   Sally Mountcastle and colleagues, "Gender Differences in Anterior Cruciate Ligament Injury Vary with Activity: Epidemiology of Anterior Cruciate Ligament Injuries in a Young, Athletic Population," *American Journal of Sports Medicine*, volume 35 (2007), pp. 1635–1642.

32   Julie Agel, Elizabeth Arendt, and Boris Bershadsky, "Anterior Cruciate Ligament Injury in National Collegiate Athletic Association Basketball and Soccer," *American Journal of Sports Medicine*, volume 33 (2005), pp. 524–531.

33   Philippe Neyret and colleagues, "Partial Meniscectomy and Anterior Cruciate Ligament Rupture in Soccer Players: A Study with a Minimum 20-Year Followup," *American Journal of Sports Medicine*, volume 21 (1993), pp. 455–460.

34   David Swenson and colleagues, "Patterns of Recurrent Injuries among U.S. High School Athletes, 2005–2008," *American Journal of Sports Medicine*, volume 37 (2009), pp. 1586–1593.

35   Bert Mandelbaum, Holly Silvers, and colleagues, "Effectiveness of a Neuromuscular and Proprioceptive Training Program in Preventing Anterior Cruciate Ligament Injuries in Female Athletes: 2-Year Follow-up," *American Journal of Sports Medicine*, volume 33 (2005), pp. 1003–1010. The success of this program was replicated by a European team of specialists, again comparing girls who had the special warm-up compared with girls on control teams that did the usual warm-up, again with astonishing benefits for girls who had the girl-specific warm-up. See Ashkan Kiani and colleagues, "Prevention of Soccer-Related Knee Injuries in Teenaged Girls," *Archives of Internal Medicine*, volume 170 (2010), pp. 43–49. For more on this topic, including links to more description of the warm-ups, with pictures of how to do the warm-up exercises correctly—provided by the orthopedic specialists who designed the warm-up—please see my article "Girls' Knees and Gender Confusion: Does 'Equal' Mean 'the Same'?," *Psychology Today*, June 25, 2012, https://www.psychologytoday.com/us/blog/sax-sex/201206/girls-knees-and-gender-confusion.

36   I first learned of Samantha's story in Michael Sokolove's book *Warrior Girls*, which tells her story through December 2007. I am grateful to Samantha for updating me on her story through January 2020.

37   Specifically, these investigators found that the overall rate of concussion per 1,000 athlete exposures was 0.36 in girls' soccer, compared with 0.22

in boys' soccer (0.36 is 60 percent greater than 0.22); the risk was 0.21 in girls' basketball, compared with 0.07 in boys' basketball (0.21 is 300 percent greater than 0.07). See Luke Gessel, Sarah Fields, and colleagues, "Concussions among United States High School and Collegiate Athletes," *Journal of Athletic Training*, volume 42 (2007), pp. 495–503.

38 Sokolove, *Warrior Girls*, p. 254.

39 See, for example, Rhoshel Lenroot and colleagues, "Sexual Dimorphism of Brain Developmental Trajectories during Childhood and Adolescence," *NeuroImage*, volume 36 (2007), pp. 1065–1073, especially figure 2(d) on page 1068. The lateral ventricles are significantly larger in boys than girls at every age, even at ages ten through thirteen—ages at which these authors note the average girl is actually taller than the average boy (see their comment on page 1070).

40 According to the NCAA/Ohio State University study cited above, contact between the head and the soccer ball was associated with concussion in 5,350 girls and in 1,716 boys; see Luke Gessel, Sarah Fields, and colleagues, "Concussions among United States High School and Collegiate Athletes," pp. 495–503; these specific figures will be found on page 497. Of course, another explanation for this finding might simply be that girls are three times more likely than boys to hit the ball with their heads, but that explanation seems implausible.

41 See, for example, Alexis Colvin and colleagues, "The Role of Concussion History and Gender in Recovery from Soccer-Related Concussion," *American Journal of Sports Medicine*, volume 37 (2009), pp. 1699–1704. Her team found that "these differences do not appear to reflect differences in mass between genders" and that "gender appears to be more important than the mass of the player in postconcussive testing."

42 Sokolove, *Warrior Girls*, p. 256.

43 Tucker Center, *The 2007 Tucker Center Research Report*, p. 55.

44 Katherine Gunter and colleagues, "Impact Exercise Increases BMC [bone mineral content] during Growth: An 8-Year Longitudinal Study," *Journal of Bone and Mineral Research*, volume 23 (2008), pp. 986–993.

45 Kerry McKelvie and colleagues, "A School-Based Exercise Intervention Elicits Substantial Bone Health Benefits: A 2-Year Randomized Controlled Trial in Girls," *Pediatrics*, volume 112 (2003), pp. e447–e452.

46 Kathleen Janz and colleagues, "Physical Activity and Femoral Neck Bone Strength during Childhood: The Iowa Bone Development Study," *Bone*, volume 41 (2007), pp. 216–222.

47 Keith Loud, Catherine Gordon, and colleagues, "Correlates of Stress Fractures among Preadolescent and Adolescent Girls," *Pediatrics*, volume 115 (2005), pp. e399–e406.

48   In one study, 29 percent of girls who had broken a bone had a history of
      not drinking any milk, compared with 12 percent of girls who had never
      broken a bone; but among boys, there was no significant difference in the
      likelihood of drinking milk, or not drinking milk, when comparing boys
      who had broken a bone with boys who had never broken a bone. That find-
      ing comes from "Fractures during Growth: Potential Role of a Milk-Free
      Diet," *Osteoporosis International*, volume 18 (2007), pp. 1601–1607. In
      addition, C. McGartland and colleagues found that drinking soda was asso-
      ciated with brittle bones in girls but not in boys; see their article "Carbon-
      ated Soft Drink Consumption and Bone Mineral Density in Adolescence,"
      Journal of Bone and Mineral Research, volume 18 (2003), pp. 1563–1569.
      In boys, activity seems to be even more important in determining bone
      density than it is in girls; see, for example, Susi Kriemler and colleagues,
      "Weight-Bearing Bones Are More Sensitive to Physical Exercise in Boys
      Than in Girls during Pre- and Early Puberty: A Cross-Sectional Study,"
      Osteoporosis International, volume 19 (2008), pp. 1749–1758. For more
      evidence that diet is the primary determinant of bone density in females,
      whereas activity is the primary determinant of bone density in males,
      see my chapter entitled "Dietary Phosphorus as a Nutritional Toxin:
      The Influence of Age and Sex," in *Reviews in Food and Nutrition Toxicity*,
      eds. Victor Preedy and Ronald Watson (New York: CRC Press, 2003), pp.
      158–168.

49   D. Ma and G. Jones, "Soft Drink and Milk Consumption, Physical Activity,
      Bone Mass, and Upper Limb Fractures in Children: A Population-Based
      Case-Control Study," *Calcified Tissues International*, volume 75 (2004),
      pp. 286–291.

50   Katherine Tucker and colleagues, "Colas, but Not Other Carbonated Bever-
      ages, Are Associated with Low Bone Mineral Density in Older Women: The
      Framingham Osteoporosis Study," *American Journal of Clinical Nutrition*,
      volume 84 (2006), pp. 936–942.

51   C. McGartland and colleagues, "Carbonated Soft Drink Consumption and
      Bone Mineral Density in Adolescence" (see earlier reference).

52   L. Esterle and colleagues, "Milk, Rather Than Other Foods, Is Associated
      with Vertebral Bone Mass and Circulating IGF-1 in Female Adolescents,"
      Osteoporosis International, volume 20 (2009), pp. 567–575. See also Leann
      Matlik and colleagues, "Perceived Milk Intolerance Is Related to Bone Min-
      eral Content in 10- to 13-Year-Old Female Adolescents," *Pediatrics*, volume
      120 (2007), pp. e669–e677. The role of milk in building strong bones seems
      to be especially important in Caucasian girls; see, for example, another
      recent report from Esterle's group, "Higher Milk Requirements for Bone
      Mineral Accrual in Adolescent Girls Bearing Specific Caucasian Genotypes

in the VDR Promoter," *Journal of Bone and Mineral Research*, volume 24 (2009), pp. 1389–1397.

53   A. Z. Budek and colleagues, "Dietary Protein Intake and Bone Mineral Content in Adolescents," *Osteoporosis International*, volume 18 (2007), pp. 1661–1667.

54   See, for example, Oliver Franklin-Wallis, "White Gold: The Unstoppable Rise of Alternative Milks," *Guardian*, January 29, 2019, https://www.the guardian.com/news/2019/jan/29/white-gold-the-unstoppable-rise-of -alternative-milks-oat-soy-rice-coconut-plant.

55   Norman Carvalho and colleagues, "Severe Nutritional Deficiencies in Toddlers Resulting from Health Food Milk Alternatives," *Pediatrics*, volume 107 (2001), https://pediatrics.aappublications.org/content/107/4/e46.

56   Mary Murphy and colleagues, "Drinking Flavored or Plain Milk Is Positively Associated with Nutrient Intake and Is Not Associated with Adverse Effects on Weight Status in U.S. Children and Adolescents," *Journal of the American Dietetic Association*, volume 108 (2008), pp. 631–639.

57   In my experience, lactose intolerance is overdiagnosed among children. Before assuming that your child is lactose intolerant, ask whether she can eat a bowl of regular ice cream without getting severe GI symptoms. If she can, then she is not lactose intolerant. Lactose intolerance means that a child does not have enough of the enzyme *lactase*, which breaks down milk sugar (lactose) into its component sugars, glucose and galactose. Buy predigested milk such as Lactaid milk, and mix in some lactase enzymes (available at most grocery stores) into the Lactaid milk. Those simple measures will be sufficient for most children who truly have mild to moderate lactose intolerance. If in doubt about the diagnosis, ask your doctor to request a *hydrogen breath test*. As the AAP Committee on Nutrition observed in its review article on this topic, "Some patients think they are lactose intolerant when they prove not to be." The hydrogen breath test is a simple, noninvasive test that can resolve the confusion. You can read the full text of the report of the AAP's Committee on Nutrition at https://pediatrics .aappublications.org/content/118/3/1279.full. The reference is "Lactose Intolerance in Infants, Children, and Adolescents," *Pediatrics*, volume 118 (2006), pp. 1279–1286.

58   Jennifer Flynn, Stella Foley, and Graeme Jones, "Can BMD Assessed by DXA at Age 8 Predict Fracture Risk in Boys and Girls during Puberty? An Eight-Year Prospective Study," *Journal of Bone and Mineral Research*, volume 22 (2007), pp. 1463–1467.

59   Karin Allor Pfeiffer and colleagues, "Sport Participation and Physical Activity in Adolescent Females across a Four-Year Period," *Journal of Adolescent Health*, volume 39 (2006), pp. 523–529.

60   Rod Dishman and colleagues, "Physical Self-Concept and Self-Esteem Mediate Cross-Sectional Relations of Physical Activity and Sport Participation with Depression Symptoms among Adolescent Girls," *Health Psychology*, volume 25 (2006), pp. 396–407.

61   Maike ter Wolbeek and colleagues, "Predictors of Persistent and New-Onset Fatigue in Adolescent Girls," *Pediatrics*, volume 121 (2008), pp. e449–e457.

62   Elsie Taveras and colleagues, "The Influence of Wanting to Look Like Media Figures on Adolescent Physical Activity," *Journal of Adolescent Health*, volume 35 (2004), pp. 41–50.

63   Tucker Center, *The 2007 Tucker Center Research Report*, p. 21.

64   Lauren Fleshman, "I Changed My Body for My Sport. No Girl Should," *New York Times*, November 16, 2019, https://www.nytimes.com/2019/11/16/opinion/girls-sports.html.

65   Jeanne Nichols and colleagues, "Prevalence of the Female Athlete Triad Syndrome among High School Athletes," *Archives of Pediatrics and Adolescent Medicine*, volume 160 (2006), pp. 137–142.

66   M. K. Torstveit and J. Sundgot-Borgen, "Participation in Leanness Sports but Not Training Volume Is Associated with Menstrual Dysfunction," *British Journal of Sports Medicine*, volume 39 (2005), pp. 141–147.

67   If you're not familiar with group contrast effects, you will find a good introduction to the topic—including a discussion of the classic Robbers Cave experiment—in Judith Rich Harris, *The Nurture Assumption: Why Children Turn Out the Way They Do*, second edition (New York: Simon & Schuster, 2009), chapter 7, pp. 115–135.

68   See, for example, the closing paragraphs in Kelly Holleran, "Educators Report Benefits from Gender-Segregated Teaching," *Charleston Daily Mail* (West Virginia), November 7, 2007.

69   Carol Cronin Weisfeld and colleagues, "Female Inhibition in Mixed-Sex Competition among Young Adolescents," *Ethology and Sociobiology*, volume 3 (1982), pp. 29–42.

70   Kandy James, "'You Can Feel Them Looking at You': The Experiences of Adolescent Girls at Swimming Pools," *Journal of Leisure Research*, volume 32 (2000), pp. 262–280. Although this report describes girls' experience at swimming pools, I've heard similar comments made by girls in almost every other kind of physical activity when boys are present.

71   See, for example, Anna Engel, "Sex Roles and Gender Stereotyping in Young Women's Participation in Sport," *Feminism and Psychology*, volume 4 (1994), pp. 439–448. A number of schools that have adopted the single-sex format for physical education have found that the all-girls format results in more girls participating. For example, teacher Janet Fendley says that she was "astounded" by the increase in girls' participation in physical

education after her school (Smith Elementary in Martinsville, Indiana) adopted the single-sex format for physical education. See Hannah Lodge, "Some Gain Advantage from Single-Sex Education," *Reporter-Times* (Martinsville, IN), August 21, 2006, http://www.diferenciada.org/node/96. Likewise, physical education instructors noticed a big jump in participation at Andersen Junior High School in Chandler, Arizona, after that school adopted the single-sex format for physical education. See Mike Burkett, "Teachers Like Same-Sex Classes," *Mesa Independent* (Chandler, AZ), August 22, 2006.

72 Fabienne d'Arripe-Longueville and Christophe Gernigon have published several articles on this topic: see, for example, "Peer-Assisted Learning in the Physical Activity Domain: Dyad Type and Gender Differences," *Journal of Sport and Exercise Psychology*, volume 24 (2002), pp. 219–238.

73 Tucker Center, *The 2007 Tucker Center Research Report*, p. 18.

74 Richard Ryckman and Jane Hamel, "Male and Female Adolescents' Motives Related to Involvement in Organized Team Sports," *International Journal of Sport Psychology*, volume 26 (1995), pp. 383–397.

75 Kandy James, "What Designers Should Know about How Adolescent Girls Use Space," *Implications* (a newsletter from the University of Minnesota), volume 4, number 9 (2006).

76 Courtney Martin, *Perfect Girls, Starving Daughters: The Frightening New Normalcy of Hating Your Body* (New York: Free Press, 2007), p. 256.

77 Madeline Levine, *The Price of Privilege: How Parental Pressure and Material Advantage Are Creating a Generation of Disconnected and Unhappy Kids* (New York: HarperCollins, 2006), p. 183.

chapter 7

1 For a review of the scholarly evidence that girls are, on average, more concerned with pleasing their parents than boys are—not only in our species but also among juvenile chimpanzees—see my book *Boys Adrift*, second edition (2016), Chapter 2, especially the section "What Are Little Girls Made Of?," pp. 26–32.

2 Benedict Groeschel describes the years of puberty as the years of spiritual awakening in *Spiritual Passages: The Psychology of Spiritual Development* (New York: Crossroads, 1983), especially in the sections "Stages of Human Development," pp. 43–53, and "Religion of Adolescence," pp. 68–69.

3 All quotes in this paragraph are from Christian Smith and Melinda Lundquist Denton, *Soul Searching* (New York: Oxford University Press, 2005), p. 261.

4 The Honorable Carol J. Orbison, Judge, in the Court of Appeals of Indiana, *Bean v. Indiana*, September 9, 2009, https://www.in.gov/judiciary/opinions/pdf/09090902ewn.pdf.

5 The quotes from Stephanie Berry and William Pollack are found in Elizabeth Olson, "A Rise in Efforts to Spot Abuse in Youth Dating," *New York Times*, January 3, 2009, https://www.nytimes.com/2009/01/04/us/04abuse.html.

6 Robert Bly and Marion Woodman, *The Maiden King: The Reunion of Masculine and Feminine* (New York: Holt, 1998), p. xvii.

7 The breakthrough publication in this regard—the article that really changed the way scholars thought about gender, crystallizing the then-emerging understanding of gender as being two-dimensional rather than one-dimensional—was Alfred Heilbrun, "Measurement of Masculine and Feminine Sex Identities as Independent Dimensions," *Journal of Consulting and Clinical Psychology*, volume 44 (1976), pp. 183–190.

8 In Book 3, §270 of *Die Fröhliche Wissenschaft* (*The Gay Science*), Nietzsche writes, *"Du sollst der werden, der du bist"*—you should become what you are. Nietzsche understood that becoming who you are is not an easy task; the subtitle of his final book, *Ecco Homo*, was *"Wie man wird, was man ist"*—how one becomes what one is. Nietzsche himself cited the Greek poet-philosopher Pindar as his inspiration for this idea.

9 Bly and Woodman, *The Maiden King*, p. 173.

10 Bly and Woodman, *The Maiden King*, p. 22. "Disappointment" is capitalized in the original.

11 Bly and Woodman, *The Maiden King*, pp. 22, 23.

12 Courtney Martin, *Perfect Girls, Starving Daughters: The Frightening New Normalcy of Hating Your Body* (New York: Free Press, 2007), p. 251.

13 For more about the negative consequences of the hookup culture for women in college and beyond, see Kathleen Bogle, *Hooking Up: Sex, Dating, and Relationships on Campus* (New York: NYU Press, 2008), especially Chapters 6 and 7.

14 Bly and Woodman, *The Maiden King*, p. 20, cite Joseph Chilton Pearce, *Evolution's End: Claiming the Potential of Our Intelligence* (New York: HarperCollins, 1992) as the source of this idea: see Chapter 22 in Pearce's book, especially p. 190.

15 Amelia Tait, "So You Wanna Be a Kidfluencer?," *MIT Technology Review*, February 2020, pp. 38–42. The quote is on page 38.

16 For more on this point, see Kathleen Kovner Kline, ed., *Authoritative Communities: The Scientific Case for Nurturing the Whole Child* (New York: Springer, 2008), especially pp. 17–18.

17 Kate Fagan, *What Made Maddy Run: The Secret Struggles and Tragic Death of an All-American Teen* (Boston: Back Bay Books, 2018), p. 72.

18 Fagan, *What Made Maddy Run*, p. 222.

19 Fagan, *What Made Maddy Run*, p. 268.

20 Kate Fagan's story is titled "Split Image," published by ESPN on May 7, 2015. You can read it online at http://www.espn.com/espn/feature/story /_/id/12833146/instagram-account-university-pennsylvania-runner-showed -only-part-story.

21 Smith and Denton, *Soul Searching*, p. 221.

22 Smith and Denton, *Soul Searching*, Table 34, p. 222.

23 Smith and Denton, *Soul Searching*, Table 36, p. 224.

24 Smith and Denton, *Soul Searching*, p. 225.

25 Smith and Denton, *Soul Searching*, Table 37, p. 225.

26 Smith and Denton, *Soul Searching*, p. 194.

27 Smith and Denton, *Soul Searching*, p. 246.

28 Lisa Miller and Merav Gur, "Religiosity, Depression, and Physical Maturation in Adolescent Girls," *Journal of the American Academy of Child and Adolescent Psychiatry*, volume 41 (2002), pp. 206–214.

29 W. A. Mirola, "A Refuge for Some: Gender Differences in the Relationship between Religious Involvement and Depression," *Sociology of Religion*, volume 60 (1999), pp. 419–437.

30 Shirley Feldman and colleagues, "Is 'What Is Good for the Goose Good for the Gander'? Sex Differences in Relations between Adolescent Coping and Adult Adaptation," *Journal of Research on Adolescence*, volume 5 (1995), pp. 333–359.

31 Alethea Desrosiers and Lisa Miller, "Relational Spirituality and Depression in Adolescent Girls," *Journal of Clinical Psychology*, volume 63 (2007), pp. 1021–1037.

32 Desrosiers and Miller, "Relational Spirituality and Depression in Adolescent Girls," p. 1032.

33 Rabbi Sasso made these remarks to Christa Tippett on the public radio program *Speaking of Faith*, May 7, 2008.

34 This is a quotation from a teenager interviewed by Smith and Denton, *Soul Searching*, p. 133.

35 Smith and Denton, *Soul Searching*, p. 133. Italics in original.

36 Smith and Denton, *Soul Searching*, p. 135.

37 The first three sentences of this paragraph are my paraphrase of Smith and Denton, *Soul Searching*, p. 267.

38 Smith and Denton, *Soul Searching*, make this comment (p. 247): "Most American adolescents live the vast majority of their extrafamilial lives in age-stratified institutions and consuming age-targeted products and services. American youth spend about 35 to 40 waking hours per week from between 12 and 17 years in mass-education schools that sort them into classes by single-year age differences. Teens spend the greater part of their weekdays with and being socialized by their age-identical peers. In

off-school hours, they often spend many hours watching television programs that are also targeted to their specific age groups. Another major use of time by young people is in sports, hobbies, and play, also spent with other youth of similar age. Structurally, therefore, the schedules and institutions that organize youths' lives tend to isolate and limit their contacts, exposures, and ideas to those available from others their own age. In such situations, trends in and pressures from peer groups become highly influential and narrow."

39   Quoted in Sarah Kershaw, "How Much Girl Talk Is Too Much?," *New York Times*, September 11, 2008, https://www.nytimes.com/2008/09/11/health/11iht-11talk.16078388.html.

40   Quoted in Kershaw, "How Much Girl Talk Is Too Much?"

41   For an encyclopedic exposition of the decline in such groups—after a peak in the mid-twentieth century—see Robert D. Putnam, *Bowling Alone: The Collapse and Revival of American Community* (New York: Simon & Schuster, 2000).

42   Bly and Woodman, *The Maiden King*, p. 22.

43   Yollanda Zhang, personal communication (email), November 15, 2019.

44   Bly and Woodman, *The Maiden King*, p. 138.

45   Bly and Woodman, *The Maiden King*, p. 180.

46   This is, of course, my translation of Rilke's comment, which is the epigraph at the beginning of the book.

index

alcohol use: coffee and, 100; depression and, 100, 265–266n32; drunk driving and, 102–103; effects of community norms and, 100–101, 101fig; gender and, 98–99, 101–102, 264–265n24, 265–266n32; long-term effects of, 99; as obsession, 86; parental strategies and, 103–105; puberty and, 125; rates of in high school, 95; reasons for, 95–98; religion/spiritual engagement and, 213; sense of self and, 95, 97–98, 104–105; sex and, 102

Allen, Lily, 118

American Girls: Social Media and the Secret Lives of Teenagers (Sales), 7

anorexia, 71–76, 125, 269–270n15

anterior cruciate ligament (ACL) injuries, 172–173

anxiety: involuntary commitment and, 111–117; environmental toxins and, 7, 10–11; prevalence of in adolescent girls, 5–7; puberty and, 125; social media and, 49. *See also* depression; obsessions; perfectionism

appearance focus: cheerleading, 166–167; parents and, 257n19; self-objectification and, 23–24, 29–31, 62–63, 213, 259n35; sexualization of girls and, 10, 12–16, 36–37

Archie, Kimberly, 167

authoritarian parenting style, 45

authoritative parenting style, 45

Bachelor, The, 33

Barbery, Muriel, 12

Barrett, Lisa Feldman, 151

Bauerlein, Mark, 44

Baumrind, Diana, 44–45

Begin, Brittany, 108

Bennett, Jessica, 23

Berry, Stephanie, 197

Bezos, Jeff, 66

bisphenol A (BPA), 130–132, 274n40

Bleiberg, Joseph, 176

Bly, Robert, 198–203, 234

bone density, 178–182, 284n48

bovine growth hormone (BGH), 137

boys: alcohol use and, 98–99, 101–102, 264–265n24, 265–266n32; as alternate friends, 59; competitive sports and, 160–162, 171–174, 280n2; concussions and, 175–177, 283n40; desire to please parents and, 287n1; group contrast effects and, 184–187;

Mayer, John, 36
McCormick, Patty, 105–106
Mead, Margaret, 16, 256n9, 258n25
meditation, 91–92
Meeker, Meg, 4, 26–27, 255n2
menstrual periods, absence of, 74,
    80, 184. *See also* puberty
Meyrowitz, Joshua, 263n32
milk, 137–138, 180–182, 284n48
Miller, Lisa, 215
modesty, 17
monitoring software, 53–57,
    63–65, 67

name-calling, 150–155
National Center for Catastrophic
    Sports Injury Research (NCCSI),
    164–165
National Center on Addiction and
    Substance Abuse, 98
National Cheer Safety Foundation,
    167
National Eating Disorders
    Association, 74
National Institutes of Health
    (NIH), 6, 130
*No Sense of Place: The Impact
    of Electronic Media on Social
    Behavior* (Meyrowitz), 263n32
nonsuicidal self-injury (NSSI). *See*
    self-harm
Norris, Heather, 197
Nussbaum, Emily, 62, 68

Oberlin College, 152–153
obsessions: childhood dream as
    prison and, 205–212; eating
    disorders, 71–76, 269–270n15;
    excessive exercise, 76–81,
    183–184; frustrations of finding

treatment for, 110–111; increased
    possibility for, 10; links between,
    109–110; literature on, 7;
    premature adulthood, 118–119;
    self-harm, 86, 105–109, 226–227,
    266–267n42, 267n44, 268n48;
    sense of self and, 70. *See also*
    alcohol abuse; perfectionism
Ólafsdóttir, Margrét Pála, 147–148
oral sex, 19–21
Orenstein, Peggy, 7
osteoporosis. *See* bone density
overweight, 125–127, 224–227,
    274n38

PACE Centers for Girls, 224–227
"Paradise by the Dashboard Light"
    (Meat Loaf), 27–29
parenting: authoritarian parenting
    style, 45; authoritative parenting
    style, 45; Baumrind parenting
    styles and, 44–45; evolving
    style of, 240–242; permissive
    parenting style, 45
parents: appearance obsession
    and, 257n19; biological fathers
    and puberty, 138–143, 277n67;
    changing roles of, 9–10,
    240–242; competitive sports
    and, 169–171; eating disorders
    questions and, 74–75; engaging
    spirituality and, 218–220;
    gender differences in desire to
    please, 287n1; helping to explore
    spiritual beliefs, 220–222;
    maladaptive perfectionism and,
    86; modeling right-size reaction
    and, 148–150; monitoring of
    technology by, 53–56, 61–65, 67;
    puberty and, 143–144; responses

Leonard Sax, MD, PhD, is a board-certified family physician, psychologist, and the *New York Times* best-selling author of *Why Gender Matters, Boys Adrift,* and *The Collapse of Parenting.* A veteran of visits to more than 460 schools worldwide, Sax has spoken on child and adolescent development in more than a dozen countries and has appeared in many major broadcast radio and television programs, including on ABC, CBS, NBC, CNN, Fox News, PBS, the CBC, and the BBC. Sax lives with his wife and teenage daughter in Chester County, Pennsylvania.